NESTOR

ALBERT BATES LORD STUDIES IN ORAL TRADITION
VOLUME 16
GARLAND REFERENCE LIBRARY OF THE HUMANITIES
VOLUME 1923

ALBERT BATES LORD STUDIES IN ORAL TRADITION
JOHN MILES FOLEY, *Series Editor*

NESTOR
POETIC MEMORY IN GREEK EPIC

KEITH DICKSON

GARLAND PUBLISHING, INC.
NEW YORK AND LONDON
1995

Library of Congress Cataloging-in-Publication Data

Dickson, Keith.
    Nestor : poetic memory in Greek epic / by Keith Dickson.
        p.   cm. — (Albert Bates Lord studies in oral tradition ; vol. 16)
    (Garland reference library of the humanities ; vol. 1923)
    Includes bibliographical references and index.
    ISBN 0–8153–2073–6 (alk. paper)
    1. Homer—Characters—Nestor.   2. Epic poetry, Greek—History and
criticism.   3. Nestor (Greek mythology) in literature.   4. Trojan War in
literature.   5. Aged men in literature.   6. Memory in literature.   7. Homer.
Odyssey.   8. Homer. Iliad.   I. Title.   II. Series.   III. Series: Garland
reference library of the humanities ; vol. 1923.
    PA4037.D46   1995
    883'.01—dc20   95-12542
                                                                                   CIP

Printed on acid-free, 250-year-life paper
Manufactured in the United States of America

Fay & Sam

Contents

Acknowledgments

Very preliminary work on this book was begun under the auspices of a National Endowment for the Humanities Summer Seminar in the Humanities Grant in 1989. It was helped along toward completion by a Purdue Research Foundation Summer Faculty Research Grant in the following year, as well as by a research leave from the Department of Foreign Languages and Literatures at Purdue University during the Fall 1991 semester. I am grateful for this; like the best kind of support, it was timely and unobtrusive, and no strings were attached.

If there are few individuals to whom I am directly indebted, the burden of debt to each is that much greater, while the burden of responsibility of course remains mine alone. These few chiefly include John Miles Foley, for guidance in the early and fragile stages of this work, and for welcome support at the end; and John Peradotto, for a model of clarity, rigor, and intellectual vitality over the last two decades. Thanks are also due to Ann Astell, John Kirby, Anthony Tamburri, and Deborah Starewich, and to a number of anonymous editors, each in their own way, for useful comments and advice at crucial points *en route*.

Chapter 2 represents a revised and expanded version of my essay, "Kalkhas and Nestor: Two Narrative Strategies in *Iliad* 1," which appeared in *Arethusa* 25.2 (1992). I am grateful for permission to republish this material. Parts of Chapter 1 and 3 appeared earlier in less developed form in *Oral Tradition* 8.1 (1993), as "Nestor Among the Sirens," and in *Oral Tradition* 5.1 (1990), as "A Typology of Mediation in Homer."

Nestor

1

Naming Nestor:
The Muse at Pylos

1. INTRODUCTION

What better way to begin a work on storytelling than with a simple piece of narrative? Tantalizingly brief, a fragment stripped of most embellishment, sketching little more than a few iconic gestures—a name, a place, a posture struck, a swift and apparently final reaction—yet at the same time also a tale suggestively rich with allusion? Like many fragments, this one is found nested in another tale that is itself embedded in a tale that is a fragment of an even larger story. They say that the men who sailed to fight at Troy under Nestor's command hailed from the fabled towns of Pylos and lovely Arene, from Thryon and strong-built Aipy, Kyparisseeis and Amphigeneia, from Pteleos and Helos (*Il.* 2.594-600):

§1

        . . . καὶ Δώριον, ἔνθα τε Μοῦσαι
ἀντόμεναι Θάμυριν τὸν Θρήϊκα παῦσαν ἀοιδῆς,
Οἰχαλίηθεν ἰόντα παρ' Εὐρύτου Οἰχαλιῆος·
στεῦτο γὰρ εὐχόμενος νικησέμεν, εἴ περ ἂν αὐταὶ
Μοῦσαι ἀείδοιεν, κοῦραι Διὸς αἰγιόχοιο·
αἱ δὲ χολωσάμεναι πηρὸν θέσαν, αὐτὰρ ἀοιδὴν
θεσπεσίην ἀφέλοντο καὶ ἐκλέλαθον κιθαριστύν.

        . . . and Dorion, where the Muses
met Thamyris the Thracian and stopped him from singing
as he came from Oikhalie and Oikhalian Eurytos;
for he swore, boasting he would win, even if the very Muses
sang against him, the daughters of Zeus who holds the *aigis*.
But in their anger they impaired him, and took away
wondrous song, and made him utterly forget his harping.

The shortest stories are sometimes the best: they engage and empower us as readers, make us work, conscript us into the

3

task of actively generating meaning along with the narration of a tale. To this extent, they serve perhaps even better than longer tales do to thematize the tacit assumptions that guide the process by which meaning is generated in narratives, thus exposing the complicity that exists between storyteller and audience.[1] For it is ellipsis far more than embellishment that reveals the truly productive depth of narration; in what is left unsaid or else merely suggested, the implicit boundaries within which stories orient themselves come slowly into view—or into earshot, in the case of tales that are heard rather than read (as now) from a page silently. Beneath or behind or beyond or around or within every tale—no metaphor quite captures this relation properly—is the far broader context within which the tale is situated, and upon which it depends for its meaning. To be sure, this is a context whose contours are largely shaped by the prejudices and expectations of the community that makes up its audience. Such expectations constitute a receptive horizon that is in some respects fixed, in others quite pliable and open to refiguration. Aspects of its fixity concern us more at this point. For the more homogeneous the audience is in the presuppositions with which it receives a tale, the less the tale actually needs to say outright, the more it can simply take for granted as already given since already well understood.

But these assumptions in turn are themselves to a large extent influenced by prior tales received on other occasions by the same audience; it is chiefly in terms of what it has heard or read before that the audience apprehends and understands *this* story. It is with reference to this fact that we speak of the "intertextuality" of narratives. Eagleton's remarks (1983:138) on the subject of literate texts of course apply equally—perhaps even more closely—to works that are orally composed and transmitted:[2]

> All literary texts are woven out of other literary texts, not in the conventional sense that they bear the traces of "influence" but in the more radical sense that every word, phrase or segment is a reworking of other writings which precede or surround the original work. There is no such thing as literary "originality", no such thing as the "first" literary work: all literature is "intertextual". A specific piece of writing thus has no clearly defined boundaries: it spills over constantly into the works clustered around it, generating a hundred different perspectives which dwindle to vanishing point.

Καί ἐν ἀρχῆι οὐκ ἦν λόγος, ἀλλά ἔργον, ὡς ἔϱη ὁ Φάνοι

Far from being something somehow hermetically closed in on itself, even the simplest tale instead opens out—and opens dynamically, sometimes even with a *challenge*—onto a realm of other tales that the audience knows quite well, having encountered them already in one form or another. And it is to these other tales—both singly and in the form of the broad narrative background they create—that the audience attends subaudially, as it were, at the same time as it hears each new one told, or hears the "same" tale in a different telling. This is of course especially, though not exclusively, true of so-called "traditional" communities, namely communities for which narratives are privileged means of encoding those practices and values that help define the group's identity and guide its aspirations. Within such communities, even the fullest and most "rounded" of tales is itself at best only one part of a much larger narrative whole, a kind of narrative metonym. In this respect, the fragmentary nature of Thamyris' tale is less an anomaly than a true representative of what obtains in the case of all narratives.

On the other hand, a felt need for explanation is often a token of distance from the presuppositions that guide a tale's meaning, a sure sign of some break between its original context and that of its new moment of reception. This distance is variable, a function of both the extent and also the nature of the break; consequently, the means of bridging it also vary. They can range from simple epexegetic asides by the narrator of the tale—as in the gloss of a term or practice whose meaning has ceased to be immediately transparent—to extended commentary on the tale itself by other, subsequent hands. The latter generally occurs once the tale has achieved a form stable enough to allow it to survive the passing of the original community in and for which it was first composed. The fixing of an oral tale as a more or less definitive text, for instance— brought about by the advent of literacy, and by the use of writing to record what had previously been carried by word of mouth—is always something of a mixed blessing. On the one hand, it frees the tale from the spatial and temporal limits imposed by the occasions of its performance, thus giving it a life of its own and also greater longevity than that of both its original narrators and audiences. At the same time, this freedom also risks the estrangement of its meaning. For the tale's new status as an independent artifact is bought at the

price of severing the vital link it once had with its narrative
context, and so with the relatively homogenous horizon of
expectations into which it was initially received. What is lost
thereby is its transparency; its sense and import are no longer
obvious. This is so much the case that its subsequent reception on
other occasions, now often separated from its initial ones by
vast temporal distance and shifting cultural presuppositions,
can render much of the tale opaque or even quite alien, and thus
in need of interpretation. Interpretation springs from ruptured
continuity. It always begins after the tacit assumptions that
once guided the production of its meaning have ceased to be
communal property, so to speak, and the tale's once implicit
context must then be excavated, examined and discussed at a
level of explicitness unnecessary at its first reception.[3]

This partly describes the situation in which the present
fragment is received by us. *En route* from Oikhalie, they say
that the Thracian bard Thamyris encountered the Muses at
Dorion, a town then—or perhaps some later time?—under the
hegemony of Nestor's Pylos.[4] Precisely there—though where
precisely is a matter of dispute—in answer to his boast—how
motivated, we are not expressly told—to surpass even those
goddesses in singing—and why precisely on these terms?—they
permanently maimed him (πηρὸν θέσαν), rescinding their
gift of ἀοιδὴ θεσπεσίη [divine song] and—or else possibly
by?—making him forget how to play the lyre (ἐκλέλαθον
κιθαριστύν).[5] The ancient scholiasts, moved already by the
need to interpret and explain, flesh out some of the details, but
still leave it—at least to modern sensibilities—alluringly
bare. Not that the tale lacks sense for us, or strikes us as
unredeemably foreign. Cultural presuppositions indeed change
over time, but their rate of shift is often glacial. For that
matter, Thamyris' tale is of course not the only instance in
Greek legend of divine gifts punitively withdrawn from
unworthy recipients. The narrative *comparanda* are numerous—
tellingly (even disturbingly) so, in fact—and together lend
their weight to the traditional maxim that too much
prosperity too often proves "undigestible"—the metaphor is
Pindar's (cf. *Ol.* 1.55-57), but certainly not the idea—leading
mortals to usurp causality for what in fact always remains the
free gift of the gods.[6]

Any full exegesis of this fragment would first require some analysis and discussion of the syndrome of ὄλβος, κότος and ἄτη [prosperity—surfeit—self-destructive folly] in Greek thought. For it is chiefly this complex of affects—along with a number of more basic assumptions about human nature, in which these affects are grounded—that sketches the unspoken suppositions from which the tale of Thamyris gets its psychological and moral thrust. The terrain here has to a large extent already been mapped by prior scholarship,[7] and in any case it is not especially germane to the point of my study. Also required for a better grasp of his tale is some consideration of the notions that shape archaic Greek understanding of the nature and especially the source of poetic narratives. What does it mean that a tale is characterized as ἀοιδὴ θεσπεσίη? How does this characterization affect it in substance and form? How does it influence the dynamics of its reception? What precisely is the nature of this gift that the Muses can both give and withdraw, and what empowers them as donors? These issues are in fact much closer to my project, though I prefer to approach them along a somewhat oblique track.

What I propose to begin by addressing is whether it is at all significant that the tale of Thamyris is embedded in that section (*Il.* 2.591-602) of the *Catalogue of Ships* detailing the contingent that sailed under Nestor's leadership. At first glance, the reference seems no more than a piece of local history—and an apparently muddled one, at that—inserted in the *Catalogue* and motivated perhaps by the desire to celebrate now obscure traditions in which the bard's audience had some vested interest, if not by the felt need to cater to that interest.[8] In this respect alone it would resemble the legend of Erekhtheus in the list of the Athenian contingent at Troy (546-51); of the arrival of Tlepolemos at Rhodes, on the run after his murder of Likymnios (657-70); and of the battle between the "beast men" and Perithoös (740-44), the father of Polypoites, joint captain (along with Leonteus) of troops from eastern Thessaly. What distinguishes it from these other "digressions," however, is the fact that Thamyris stands in no clearly discernible relation to Nestor. This Thracian is an outlander, displaced, restless, far from his home, on the move between Thessaly and the southwestern Peloponnese—or else, alternately, between towns within the borders of Messenia itself.[9] In either case, nothing dynastic or genealogical associates him with the Gerenian horseman, nor is there even any less direct connection stated or implied, any vaguer mythic affiliation between the two figures. Mere topography seems to provide the link.

To be sure, contiguity in space may well suffice; it may simply be enough that Thamyris wandered into Nestor's neighborhood once and there met with considerably more than his match.[10] By this account, his link with Nestor is wholly accidental, possibly even the result of mere homonomy of place-names, thanks to which a false signpost or a strange bend in the narrative path somehow translates the traveller from Thessaly to Messenia. Whatever the case, such a detour would of course be extrinsic and so unrelated to both the origin and the destination of Thamyris and his story. In a move that seems to mirror the Thracian bard's own itinerary, the singer jogs a little off the track here, straying from his straighter course; and the catalogue of the old man's ships merely provides the site— simultaneously topographic and textual—for an *obiter* reference to his punishment. On this account, what we have here is just an aside, the narrative equivalent of some passing allusion, a stray remark made on the road.[11]

But as I have already suggested, places in texts occupy a very different kind of space than do places in the cartographer's world, and occupy them in very different ways. The assumption of a chance link—even granting, for argument's sake, its status as the product of now hopelessly conflated towns and tales—still leaves unaddressed, at very least, the issue of what significance the association of Thamyris and Nestor gains in the *Iliad* narrative once this connection is made. Painstaking archaeological finds, worn lumps of rock that were trophies once, citations from Pausanias and Strabo, tentative maps of vanished kingdoms, conflicting claims about Oikhalie may well help situate the legend in a kind of reclaimed archaic space, but they have little to say about its *textual* orientation and so too, at a deeper level, about the implicit assumptions that could justify its bearings. The link between Nestor and Thamyris raises questions of effect (if not also of intention) that cannot be answered adequately, if at all, by pointing out ruins in the modern Greek landscape. Presuppositions may well shift glacially, and far more slowly than topographic borders, but shift they do; and they are generally harder to retrace than lines in the dirt. The narrative space through which Thamyris moves and in which he incurs his punishment must instead be plotted by reference to other cardinal points; its bearings must be taken not from digs along the banks of "a spring called Achaia" (Simpson-Lazenby 1970:85), but instead from the excavation of a qualitatively unique kind of terrain. The landscape here is more properly a cultural or *epistemic* one, a space traversed by communal memory, a territory with landmarks fixed and boundaries drawn by traditional habits of practice and thought, and also by the expectations these habits engender.

What I would like to entertain in what follows is the chance that this link is not an arbitrary but instead a well motivated one, that more than physical topography brings Nestor and Thamyris together in the *Catalogue of Ships*. Specifically, I will argue that what structures their relation is the issue of authority in oral narrative traditions. This is an issue that is certainly neither indifferent nor incidental to a bard whose own claim to be heard and believed rests on an explicit appeal to the very Muses who are said to have maimed the Thracian. Thamyris' stupid arrogance clearly offers a negative paradigm, an *exemplum* implicitly pointing to what the proper relation between singer and divine source should be, and also to how narratives mean to be understood in "traditional" communities. The power of epic memory is purportedly a gift, not something over which mere mortals can claim any right of ownership, and its origin must always be respectfully acknowledged—as Homer himself has indeed just done some one hundred lines earlier (*Il.* 2.484-92), in the celebrated invocation preceding the *Catalogue*. What motivates the association of Thamyris with Nestor is the fact that the old man too in his own way embodies a connection to these issues and consequently moves through an analogous terrain. The road they share is no arbitrary one. At a level much deeper than physical maps represent, both figures chart contrasting models of how the problem of veracity in storytelling is addressed in Greek oral tradition.

2. A TYPOLOGY OF ELDERS

At first glance, two features serve to characterize Nestor in the Homeric poems, and even to characterize him uniquely: longevity and the command of persuasive speech. Not only is the venerable Pylian as much as two generations older than his associates at Troy (*Il*. 1.250-53; cf. *Od*. 3.245-46), but he is also the speaker whose counsel is most often styled "best" (ἀρίστη) in the *Iliad* (*Il*. 2.370-72; 7.324-25 = 9.93-94),[12] and whose advice—for better and sometimes for worse—most consistently earns the respect, approval and obedience of his fellow Akhaians. Agamemnon, not usually liberal with praise, wishes that he had ten men such as Nestor (*Il*. 3.371-74); others praise him (*Il*. 1.286, 8.146, *Od*. 3.331) for words that are always "right and fitting" (κατὰ μοῖραν); and posterity will even enshrine him as a paradigm of wisdom whose worth is a function of his age, an *exemplum* to which the later rhetorical tradition will appeal in order to show that years diminish physical strength but only strengthen the powers of the mind.[13] These two features are by no means peculiar to Nestor, however, but instead are common to the *type* of figure he represents within the narrative tradition that supports him. At issue here is the degree to which characterization in oral tales gets its bearings from certain generic and typological representations that are closely linked to the functions such characters play in the narrative.[14] The full weight of this issue will grow more apparent in the course of the following discussion.

The influence of generic types on how Nestor's character is formulated becomes clear if we consider the extent to which that formulation is controlled by the values that shape the moral horizon of the tales he inhabits.[15] Especially in the society of warrior elite in the *Iliad*, in which the highest premium is put on physical prowess, the weak either die ingloriously—the stuff of which others' *kleos* [fame] is made— or else they learn how to *talk*. What in fact traditionally distinguishes old men and women from young ones is the contrast between verbal skill and physical strength. Elder and Counselor are virtually isomorphic types, traversed and defined by the same set of attributes: Nestor himself, Priam, Phoinix and heralds like Periphas in the *Iliad*, along with

Aigyptios, Halitherses, Mentor, Ekheneos, Euryklea, Eurynome in the *Odyssey*—all are elderly, all affect things almost exclusively through their choice of words. Another token of the generic nature of their characterization is the fact that elderly figures are assigned their places in Homer's tales through reference to a relatively narrow constellation of roles, around which an equally well-defined cluster of traits tends to gravitate. The figures of Counselor, Herald, Prophet and Nurse are consistently formulated in terms of such predicates as memory, sorrow, rhetorical skill, sagacity, goodwill and circumspection. Nor is this conjunction an accidental one. Characters in traditional narratives essentially *are* what they *do*; their attributes and functions determine each other reciprocally.

The link between diminished capacity for action and increased capacity for speech of course in turn rests on the familiar contrast between *mythos* and *ergon* [word and deed] in the Homeric poems.[16] Moreover, the terms of this opposition are parallelled by the equally widespread antithesis of persuasion and force—*peitho* and *bia*—throughout Greek culture as a whole.[17] To be sure, the extent of this bare contrast should not be exaggerated, especially as it applies to Greek epic tradition. As Martin has reminded us, *mythos* and *ergon* need not always embody mutually exclusive values.[18] Heroic excellence in Homer instead ideally comprises the seamless unity of excellent action and excellent speech. The best warrior is the one who combines the power to fight effectively with the skill to persuade others by means other than sheer force. The aim of his education, as Phoinix reminds Akhilleus during the *Embassy* scene (*Il.* 9.440-43), is to excel in debate no less than in battle, hence "to be *both* a speaker of words and *also* a doer of deeds" (μύθων τε ῥητῆρ' ἔμεναι πρηκτῆρά τε ἔργων).

At the same time, the *mythos-ergon* contrast must not be scanted, either. The antithesis between physical strength and authoritative speech remains fundamental to the representation of elderly figures in Homer; it is the template on which their characters are formed. The power of this contrast in fact becomes clearest of all when it seems to be violated, namely in those cases in which young men like Poulydamas (*Il.* 18.249-53), Thoas (*Il.* 15.281-85) and Diomedes (*Il.* 9.53-59) enjoy effective command of speech. Here their ability always calls for explicit comment as something unexpected, out of the ordinary and thus truly exceptional. For that matter, precocious exhibition of rhetorical skill can even provoke suspicion and outright censure from other characters on the ground that it manifests cowardice, a predilection for *talk* when swift *action* seems called for instead. This is of course most evident in the highly formulaic tension that structures all interaction between Poulydamas and Hektor in the *Iliad*. The four scenes in which they are paired (*Il.* 12.60-81;210-50, 13.722-53, 18.249-313) indeed exhibit an interlocking pattern of sound advice offered by Hektor's Trojan "double" and either approved or rejected by the hero—in the last scene, to his ultimate demise.[19]

Thoas, the Aitolian fighter in *Iliad* 15, offers another case in point. Along with his prowess in war—ἐπιστάμενος μὲν ἄκοντι | ἐσθλὸς δ' ἐν σταδίῃ [skilled in the spear's throw and brave in close fight] (283-84)—his skills in debate are remarkable for one so young—ἀγορῇ δέ ἑ παῦροι Ἀχαιῶν | νίκων, ὁππότε κοῦροι ἐρίσσειαν περὶ μῦθον [In assembly few of the Akhaians could outdo him when the young men contended in debate] (284-85). The status he enjoys is in fact implicitly marked in an earlier passage (*Il.* 13.215-18), in which no less than Poseidon assumes his voice (#εἰσάμενος φθογγήν) to address Idomeneus and incite him to avenge the death of Imbrios.[20]

Similar features characterize the "good suitor" Amphinomos in the *Odyssey* (*Od.* 16.394-99). His way with words more than that of any other pleased Penelope, since his intentions (on the narrator's account) were the best: μάλιστα δὲ Πηνελοπείῃ | ἥνδανε μύθοισι, φρεσὶ γὰρ κέχρητ' ἀγαθῇσιν [and he pleased Penelope more than the others in talk, for he had good sense and discretion] (397-98). The end-line formula φρεσὶ γὰρ κέχρητ' ἀγαθῇσιν# is elsewhere used only of Klytaimestra before she yields to Aigisthos' seduction (*Od.* 3.266), and also of Eumaios (*Od.* 14.421), to describe his deep reverence for the gods. This explicit link between persuasive speech and the motives—goodwill, discretion, propriety, respect for traditional ways—that are attributed to the speaker by his audience is an important one. Insofar as these motives help delineate the *ethos* of the accomplished speaker in Homer, at the same time as they suggest the rhetorical strategies to which such a speaker frequently has recourse, they will demand attention at a later point (Chapter 3).

Despite these and similar instances in which young men exhibit an effective control over language, speech nonetheless remains the proper domain of the elderly. The close association between rhetoric and traditional values suggests as much, since the advice offered by aged figures more often than not amounts to conventional and often highly conservative wisdom; but even in rhetorical technique, the paradigm is still one set by old women and men. In this light—and especially as it expressly evokes the contrast between *mythos* and *ergon*—the way in which Nestor qualifies his praise of Diomedes in *Iliad* 9 is worth quoting in full. The young warrior has just finished chastising Agamemnon's cowardice in no uncertain terms, claiming that he and Sthenelos alone, if need be, would fight until Troy is finally brought down. His boast wins loud approval from the assembled Akhaians; and then Nestor rises to speak in turn (*Il.* 9.53f.; 56-59):

§2

Τυδεΐδη, περὶ μὲν πολέμῳ, ἔνι καρτερός ἐσσι
καὶ βουλῇ μετὰ πάντας ὁμήλικας ἔπλευ ἄριστος
        . . . ἀτὰρ οὐ τέλος ἵκεο μύθων.
ἦ μὲν καὶ νέος ἐσσί, ἐμὸς δέ κε καὶ πάϊς εἴης
ὁπλότατος γενεῆφιν· ἀτὰρ πεπνυμένα βάζεις
Ἀργείων βασιλῆας, ἐπεὶ κατὰ μοῖραν ἔειπες.

Son of Tydeus, beyond others you are strong in battle,
and in counsel also are noblest among all men of your own age.
    ... Yet you have not perfected your argument,
since you are a young man still and could even be my own son
and my youngest born of all; yet still you argue in wisdom
with the Argive kings, for you have spoken right and fittingly.

The specific terms of his qualification—in particular, the sense of the participle πεπνυμένα and the full range of the phrase κατὰ μοῖραν ἔειπες# [you have spoken properly]—will be examined in more detail shortly. Here it is enough to note that however closely Diomedes may come to realizing the ideal of being "both a speaker of words and a doer of deeds," his age apparently makes him a deficient rhetorician.[21] The kind of mastery needed in order to identify and reach the τέλος μύθων [perfection of an argument] instead more appropriately belongs to older men, next to whom even an accomplished warrior is at best like a son (παῖς)—and a youngest one at that. It is therefore unsurprising that Nestor is at no loss for words when it comes to finishing what Diomedes has only begun, and that he does so with "a simple proposal in elegant form" (Martin 1990:25) that wins the unanimous assent of his audience. Much the same implication informs Nestor's compliment to Telemakhos at Pylos: he could only be Odysseus' child, gifted early with the power of speech, for his words were all fitting (ἐοικότες), and otherwise οὐδέ κε φαίης | ἄνδρα νεώτερον ὧδε ἐοικότα μυθήσασθαι [no young man could talk as fittingly] (*Od.* 3.124-25). Menelaos remarks on precisely the same quality (*Od.* 4.204-05), and in much the same terms, after Peisistratos has spoken "just as a wise man would speak and do, *and one who was older*" (καὶ ὃς προγενέστερος εἴη#).

Rhetorical prowess is thus clearly a domain over which the elderly conventionally exercise control. Their exhibition of this trait accordingly often passes without special notice, for it is deemed natural to their character, and therefore central to their characterization. Once again, the values endorsed by a warrior elite go a long way towards explaining this conjunction of attributes, as well as the degree to which attribute and function work as correlative features. In a world in which a harsh but lucid economics of *kleos* prevails, enjoining the violent exchange of life here and now for brave death with everliving fame in the speech of the community, old people are either entirely peripheral to the main events—the superannuated Trojan elders who chirp like cicadas in the *Teikhoskopia* (*Il.* 3.146-53) come to mind as the extreme example of sweet but impotent speech—or else they influence them through speech alone. Given the limitations of their age, they can *do* no more than talk; and, more than any other type of character in the narrative, the elderly *are* as they *say*.

If the attribution of advanced age and command of speech is not an especially unique one, then, it still remains true that Nestor is the most conspicuous embodiment of these traits in the poems. Both in fact are represented in his person in almost exaggerated form, and to complementary degrees of exaggeration. To his extraordinary longevity—at least doubling that of his peers—corresponds his no less remarkable tendency to indulge in seemingly interminable talk, namely in an almost chronic logorrhea.[22] These characteristics are homologous. As a member of a group in which exceptional action in war wins undying glory in what others say, Nestor has clearly outlived his prime on this and any field of battle. All his strength has left him (*Il.* 8.103); never again will he fight with fists or wrestle, compete in spear-throwing or swiftness of feet (*Il.* 23.621-23), since his limbs are unsteady and his arms "no longer swing light" from his shoulders (626-28). His sole *aristeia* on the battlefield nearly ends in disaster, and would have cost him his life but for the timely intervention of Diomedes (*Il.* 8.78-112)—who in some respects figures as the image of Nestor as he claims to have been in his own vanished youth.[23]

On the one hand, the formulas used to describe him emphasize his diminished powers. To Nestor alone in the *Iliad* is the hemistich χαλεπὸν δέ σε γῆρας ὀπάζει# [hard old age attends you] (*Il.* 8.103) applied, along with its allomorph χαλεπὸν κατὰ γῆρας ἐπείγει# [hard old age presses you down] (*Il.* 23.623). In the earlier passage, Nestor's metaphorical bondage to age is even reflected in the concrete situation in which Diomedes finds him, stranded vulnerably on the field after his lead horse has fallen and tangled the reins of the chariot, throwing the whole team into confusion as a menacing Hektor bears down hard upon him. In the second, the phrase draws attention to the infirmities that prevent him from participating even in the somewhat more genteel competition of Patroklos' funeral games. An alternate version of the same formula—χαλεπὸν δ' ἐπὶ γῆρας ἱκάνει# [hard old age has come upon him]—appears once in the *Odyssey* (*Od.* 11.196), where it is used of the aged Laertes, who now lies down among slaves with tattered rags for cover, aching for his son's return. The related phrase χαλεπὸς δέ ἑ δεσμὸς ἐδάμνα# [hard bondage was breaking him] is found (*Il.* 5.391) with reference to the god Ares subdued by just as strong a necessity, bound to his death in the unbreakable chains of the giants Ephialtes and Otis.

The image of age (γῆρας) as an agent that binds figures also in Akhilleus' description (*Od.* 11.497) of the waning rule of his father Peleus, his authority spurned οὕνεκά μιν κατὰ γῆρας ἔχει χεῖράς τε πόδας τε [since age fetters him hand and foot] and himself now prey to unanswered outrage. The bondage to which age subjects the elderly, along with the pity—sometimes even a little contemptuous—in which they are often held by other members of society, is reflected in the epithets traditionally predicated of γῆρας. It is consistently a woeful (λυγρόν: *Il.* 5.153, 10.179, 18.434, 23.644; *Od.* 24.249-50), harsh (στυγερόν: *Il.* 19.336) and grievous (ὁλοόν: *Il.* 24.487) affliction that seizes (μάρπτειν: *Od.* 24.390) its prey, holds (ἔχειν: *Od.* 11.497), burdens (ὁπάζειν: *Il.* 4.321, 8.103) and wears (τείρειν: *Il.* 4.315, 24.233) them down ineluctably. Moreover, given the simple cruelty of a world in which only the strong can thrive, the powerlessness of the aged leaves them acutely vulnerable to hosts of other wrongs, chief among which are the outrages perpetrated by the arrogance of youth.[24] Age makes them victims of such scandals as the mistreatment that feeble Khryses suffers and may yet live to suffer at Agamemnon's hands (*Il.* 1.26-33), or the "meager life grieving in harsh old age" (τυτθὸν ἔτι ζώοντ' ἀκάχησθαι | γηραΐ τε στυγερῷ) that Akhilleus fears his father Peleus now endures in his mighty son's long absence (*Il.* 19.335-37)—already on the sorrowful threshold of age (ὁλοῷ ἐπὶ γήραος οὐδῷ#), encompassed and afflicted by enemies, defenseless against their threats (*Il.* 24.486-89).[25]

The logorrhea that matches Nestor's longevity is the focus of a later section of this chapter; at this point, it will be helpful to provide a brief sketch of other attributes involved in the formulation of elderly characters. The generic type of the Elder in fact comes to expression through a constellation of predicates that include, among other things, a broader than average depth and range of knowledge, along with the capacity for what can be called circumspection or prudence.

Old Halitherses (*Od.* 2.188), Ekheneos (*Od.* 7.157) and Nestor himself (*Od.* 24.51) are all qualified by the closing hemistich παλαιά τε πολλά τε εἰδώς# [knowing many ancient things]. Although based on the ubiquitous endline formula — u u εἰδώς#, the phrase as such appears nowhere else in either poem; but πάλαι πολέμων ἐῢ εἰδώς# [wise in fighting from of old], used with reference to Nestor (*Il.* 4.310), should also be noted. Moreover, the formula adverting to the trait of circumspection—ὁ γὰρ οἶος ὅρα πρόσσω καὶ ὀπίσσω# [who alone looked both ahead and behind]—is used only with reference to Halitherses (*Od.* 24.452) and the Trojan Poulydamas (*Il.* 18.250); the latter's enjoyment of traits well in advance of his years has already been mentioned. An enjambed line with the same formula also characterizes Halitherses in the *Odyssey* (*Od.* 2.158-59): Μαστορίδης· ὁ γὰρ οἶος ὁμιλικίην ἐκέκαστο | ὄρνιθας γνῶναι [Mastor's son, for he alone of his generation knew the meaning of birdflight]. Finally, a slightly different version of the line in one instance (*Il.* 1.343) denies precisely this capacity to Agamemnon (οὐδέ τι οἶδε νοῆσαι ἅμα πρόσσω καὶ ὀπίσσω [and has not wit enough to look before and behind]). In the other, it serves to represent Priam as an exemplary elder, explicitly contrasting his prudence with the impetuousness of youth. These lines have a distinctly gnomic ring (*Il.* 3.108-10):

§3

αἰεὶ δ' ὁπλοτέρων ἀνδρῶν φρένες ἠερέθονται·
οἶς δ' ὁ γέρων μετέῃσιν, ἅμα πρόσσω καὶ ὀπίσσω
λεύσσει, ὅπως ὄχ' ἄριστα μετ' ἀμφοτέροισι γένηται.

The minds of younger men are always frivolous,
but when an elder is among them, he looks behind him
and in front, so that all comes out far better for both sides.

The intersection of the traits of rhetorical prowess and advanced age in the figure of the herald (*kêryx*) should be noted. Of the eighty-eight instances of the noun in its various inflections, only one-fifth exhibit adjectival or clausal modification. This ranges from simple epithets—most of which survive as *hapax legomena*—such as λιγυφθόγγοισι [clear-voiced] (5X), ἀγαυοί# [splendid] (2X), ἀστυβοώτην# [calling throughout the city], ἠπύτα [loud] and ἠεροφώνων# [raising the voice], to clauses like Διὸς ἄγγελοι ἠδὲ καὶ ἀνδρῶν# [messengers of gods and men] (2X) or οἳ δημιοεργοὶ ἔασιν# [who serve the *dêmos*] (2X).[26] The largest group of modifiers—to which must be added a few

additional instances in which the noun is replaced by the
herald's proper name—seems to cluster around the trait of
"sagacity" or "soundness of mind" that comes to expression
uniquely in formulas built upon the participle πεπνυμεν-:[27]

§4

A	. . .πεπνυμένω ἄμφω#	(2X)
B	. . .πεπνυμένα εἰδώς#	(4X, of Medon)
C	. . .πεπνυμένα μήδεα εἰδώς#	(2X)
D	. . .φίλα φρεσὶ μήδεα εἰδώς#	(1X)
and cf. E	. . .πυκινὰ φρεσὶ μήδε' ἔχοντες#	(2X)

The last example in this series (E) is used on both occasions
of Priam and his aged *kêryx*, and should be compared with the
allomorph ἔστι δέ μοι γρῆϋς πυκινὰ φρεσὶ μήδε'
ἔχουσα [I have an old woman, whose thoughts are prudent]
(*Od.* 19.353), spoken with reference Eurykleia, Odysseus' old
nurse. The "wisdom" or "compactness of mind" that
characterizes the herald is indeed a trait most often associated
with maturity; compare the midline formula πυκινὸν ἔπος
[sound word] used only of Priam (*Il.* 7.375), Nestor (*Il.* 11.787)
and Zeus (*Il.* 24.74), and once (*Il.* 24.744) of Hektor by
Andromakhe.[28] The advanced age of the herald—or of the best
kind of herald—is in fact an abiding characteristic of the type.
For his mission to Akhilleus in *Iliad* 24, Priam chooses Idaios
as his charioteer. The *kêryx* is twice described (*Il.* 24.282;674),
along with Priam, by the E-formula; and he is characterized
earlier by formulas A (*Il.* 7.276) and C (*Il.* 7.278). His age is
emphasized in the virtually identical lines #κῆρυξ τίς οἱ
ἕποιτο γεραίτερος [Let some elder herald attend him] (*Il.*
24.149;178), and also in Hermes' comment οὔτ' αὐτὸς νέος
ἐσσί, γέρων δέ τοι οὗτος ὁπηδεῖ [You are not young
yourself, and he who attends you is aged] later in the same book
(368).

In a passage striking for its *hapax legomena*—whose
details contribute much to the Beggar's credibility—the
disguised Odysseus describes the herald Eurybates as κῆρύξ
ὀλίγον προγενέστερος αὐτοῦ [a herald, a little older
than he was] (*Od.* 19.244). Elsewhere, the adjective

προγενέστερος (7X) is restricted to the description of figures such as Nestor (*Il.* 2.555, 9.161) and the Phaiakian Ekheneos (*Od.* 7.156, [11.342]). The Eurybates passage (*Od.* 19.248) also associates age with the trait of sound-mindedness—οἱ φρεσὶν ἄρτια ᾔδη# [his thoughts were sensible]—in a formula directly echoed in the phrase φρεσὶν ἄρτια βάζειν# used by Alkinoos of the sensible man (*Od.* 8.240). Closely related in turn, and to come full circle, is the use of the phrase πεπνυμένα βάζεις# in Menelaos' compliment to Nestor's son Peisistratos (*Od.* 4.204-06)—

§5

> ὦ φίλ', ἐπεὶ τόσα εἶπες ὅσ' ἂν πεπνυμένος ἀνὴρ
> εἴποι καὶ ῥέξειε, καὶ ὃς προγενέστερος εἴη·
> τοίου γὰρ καὶ πατρός, ὅ καὶ πεπνυμένα βάζεις

> Friend, since you have said all that a man who is thoughtful
> could say or do, even one who was older than you are—
> for this is the way your father is; so you too speak thoughtfully.

—as well as in Nestor's praise of Diomedes (πεπνυμένα βάζεις#) in the lines quoted earlier from *Iliad* 9 (§2). To these may finally be added the description of Periphas, Ankhises' herald, whom Apollo impersonates to encourage the terrified Aineias in Book 17 (*Il.* 17.322-25):

§6

> . . .ἀλλ' αὐτὸς Ἀπόλλων
> Αἰνείαν ὄτρυνε, δέμας Περίφαντι ἐοικώς,
> κήρυκι Ἠπυτίδη, ὅς οἱ παρὰ πατρὶ γέροντι
> κηρύσσων γήρασκε, φίλα φρεσὶ μήδεα εἰδώς.

> . . . but Apollo himself
> stirred on Aineias, assuming the form of the herald
> Periphas, Epytos' son, who grew old in his herald's office
> by his aged father, and a man whose thoughts were of kindness.

Almost dreamlike, through a kind of condensation of *personae*, the son ages gradually into the figure of his father. This image succinctly nests the herald in an associative web of old age, paternity and the closely related trait of goodwill. The clustering of these attributes, along with the others

mentioned above, defines the ethical terms within whose
contours elderly figures take their shape in Homer. Despite
implicit generational tensions, elders occupy a space ideally
marked by its calmness of heart and gentle motives, a space of
prudent counsel elegantly phrased, a space that—unlike the
harshly lit field of battle, where young warriors strive for
sudden glory from the flash of a spear—shades off at its edges,
blurring present with past, immediacy with circumspection,
and action (*ergon*) with memory that comes to expression in the
word (*mythos*).

3. NAME AND CHARACTER

In Nestor's case, the link between longevity and command
of rhetoric is thematic in the lines used to describe him when
he first appears in the *Iliad* (*Il*. 1.247-49). The individual
elements of his characterization warrant close analysis. Its
final aim is to identify a cluster of shared qualities, an
associative set of traits predicated of Nestor in the narrative
tradition out of which the Homeric poems arise. Before this can
be undertaken, however, a few methodological assumptions
first need to be addressed.

Let me take as my point of departure a modern discussion of
how character or *ethos* is constructed in narratives.[29] In this
context, Roland Barthes (1974:190-91) makes an observation
that is perhaps even more valid for oral texts than for the text
of Balzac's *Sarrasine*, which inspires his comment:

> Character is an adjective, an attribute, a predicate (for example:
> *unnatural, shadowy, star, composite, excessive, impious*, etc.).
> Even though the connotation may be clear, the nomination of its
> signified is uncertain, approximate, unstable: to fasten a name to
> this signified depends in large part on the critical pertinence to
> which we adhere: the seme is only a *departure*, an avenue of
> meaning. . . . [W]hat is constant is that the seme is linked to an
> ideology of the person (to inventory the semes in a classic text is
> therefore merely to observe this ideology): the person is no more
> than a collection of semes. . . . What gives the illusion that the
> sum [of traits predicated of a character] is supplemented by a
> precious remainder (something like *individuality*, in that,
> qualitative and ineffable, it may escape the vulgar bookkeeping
> of compositional characters) is the Proper Name, the difference
> completed by what is *proper* to it. The proper name enables the

person to exist outside the semes, whose sum nonetheless constitutes it entirely. As soon as a Name exists (even a pronoun) to flow toward and fasten onto, the semes become predicates, inductors of truth, and the Name becomes a subject.

On this account, the substantiality enjoyed by characters in stories—their "roundedness," as we say, their "depth" or overall "weight"—is largely the result of habitual inferences we make from the shadow cast by the clusters of "semes" to which their Proper Names are attached. Someone is *prudent* or *sly*, *swift-footed* or *honey-tongued*. In their specificity, such adjectives offer a description that supplies content for an otherwise "empty" name; it gives connotative value or *sense* to supplement the mere denotation or *reference* that the name alone provides.[30] This of course excludes those names which themselves incorporate some descriptive element, ranging from so-called "speaking names" (*Redende Namen*), such as "Elpenor" and "Kalypso," to the generic and functional names (Sleeping Beauty, The Witch) of many folktale characters. Strictly speaking, the "person" or character is "entirely constituted" by the descriptive predicates that make it up; it is in sum "no more than a collection of semes." Despite our strong temptation (in narrative as perhaps elsewhere) to privilege the Subject as a primary thing to which qualities somehow accrue secondarily—a temptation as old at least as Aristotle's ontology of substance—*ethos* might thus be better understood as little more than a nesting of adjectives. Apart from being a sublime essence somehow ineffable and qualitatively distinct from the events that swirl around, impinge upon and flow from it, a character may instead be simply the dimensionless point at which certain attributes converge, something created at the site and also by the fact of their intersection.

I would argue that what contributes the most to lend characters what Barthes calls the "illusion" of individuality is that these attributes are indices of narrative potential.[31] Someone is *prudent* or *sly*, *swift-footed* or *honey-tongued*. These are not "static" predicates, fixed pegs onto which a Proper Name can be hung; instead, they are dynamic tokens. Each adjective promotes the possibility and therefore engenders the expectation of a certain kind of action. *Sly is as sly does.* The attribute creates a "personality" for the name by hinting at a history of prior actions that have coalesced into a distinct *ethos* marked by this epithet. Moreover, such a history also now implicitly motivates the character's subsequent actions. It is precisely because it is emblematic of a past that the attribute can additionally promise a certain kind of future for its character. This is because it traces the arc of a probable or "characteristic" narrative, plots "an avenue of meaning," and thus *a fortiori* suggests the presence of a unique and self-consistent agent at its point of origin—a suggestion legitimized by the *imprimatur* of a Proper Name.

The value Barthes' insight lends to an appreciation of Homeric names and characters should be clear. This is especially so in light of claims made about the connotational, metonymic or *anaphoric* depth perceived as the benchmark of traditional oral poetry. Foley is both the most recent and also the most lucid scholar to address this issue. He introduces it by contrasting modern literary works, in which "an author (not a tradition) *confers* meaning on his or her creation," with traditional ones, where meaning is largely inherited or *inherent* (1991:9-10):[32]

> . . . a traditional work depends primarily on elements and strategies that were in place long before the execution of the present version or text, long before the present nominal author learned the inherited craft. Because the idiom is metonymic, summoning conventional connotations to conventional structures, we may say that the meaning it conveys is principally *inherent*. . . . If the oral traditional equivalent of the textual echo characteristic of a literary work is the text-to-tradition reverberation legislated by metonymy, then we can also describe inherent meaning as the fulfillment of a figure of anaphora. . . . When we "read" any traditional performance or text with attention to the inherent meaning it necessarily summons, we are, in effect, recontextualizing that work, reaffirming contiguity with other performances or texts, or, better, with the ever-immanent tradition itself . . .

It is through traditional anaphora that each performance of a story stands related as figure to the background defined by every prior telling. Though every performance produces a uniquely different tale, its narration is always situated and orients itself within this common narrative space. The tale that evolves in the course of a single telling is thus interwoven with a tacit narrative whole of which it forms only a part.[33] To return to an issue raised earlier, it is a radically *intertextual* thing, in the sense that much of its meaning comes to it not from within its own textual parameters but instead extrinsically, from the absent narratives to which it implicitly refers. This absence is by no means absolute, of course, since these prior narratives are held fast in the shared and regulative memories of bard and audience—as the singer of many such tales before, and as the listeners to whom many such tales have already been sung—and as such they are always subject to allusive or even to full evocation.

This shared narrative space is much like a communal map in whose terms both audience and teller can plot their bearings *vis-à-vis* the tale. Within such a space, moreover, traditional phraseology clearly enjoys rich connotative value.[34] At virtually all levels—colon, phrase, scene, narrative motif— the storyteller works with, and the audience responds to, material that is ready at hand and already charged with conventional meanings. Even the barest formulaic gesture on a singer's part can suffice to evoke for his listeners a plethora of specific associations shaped by other, earlier performances in which that same formula was spoken—and spoken perhaps with more explicit motivation—or in which an identical narrative pattern was engaged. Hence the primacy of anaphora and allusion in oral texts, as keys to interpretation no less than as compositional principles. For if the text from which a traditional expression gets its full sense is not simply or even chiefly the particular text that arises in the course of a single telling, but rather the traditional narrative *context* in which that performance evolves, the formula becomes a privileged site of meaning. I mean this not just in a "soft" sense, according to which *any* use of traditional language in *any* text whatsoever always resonates with a kind of archaic tonality, thus evoking a special sanction for what it says now from what seems to have been said since the beginning of storied time. Even Parry himself was willing to grant this much—what could be called a "chromatic" significance—to the fixed or "ornamental" epithet, acknowledging that it "adds to the combination of substantive and epithet an element of nobility and grandeur, but no more than that."[35] Romantic and New Critical interpretations of Homer incidentally win something of a toehold here, at least to the extent that Parry's admission allows room for talk, often vague, of the so-called "poetic effect" of formulas.[36]

Far from exhibiting merely chromatic tonalities, formulaic expressions instead resonate back through specific traditions of

storytelling. The "swift feet" (πόδας ὠκύς) of Akhilleus, for
instance, have "existential weight" precisely because they
have already run other narrative paths before, and as a result
embody the potential for running them again. However
incongruent the epithet may sometimes appear in the text of
one performance or another—as when "Homer *nods*," as they
say, and "swift" Akhilleus *sleeps*—it may in fact tacitly evoke
other narrative contexts in which it had better motivation,
namely in which the grounds for its predication were more
explicit, in which swiftness was essential to the tale that
formulates his heroic identity.[37] The formula would thus
indeed function as a kind of mnemonic, but not just in the sense of
a technical aid to help a singer fill the metrical pattern of a
line after one or another caesural break. Instead, it would
enable the singer *and also the audience* to develop a character
more fully by filling it out with the flesh of that character's
prior narrative history, invoking a potential implicit in each
individual telling. The "semes" or predicates that converge to
formulate *ethos* in oral tales are thus privileged vehicles of
tradition, each rich with anaphora, suggesting "avenues of
meaning" along which the character can be expected to travel.
To ignore this is to consign them to a merely metrical role, from
which the only escape route leads mapless into a foggy marsh
of "poetic effect."

To be sure, the range of formulaic anaphora is not limited
solely or even principally to the evocation of specific narrative
events. Anaphora also and more fundamentally incorporates
reference to the network of implicit associations and judgements
on whose basis a community's values are structured, and
through which they are maintained over time. Narratives are
indeed privileged vehicles for articulating and transmitting
how "traditional" societies in particular understand their
world, as well as how they deem it proper to act on the basis of
this understanding. In this respect, the metonymy that gives
formulaic expressions their depth of meaning is just one instance
of a far more extensive anaphoric work. That work, as I
suggested earlier, is at one and the same time *epistemic* and
ideological. By gesturing in certain moral directions—
associating swiftness to act (say) with rashness, and by
contrasting it with a success that results from taking time to
deliberate over options—certain kinds of conventional

behavior are implicitly valorized at the expense of others. The antagonism between Hektor and Poulydamas is of course a prime instance of this specific conflict of practical values, as Chapter 3 will show. At an even deeper level, the formulaic linking of certain predicates with certain generic characters in narrative—action with youth, talk with the elderly—helps reinforce and canonize a rough ethical typology to which the community in general subscribes, and whose confirmation it expects from the stories it hears. And by retraversing, at a lower level still, the basic associations between things that the group experiences as somehow "naturally" related—the human voice with sweetness, for instance, or else (to compound similes) with the flow of sweet water or wine—narratives etch those metaphors, along with the values they support, even more deeply in communal memory and practice. It is at this deeper, anaphoric level that the attributes that constitute Nestor's proper name must now be considered.

4. NAMING NESTOR

Let me return to the lines with which Nestor is first introduced in the *Iliad*. Akhilleus has just answered Agamemnon threat for threat, and dashes the scepter to the ground (*Il.* 1.247-52):

§7

           τοῖσι δὲ Νέστωρ
ἡδυεπὴς ἀνόρουσε, λιγὺς Πυλίων ἀγορητής,
τοῦ καὶ ἀπὸ γλώσσης μέλιτος γλυκίων ῥέεν αὐδή·
τῷ δ' ἤδη δύο μὲν γενεαὶ μερόπων ἀνθρώπων
ἐφθίαθ', οἵ οἱ πρόσθεν ἅμα τράφεν ἠδ' ἐγένοντο
ἐν Πύλῳ ἠγαθέῃ, μετὰ δὲ τριτάτοισιν ἄνασσεν.

             ... and between them Nestor
the sweet-spoken rose up, lucid speaker of Pylos,
from whose lips the voice flowed sweeter than honey.
In his time two generations of mortals had already died—
those who had before grown up with him, and the ones born to
    them
in sacred Pylos—and he was ruling among the third.

   This cluster of epithets in the old man's characterization
needs to be unpicked, as it were, the better to appreciate the
range of connotation each may enjoy. To begin with, it is
important to note the resonance of the adjective ἡδυεπής
[sweet-speaking] in the epic tradition. For although a *hapax* in
Homer, it is taken up and repeated in the *Hymns* with explicit
reference to the Muses (*Hym.* 32.2)—Μοῦσαι, | ἡδυεπεῖς
κοῦραι Κρονίδεω Διός, ἵστορες ᾠδῆς [Muses, *sweet-
speaking* daughters of Kronian Zeus, adepts of song]—and the
singer himself (*Hym.* 21.4)—<sc. ἀοιδὸς> ἡδυεπὴς
πρῶτόν τε καὶ ὕστατον αἰὲν ἀείδει [(the) *sweet-
speaking* (bard) always sings (of you) first and last]. Neither of
these citations is idiosyncratic to the *Hymns*, but instead both
are guided by the same traditional associations. What tends to
confirm this is their formulaic rigor. In all three cases, the
epithet occupies the same line-initial position; and in the case
of both Nestor and the Muses in *Hymn* 32, ἡδυεπής appears at
the beginning of a line that is enjambed with the line in which
proper name to which it refers is mentioned. The link between
"sweet" speech and poetry will emerge as an abiding theme in
what follows.
   As a predicate, the sweetness to which the first element in
the compound ἡδυ-επής refers has a broad connotative range
in Homer. In a great number of the occurrences of the adjective
ἡδύς, including the compound ἡδύποτος [sweet-tasting] (*Od.*
2.340, 3.391, 14.507), the adjective is predicated of wine
(οἶνος)—the releaser from troubles, the bringer of joy—and
also of sleep (ὕπνος), whose own sweetness is likewise
formulaic (*Il.* 1.610, 2.71, 10.4, 23.232, *Od.* 5.472, 7.289, 9.333,
18.149, 19.49). The suggestion here is that whatever is sweet is
at least potentially also intoxicating, and at the outer limit of
the rapture it brings is an oblivion for which sleep may serve as
an apt metaphor. More obviously relevant to the
characterization of Nestor's voice as ἡδυεπής is the fact that
on nine occasions "sweet" also describes the sound of laughter—
most often (*Il.* 2.270, 11.378, 21.508, 23.784, *Od.* 20.358, 21.376) in
the formula ἡδὺ γέλασσα-# [sweetly laughing], three times
(*Od.* 16.354, 18.35;111) with the adverb in line-initial position.
In none of these cases is the laughter at issue represented as

derisive; instead, it is disarming: it lulls suspicion and encourages trust.

The hemistich λιγὺς Πυλίων ἀγορητής# [lucid speaker of Pylos] is repeated once elsewhere (Il. 4.293), when Nestor calls his troops to order. Its covariant formula, λιγύς περ ἐὼν ἀγορητής# [although a lucid speaker], appears on three occasions (Il. 2.246, 19.82, Od. 20.274); here the sense is concessive, and its contrast with the phrase used of Nestor is an interesting one. These versions all occur in direct speech, not in the narrative portion of the text, and advert to a speaker's *failure* to command the attention or respect of his audience. In *Iliad* 19, Agamemnon acknowledges the difficulty faced by even the best orator when confronted by an unruly crowd— ἀνδρῶν δ' ἐν πολλῷ ὁμάδῳ πῶς κέν τις ἀκούσαι | ἢ εἴποι; βλάβεται δὲ λιγύς περ ἐὼν ἀγορητής [How in the great murmuring of men could anyone listen or even speak? Even a lucid speaker is baffled.] (Il. 19.81-82). This is by way of a preface to his public apology to Akhilleus, whose own speech has just won the loud approval of the mustered troops. In the *Odyssey* passage, its tone is sarcastic: Antinoos taunts Telemakhos and threatens to shut his mouth permanently, "lucid speaker" that he is. Equally biting is its use by Odysseus in *Iliad* 2 to refer to Thersites, whose role in the narrative is precisely the opposite of Nestor's.[38] To Nestor alone is the epithet applied without any semblance of irony.[39]

In turn, the range of the adjective λιγύς [lucid], either alone or else in its various compounds (λιγύφθογγος, λιγύφωνος), is an extensive and at first glance even a heterogeneous one. It comprises reference to the sound of whip (1X) and wind (6X), birdsong (2X) and the chirping of cicadas (1X), shrill weeping (5X), the song of Sirens (1X) and Muses (1X), the lyre's piercing tone (7X) and the clear voice of heralds (6X).[40] The underlying basis for these uses seems to be the high pitch and amplitude of certain sounds. Clear or "lucid" describes the noise that pierces, the voice that carries far to penetrate the ear and to command attention. Moreover, in the case of cicadas, birds, Sirens (themselves birdlike), Muses, mourners, heralds and lyres, it also designates a pitch of sound that Greek culture seems to have found aesthetically pleasing and even seductive.[41] The association of pleasure with weeping

and the dirge may seem anomalous in this group, until it is
remembered how much less tentative Homeric culture is than
ours in acknowledging the genuine satisfaction that comes from
public expression of sorrow. Grief is no less sustenance than food
or drink, and as such no less fully enjoyed, as the formulaic
responsion between dining and lamentation clearly suggests.
With a line such as αὐτὰρ ἐπεὶ τάρπημεν ἐδητύος ἠδὲ
ποτῆτος [Now when we had taken our pleasure of eating and
drinking] (Il. 11.780; Od. 5.201) compare, for example, both
αὐτὰρ ἐπεὶ ῥα γόοιο τετάρπετο δῖος 'Αχιλλεύς | καί
οἱ ἀπὸ πραπίδων ἦλθ' ἵμερος ἠδ' ἀπὸ γυίων [When
brilliant Akhilleus had taken his pleasure of sorrow and the
passion for it had left his mind and body] (Il. 24.513), and ἡ δ'
ἐπεὶ οὖν τάρφθη πολυδακρύτοιο γόοιο [But when she
had taken her pleasure of tear-filled sorrow] (Od. 19.213;251,
21.57).[42] A similar need is apparently fulfilled in both cases.

   The specifically aesthetic pleasure produced by things
qualified as λιγύς deserves further comment; the term's
reference to (human or divine) voice and music in fact amounts
to well over three-quarters of its uses. Speakers such as Nestor
(2X), Menelaos (Il. 3.214) and heralds in general—often in the
colon κηρύκεσσι λιγυφθόγγοισι—account for twelve of its
occurrences; twice it modifies the song of Sirens (Od. 12.44) and
Muses (Od. 24.62), respectively; and seven instances describe
the lyre. Its use with the formix or lyre shows the highest
degree of regularity, appearing always in the endline formula
φόρμιγγι λιγείῃ# (Il. 9.186, 18.569, Od. 4.254) or, with
change of case, φόρμιγγα λίγειαν# (Od. 8.261;537, 22.332,
23.133). The reference to the Muse in Odyssey 24 combines
keening with poetic song, since the passage recounts the divine
threnody heard by the Akhaians at the funeral of Akhilleus
(Od. 24.60-61), and so once again raises the issue of the pleasure
produced by the transmutation of grief into ritual utterance.
The attribution of λιγυρὴ ἀοιδή [lucid song] to the deadly
Sirens in Book 12 of the same poem is an interesting one; as
others have pointed out, the terms in which they are described
are precisely those elsewhere reserved for the Muses
themselves.[43]

   In this context, the characterization of the speech of the
Trojan elders (δημογέροντες) in the Teikhoskopia (Il.

3.146-53) is especially noteworthy. Even old men who do
nothing but sit at the Skaian Gates to watch the lovely Helen
pass, to watch troops passing on the plain below, to witness the
passing of empire, enjoy a distinct voice in Homer. What they
say is well known: they exonerate her beauty, along with any
man's desire to kill for it, but also recognize the worthless grief
(πῆμα) such beauty visits on the innocent. Old Priam himself,
in the lines that immediately follow (164-65), is no less quick to
absolve her. But less attention has been paid to *how* these
elders speak their mind or, better, to how they give it *voice*.
Too old now to fight in defense of Ilion, they are nonetheless
"excellent speakers" still—γήραϊ δὴ πολέμοιο
πεπαυμένοι, ἀλλ' ἀγορηταὶ | ἐσθλοί—just "like cicadas
(τεττίγεσσιν ἐοικότες) who throughout the forest settle
in trees and send forth their delicate voice" (δενδρέῳ
ἐφεζόμενοι ὄπα λειριόεσσαν ἱεῖσι).[44] Hesiod's
description of the insect in *Works and Days*—καὶ ἠχέτα
τέττιξ | δενδρέῳ ἐφεζόμενος λιγυρὴν καταχεύετ'
ἀοιδήν [and the chirping cicada settles in a tree and pours
down its clear song] (*Erga* 582-83)—is obviously modelled
either on this passage or else on some template common to both;
compare also the lines in *The Shield* (*Aspis* 393f.), where the
echoing cicada "perches on a green shoot to begin singing
summer to men" (ἠχέτα τέττιξ | ὄζῳ ἐφεζόμενος θέρος
ἀνθρώποισιν ἀείδειν | ἄρχεται).[45] The Trojan Elders'
characterization is therefore a point at which three
metaphorical streams—old age, lucid speech and poetry—all
intersect. Their physical prowess has withered along with
their bodies. They are mere wasted husks of men, unfit for the
rigors of war; but what compensates for this loss is their ability
to bring pleasure by means of the finer, sublimated body of their
voices. In fact, in the extremity of their years they may even
approach a kind of immortality, at least to the degree to
which Greek myth associates the cicada with the endless flow
of song, as if with a kind of divine logorrhea.[46] Moreover, the
terms in which that song is formulated (ὄπα λειριόεσσαν,
λιγυρὴν ἀοιδήν, ἀείδειν) are precisely those elsewhere
reserved for the description of poetic utterance. For Plato (cf.
Phaedr. 262d), of course, cicadas are οἱ τῶν Μουσῶν

προφῆται [the Muses' prophets]—by which this link is further strengthened; he also exploits the analogy between cicadas and Sirens (*Phaedr*. 257e7), which makes the link potentially all the more troubling.[47]

One might in fact be tempted to propose an implicit, "epistemic" structure that controls their representation. In such a schema, the Elders—Panthoös and Thymoites, Lampos and Klytios, Hiketaon, Agenor and Oukalegon (*Il*. 3.146-48)—would occupy one extreme of a continuum drawn by reference to the traditional contrast between *mythos* and *ergon*, word and deed. Their time for action is now long past, and virtually all that remains of them is "the seductive pleasure of language stripped down to a mantra's hum" (Ferrari 1987:28). At the other extreme is the nameless, babbling infant (νήπιος) cradled in its parent's arms (*Od*. 19.530)—the weak, humanlike but still somewhat less than human creature not yet endowed with mastery of speech or thought (cf. χαλίφρων [slack-minded] at *Od*. 4.371) or even a name to give to its desire. To the extent to which feebleness characterizes both Elder and Infant, this continuum might in fact more closely resemble an arc that verges on closure, as elderly speech slurs its articulation, passing gradually—first senescent, then senile—back into the sweet but meaningless liquid burble of the child. At the arc's apogee stands the idealized figure of the hero, combining excellent action and excellent speech in a seamless unity, thus fulfilling the aim (*Il*. 9.443) "to be both a speaker of words and a doer of deeds." And roughly midway between this heroic ideal and the Trojan Elders—halfway between the harsh battlefield light and the gathering shade at the Skaian Gates—would be the place occupied by ancient, "sweet-speaking" Nestor, whose words flow like honey.

The sweet pleasure of the old man's voice also figures in the formulaic claim τοῦ καὶ ἀπὸ γλώσσης μέλιτος γλυκίων ῥέεν αὐδή [from whose lips the voice flowed sweeter than honey] (*Il*. 1.249). This line as such is unique in Homer, though it finds an echo in the *Hymn to the Muses and Apollo* (*Hym*. 25.5), in the reference to whomever the Muses love, "from whose mouth the voice flows sweet" (γλυκερή οἱ ἀπὸ στόματος ῥέεν αὐδή#). Hesiod attributes the flow of honeyed voice from the mouth of kings to the fact that the

Muses honor and anoint them with "sweet dew," in a passage that links the persuasiveness of political rhetoric to expressly poetic origins (*Thg.* 81-84):[48]

§8

ὅν τινα τιμήσωσι Διὸς κοῦραι μεγάλοιο
γεινόμενόν τε ἴδωσι διοτρεφέων βασιλήων,
τῷ μὲν ἐπὶ γλώσσῃ γλυκερὴν χείουσιν ἐέρσην,
του δ' ἔπε' ἐκ στόματος ῥεῖ μείλιχα. . .

When the daughters of great Zeus see the birth
of one the gods will nourish to be king,
they pour sweet dew upon his tongue,
and from his mouth the sweet words flow. . .

The association of Nestor's own voice with honey (μέλι, adj. μελιηδής)—to which wine, food, life and sleep are also compared—recalls yet another, more direct connection between his speech and poetic utterance, since the voice of the Sirens themselves enjoys the same qualification. The deadly creatures lure Odysseus by claiming (*Od.* 12.187) that no travelers leave their isle "before hearing the honeyed voice from our mouths" (πρὶν γ' ἡμέων μελίγηρυν ἀπὸ στομάτων ὄπ' ἀκοῦσαι). Honey as a metaphor for poetry of course frequently recurs as a trope in the later Greek tradition.[49]

I will return to the Sirens shortly, but turn now to the comparison in the statement τοῦ καὶ ἀπὸ γλώσσης μέλιτος γλυκίων ῥέεν αὐδή [from whose lips the voice flowed sweeter than honey]. Within Homer, this line bears the closest formulaic resemblance, even if its content may at first seem unrelated, to a pair of lines that both refer to the incomparable sweetness of certain passions. In a passage from *Iliad* 2, repeated nine books later (*Il.* 2.452-54 = 11.12-14) with Eris as the agent, Athene moves swiftly among the Akhaian host, putting strength into each man's heart to fight without respite. As a result of her activity (*Il.* 2.453-54):

§9

τοῖσι δ' ἄφαρ πόλεμος γλυκίων γένετ' ἠὲ νέεσθαι
ἐν νηυσὶ γλαφυρῇσι φίλην ἐς πατρίδα γαῖαν.

Now battle became sweeter to them than to sail
in hollow ships to the dear land of their fathers.

A certain irony rounds this passage off, for it precedes the
famous *Catalogue* of men who left that land in ships to wage
sweet war at Troy, and directly follows the nearly disastrous
Peira of Agamemnon, whose immediate effect was to send the
troops running back to their ships to set sail again, this time in
pursuit of a "homecoming beyond fate" (*Il.* 2.155: ὑπέρμορα
νόστος). The second passage—with μέλιτος in the same
metrical position, though its order in relation to γλυκίων
inverted—occurs in the course of Akhilleus' bitter rejection of
the anger (χόλος) that precipitated the death of his friend.
May strife vanish from among gods and men, he says (*Il.* 18.106-
08), and especially anger (109-10):[50]

§10
   ὅς τε πολὺ γλυκίων μέλιτος καταλειβομένοιο
   ἀνδρῶν ἐν στήθεσσιν ἀέξεται ἠύτε καπνός.

... which far sweeter than honey dripping down
swells like smoke in the hearts of men.

These passages appear to have little bearing on the voice
that "sweeter than honey" flows from Nestor's mouth; and in
fact, closer parallels than these do exist. What is significant
about them, however, is the explicit link both make between
pleasure and forgetfulness of aim. Sweet lust for battle banishes
all thought of *nostos* in men who only a few hundred lines
earlier (*Il.* 2.142-54) scrambled down the beach to flee σὺν
νηυσὶ φίλην ἐς πατρίδα γαῖαν# [in ships to the dear
land of their fathers] (140; cf. 454). The seductiveness of
anger—smooth as liquid, fragrant as smoke—fills the breast
and blinds it to the havoc it wreaks on friends, "who in their
numbers went down before glorious Hektor" (*Il.* 18.103). The
sweet passion that causes a deferral of return home raises issues
that will later (Chapter 4.3) call for more extensive attention.
   The representation of speech (αὐδή) as a quasi-material
stuff that flows (ῥέεν) from the mouth in turn engages a wide
host of associations, some of which have already been noted.[51]
The formula μέλιτος γλυκίων ῥέεν αὐδή# [the voice

flowed sweeter than honey] responds with a variety of endline formulas of various lengths, all descriptive of the natural flow of liquids. The following sample is representative:

§11

(Il. 23.24)	. . .ἔρρεεν αἷμα#
(Il. 23.688)	. . .ἔρρεε δ᾽ ἱδρὼς#
(Il. 2.752)	. . .προΐει καλλίροον ὕδωρ#
(Il. 2.307)	. . .ὅθεν ῥέεν ἀγλαὸν ὕδωρ#
(Od. 9.140)	. . .λιμένος ῥέει ἀγλαὸν ὕδωρ#
(Od. 17.209)	. . .κατὰ δὲ ψυχρὸν ῥέεν ὕδωρ#
(Il. 11.810, 23.715)	. . .κατὰ δὲ νότιος ῥέεν ἱδρώς#
(Il. 12.33)	. . .πρόσθεν ἵεν καλλίροον ὕδωρ#

To this inventory should probably also be added the wine (Il. 6.266, 10.579, 16.231, 24.306) and tears (Il. 13.88;658, 18.32, Od. 5.84;158, 8.86;93 = 532, 16.214) that drip (λείβειν) along with honey and gall (Il. 18.108-10); and note too the frequent use of the image of pouring (χεύειν) to describe the approach of sleep (Il. 14.253, 23.63, Od. 2.395, 18.188) and the dark, final mist (ἀχλύς) of death (Il. 5.696, 16.344, 20.321;421, Od. 22.88). Together they suggest that the voice too is implicitly perceived as a kind of palpable substance, a smooth liquid body that pours from the speaker's lips into the ears of the listener, thereby inspiring there an almost tactile pleasure.[52] At the same time, these metaphors also embody an intriguing ambivalence. On the one hand, and like the pleasures of water, honey and even of tears—at least when they serve as the concomitants of ritualized grief—the smoothly flowing voice produces a delight that tantalizes, fills and satiates. On the other, in the pouring of anger, lust for battle, wine, sweet sleep and misty death, this same pleasure modulates into a thick, honeylike forgetfulness and, at the extreme, into total and permanent oblivion.

Nestor's liquid speech also exhibits honeyed sweetness: it is μέλιτος γλυκίων. Sweet in Homer are chiefly the things that soothe and lull and sate, or else that move one towards such fulfillment. Nearly half of the occurrences of the adjective γλυκερός in its various inflections are predicated of sleep,

with the remainder distributed among music (*Il.* 13.637, *Od.*
23.145), food (*Il.* 11.89), water (*Od.* 12.306), homecoming (*Od.*
22.323) and milk (*Od.* 4.88). Here again in most cases the image
of liquid softness prevails. This is especially true of sleep
(ὕπνος), which additionally accounts for nearly two-thirds of
the instances of γλυκύς and its forms. Sweet sleep not only
comes upon one, wells up, holds and releases,[53] but it is also
something poured out over sleepers—cf. ἐπὶ {κατὰ} ὕπνον
ἔχευεν# [poured sleep upon {down over}] (*Od.* 2.395, 18.188; cf.
12.338) and [ὕπνος] #νήδυμος ἀμφιχυθείς [painless
{sleep} poured all around] (*Il.* 14.253, 23.63)—like thick fluid,
like the sinister mist (ἀχλύς) that covers the eyes of the
dying (*Il.* 5.696, 16.344, 20.321;421, *Od.* 22.88). Its smooth touch
brings delight, no less than water slaking thirst or song that
fills the ear; mortals rest "taking pleasure of sweet sleep"—
#ὕπνῳ ὑπὸ γλυκερῷ ταρπώμεθα {ταρπήμεναι} —just as
of food and lamentation.

Sweet too is yearning or desire (ἵμερος), which amounts to
one-fifth of the uses of the adjective γλυκύς. Here once again
we find acknowledgment of the pleasure of giving expression to
sorrow, for the largest share of all instances of ἵμερος and its
forms in Homer are limited by the noun γόος [lamentation] in
the Genitive case—usually (6X) in the formula τοῖσι δὲ
πᾶσιν ὑφ' ἵμερον ὦρσε γόοιο# [stirred in all of them
desire for mourning].[54] Sexual passion (*Il.* 3.139;446 = 14.328
=*Od.* 22.500, *Il.* 5.429, 14.198) and music (*Il.* 18.570;603, *Od.*
1.421 = 18.304, 18.194) account for six and five occurrences,
respectively, with the rest given over to food (*Il.* 11.89) and the
exquisite skin of gods (*Il.* 3.397, 14.170).

Finally, Nestor's voice is "honeyed" or surpasses even
honey's sweetness. Most of the connotations honey
traditionally enjoys have already been touched on: its taste,
the pleasure it gives, the flow of its dense liquid body. Once
more, the distribution of the noun μέλι and its adjective
μελιηδής follows what should by now be a familiar pattern.
Fully half of the time, wine is the referent; food—fruit, cheese,
grass, honey itself—amounts to more than a quarter of the uses,
with the remainder given over to life, sleep and twice to the
voice. The first of these two instances (*Il.* 1.249) is the one that

served as a point of departure, namely the "voice sweeter than honey" that flows from Nestor's mouth. The second comes full circle to return to the issue of poetry and the Sirens, since it appears in a passage (*Od.* 12.187) in which they call their own sweet-toned (μελίγηρυς) voices "honeyed."

The individual elements in the lines λιγὺς Πυλίων ἀγορητής | τοῦ καὶ ἀπὸ γλώσσης μέλιτος γλυκίων ῥέεν αὐδή (*Il.* 1.248-49) open out on an extensive network of associations. Among the most prominent are images of clarity of tone, sweetness, fluidity and seductive allure. The old man's voice is a bright, honeylike stuff poured out, and in this respect resembles the flow of sleep no less than poured water or wine. In its clarity and liquid sweetness lies the pleasure it brings—again like sleep, food and drink, but also with affinities to music, laughter, lamentation and erotic desire. What cannot escape notice is the degree to which the formulaic attributes that configure him assimilate Nestor to singers, Muses and Sirens in the epic tradition. At least with respect to the quality of voice each enjoys, their characterization is traversed by the same set of predicates.

The link between longevity and honeyed, fluent speech—if not indeed uncontrolled speech or chronic logorrhea, when its flow becomes unremitting as the course of life from Infant to Elder nears the closure of its arc—points once more to a social and "ethical" basis for the characterization of Nestor and the aged in general as masters of sweet talk. More crucial than that his limbs are now unsteady and his arms "no longer swing light" is the fact that Nestor has outlived every witness to his former glory as a fighter, and so too any chance that his deeds will be transformed into the undying stuff of song by some *other* voice. At issue here is the dynamics of *kleos* in Greek epic, along with the peculiar mechanism of its acknowledgment and preservation. Although transmitted by word of mouth, in the form of tales handed down through subsequent generations, the fame to which all heroes aspire originates in actions first subject to another's eyewitnessing gaze. Before his achievements can be *heard* and "rumored," they must first be *seen*, since *kleos* always arises from direct *autopsis*.[55] For a warrior elite, there is even a sense in which deeds unseen, anonymous and unratified by public witness may as well have never been done at all. Their memorialization depends first on their *visibility;* only then can they undergo their strange transformation into narratives that confer on the hero a kind of vicarious immortality by being told and retold over time—first within his own group, and later even within that of others.

Moreover, what permanently seals heroic achievement is its stark finality; generally speaking, this takes the form of the warrior's death at the height of his valor. Mortality defines the hero as the very condition of his possibility. His biological end is the beginning of his greater narrative life, the point at which *autopsis* ceases and everlasting *kleos* begins. Hence the anguish implicit in Nestor's condition.[56] The old man cuts a solitary and sometimes even pathetic figure, a character defined by his temporal distension, strung out between the contrafactual mode of εἴθ' ὣς ἡβώοιμι βίη δέ μοι ἔμπεδος εἴη [If only I were young now, and the strength were still steady within me] (*Il.* 7.157, 11.669, 23.629; cf. *Od.* 14.468;503) on the one hand, and seemingly endless runs of autocitation on the other. For in cheating death, he at one and the same time risks cheating himself of *kleos* as well. Since he has lived well beyond his heroism and also beyond its original witnesses, Nestor is compelled to be *the singer of his own tale.*[57] This accounts for his addiction to relentless reminiscence. Because he can no longer *fight,* he must continue to *speak* in order to keep his own *kleos* alive, and to *speak* in as epic a dimension as the younger, more powerful men at Troy aspire to *act.* As Falkner remarks (1989:31):

> Nestor's rhetoric, perhaps the most clearly marked in the poem, is characterized by its lengthy digressions and emulation of a past of which he is the sole representative. As has been shown, the epyllia of the *Iliad* are not senile garrulity. They serve, on the one hand, to bolster morale and calm tempers among the younger warriors by putting the present in the light of history. But on the other hand, Nestor repeatedly grounds his authority in his youthful achievement and the respect he commanded rather than his age per se, implying that the latter in itself is no guarantee of his status. . . . Gutmann [1977:315-16] sees in the so-called nostalgia and reminiscing of the elderly an attempt to avoid being viewed as "other" and to secure their well-being by recalling to others their personal history. Nestor's digressions provide such occasions for life review and explicit arguments for continued self-value . . .

In a word, the fame that a glorious end in battle would have won for him in the narrative memory of his group is one that he himself now must cultivate by recourse to his own personal memory, and through the traditional mechanism of oral tales defined as the κλέα ἀνδρῶν. Aged and feeble now, strength gone but voice still fluent and compelling—like the lucid but somewhat maudlin cicadas at the gates of Troy—he is a "self-singer," simultaneously bard and subject of the tales he recounts. Whatever specific rhetorical functions they may serve on each occasion they are told,[58] Nestor's recollections of his own bygone *kleos*—in war against the Kentaurs (*Il.* 1.262-72), in the battle with Arkadians (*Il.* 7. 132-156), in Elean cattle-raids (*Il.* 11.670-762) and in the funeral games of Amarynkeus the Kretan (*Il.* 23.629-762)—also (and perhaps even chiefly) aim to perpetuate narratives in which he is himself the protagonist, thus to transform himself into precisely the stuff of those everliving stories that more vigorous heroes strive to purchase at the cost of their own splendid demise. Nestor occupies a place somewhere midway between a present in which only his words command attention any longer and a past that stretches back to some vanishing point in otherwise unsung heroics, namely into the vast and unrecorded realm of his society's oral tradition. From this place pours a voice like honey, both lucid and sweet, consistent but nonetheless fluid, touched by implicit sorrow for the irretrievability of youth, and at one and the same time alluring and also interminable.

It should be clear that to a significant extent Nestor's characterization draws on traits that identify him as an *aoidos* in his own right. Specifically, his character is formulated in terms supplied by an implicit network of semes linking the human voice to the clarity of birdsong, cicada and lyre; to the rich taste of honey and other sweet things; and to the supple flow of water, blood and wine. The basis for this last link may well also encompass the *continuous* nature of their flow; if true, it would help further motivate the connection between the fluid speech of bards and the logorrhea of the elderly. At the same time, however, the quality of voice they all share also has a potentially sinister aspect. Sweet and clear as cicadas in summer, as honey and wine, sweeter even than memories of homeland, and smooth as liquid poured out to slake thirst—their voice at one and the same time embodies a certain danger. For just like wine and sleep and mist of death, like battlelust and other kinds of wrath, like Sirens' tempting song and the nourishment that comes from the ritual expression of grief—all no less sweet and clear, all no less fluid—it might also have the power to cause pleasure that verges on forgetfulness. This darker potential will need to be explored in some detail in the following pages.

NOTES

1. The complicity between storyteller (or narrator) and audience is a fundamental tenet of so-called *Rezeptionstheorie;* see e.g. Iser 1974 and 1978, Eco 1979 (esp. 47-66) and Jauss 1982.

2. See further Ducrot and Todorov 1979:356-61.

3. Gadamer 1975:245-67, Ricoeur 1976:25-44, Bleicher 1980:108-16.

4. See the article by Höfer in Roscher 1924-1937, s.v. "Thamyris"; and Simpson-Lazenby 1970:85-86.

5. Atchity 1978:98-99, MacLeod 1983:5, Thalmann 1984: 133; Kirk 1985:217.

6. On the Thamyris story in the context of other contest-myths in Homer, see Ford 1992:96-101.

7. Gundert 1935:67-70, Ramnoux 1960, Young 1968:35-37 and 116-20, Doyle 1970, Medda 1981.

8. Svenbro 1974:16-35, Gentili 1988:3-23.

9. Simpson-Lazenby 1970:85, Kirk 1985:216.

10. Compare Kirk's remarks (1985:216) on the passage: "But why in any case did Homer choose to introduce this diversion here? It serves no purpose beyond that of attaching some elaboration to Dorion, which could have been done with a simple epithet. Other expansions in the catalogue have some distinct purpose. . . . Perhaps it was professional singer's pride, more conspicuous in the *Odyssey* than the *Iliad,* that motivated an otherwise rather gratuitous elaboration; Thamuris went too far, but at least an almost divine power in song is suggested by his story."

11. This is not, of course, to dismiss the power of the metaphor of the road (οἴμη) in how poetry is represented in archaic Greece, especially insofar as it suggests what has been called (Ong 1977) a "topical poetic" at work. See Ford 1992:40-48.

12. The quality of Nestor's counsels and the strength of his powers of mind are themselves of course expressly embodied in the names of two of his sons, Ekhephron ("who has intelligence") and Thrasymedes ("ambitious planner"), and implied in that of the third, namely Peisistratos ("who persuades the army"); see Svenbro 1993:72, quoting Sulzberger 1926.

13. Compare Cicero, *De senectute* 10.

14. Fenik 1974:172-207, Chatman 1978:107-38, Docherty 1983 and the discussion in Rimmon-Kenan 1983:59-70.

15. For a general overview, Schein 1984:67-88 and Edwards 1987:149-58.

16. Barck 1976.

17. Kirby 1990.

18. Martin (1989:27) remarks that ". . . we must remember that the heroic ideal of speaking and fighting virtuosity is always being propounded in the poem. 'Word and deed' becomes a merismus, expressing an ideal totality by reference to the extremes which shape it." He acknowledges, however, the primary role of action in this totality (76): "A hero's status as a warrior requires him to value fighting over flyting; to speak, if at all, laconically."

19. See Dickson 1990:58-61 and below, Chapter 3.4.

20. Note the allomorphic phrase #εἴσατο δὲ φθογγήν used of Iris' impersonation of Polites at *Il.* 2.791. On the impersonation of mortals by gods in Homer, see de Jong 1987:211-14. (Here and throughout this study, I have adopted Muellner's [1976] use of the sign "#" at the beginning and the end of a quotation from Homer to indicate line-initial and line-final position, respectively.)

21. On the clumsy rhetoric of Diomedes' speech in Book 9, "as if Homer were characterizing the inexperience of Diomedes through his style," see Martin 1990:124-30.

22. Mugler 1976, Atchity 1978:260, Falkner 1989:21-67.

23. Andersen 1978:111-24.

24. Querbach 1976.

25. Falkner 1989.

26. "Clear-voiced": *Il.* 2.50;442, 9.10, 23.39, *Od.* 2.6; "splendid": *Il.* 3.268, *Od.* 8.418; "calling throughout the city": *Il.* 24.701; "loud": *Il.* 7.384; "raising the voice": *Il.* 18.505; "messengers of gods and men": *Il.* 1.334, 7.274; "who serve the *dêmos*": *Od.* 17.383, 19.135.

27. **A**: *Il.* 3.148, 7.276, 9.685; **B**: *Od.* 4.696;711, 22.361, 24.442; **C**: *Il.* 2.38, *Od.* 7.278; **D**: *Il.* 17.325; **E**: *Il.* 24.282;674.

28. Foley 1991:168-74.

29. See Chatman 1978, Cixous 1974, Docherty 1983 and Rimmon-Kenan 1983; for specific application to Greek literature, Whallon 1969, Collins 1988 and Pelling 1990. For a

concise review of scholarship on the issues of naming and character, Peradotto 1990:94-119.

30. Compare Peradotto (1990:101): "Before being supplied with a 'character,' a 'personality,' what the linguist would call an 'identifying description,' what Barthes (1974:94) would call a 'figure' ('an impersonal network of symbols combined under the proper name'), the name would be inflated currency, an instrument of questionable exchange value, or in Searle's terms, an attempt at denotation without description."

31. In this I take issue with Barthes' conclusion (1974:191) to the passage quoted above: ". . . we can say that what is proper to narrative is not action but the character as a Proper Name: the semic raw material (corresponding to a certain moment of our history of the narrative) *completes* what is proper to its being, *fills* the name with adjectives."

32. See especially Foley 1988, 1990, 1991.

33. In this respect, the relation between the "narrative whole" and each individual performance resembles that between "story" and "narrative," *"fabula"* and *"récit"* in narratological theory. Genette (1980:25-29) offers the following working definition: "I propose . . . to use the word *story* for the signified or narrative content," which he specifies as the "totality of actions and situations taken in themselves, without regard to the medium, linguistic or other, through which knowledge of that totality comes to us: an example would be the adventures experienced by Ulysses from the fall of Troy to his arrival on Calypso's island." The term *narrative* is reserved by him to denote "the signifier, statement, discourse or narrative text itself," that is, "the oral or written discourse that undertakes to tell of an event or series of events: thus we would term *narrative of Ulysses* the speech given by the hero to the Phaeacians in Books IX-XII of the *Odyssey*, and also these four books themselves, that is, the section of Homeric text that purports to be the faithful transcription of that speech." On *"fabula"* and *"récit,"* see Bal 1985:5-10.

34. See Foley 1991:17-37 for numerous examples, at the level of both diction and narrative patterning, drawn from Serbo-Croatian, Greek and Old English oral poetry.

35. Parry 1971:127: "An epithet is not ornamental in itself, whatever may be its signification: it is only by dint of being used over and again with a certain substantive or group of

substantives that it acquires this quality. It becomes ornamental when its meaning loses any value of its own and becomes so involved with the idea of its substantive that the two can no longer be separated. The fixed epithet then adds to the combination of substantive and epithet an element of nobility and grandeur, but no more than that. Its sole effect is to form, with its substantive, a heroic expression of the idea of that substantive."

36. Compare Vivante 1982:129-30 on the personal epithet as the vehicle of merely "existential weight," "nothing but [an] inevitable fact of [a character's] existence," which functions "without conditioning the dramatic . . . values of the action"— as if "inevitable facts" of character were somehow independent of its dispositions for action. He concludes by remarking: "The lack of meaningful characterization in the epithets, which might be regarded as a defect, is really most effective poetically. The hero, as he is shown in action, is left free of all burdening qualification. At the same time he is not a mere name. He is there before us in the might of his nature."

37. Compare Whallon's (1969:63-70) understanding of epithets as "significantly true to individual character" in the poems. He too, however, approaches the issue from the perspective of "the poetic imagination," by asking whether fixed epithets "may not have stimulated the mind of the poet" (64), and ignores the anaphoric dimension of oral narratives as received by an audience. Despite this, his suggestion (69) that fixed epithets over the course of their transmission may themselves have come to influence the direction of the narrative—"if the epithets were not usually determined by their contexts, they may now and then have determined those contexts"—is an important one; see now Nagy 1990:18-35.

38. On the sarcasm, Kirk 1985:142; for a different interpretation, Martin 1989:109-10.

39. *Pace* Pucci, who remarks (1977:40, note 34) that "the ironic portrait of Nestor in *Il.* 1.247ff. . . . suggests a mild devaluation of this rhetoric [i.e. the traditional association of speech with honey]." He concludes that the "accumulated series of 'sweet' epithets" used of Nestor amounts to a "hyperbole [that] seems to make fun of the simile in its positive form." See Austin (1966:301, with note 11), however, on the

difference between modern perceptions of Nestor and the apparently unqualified respect he receives from his peers.

40. **Whip:** *Il.* 11.532; **wind:** *Il.* 5.526, 13.334;590, 14.17, 15.620, 23.215; **bird:***Il.* 14.290, 19.350; **cicadas:** *Il.* 3.152; **weeping:** *Il.* 19.5, *Od.* 10.201, 11.391, 18.216, 21.56; **Sirens:** *Od.* 12.44; **Muses:** *Od.* 24.62; **lyre:** *Il.* 9.186, 18.569, *Od.* 4.252, 8.261;537, 22.332, 24.133; **heralds:** *Il.* 2.50;442, 9.10, 11.684, 23.39, *Od.* 2.6.

41. See Stanford's note (1959:407) on *Od.* 12.44: "λιγυρός and λιγύς describe the kind of sound that the Greeks liked best: it is defined by Aristotle in *De Audibilibus* 804a25ff. as consisting of sharpness (ὀξύτης), fineness (λεπτότης) and precision (ἀκρίβεια)." Compare also West 1978:304 (*ad* 583).

42. Compare also ὀλοοῖο τεταρπώμεσθα γόοιο# [we had taken our fill of sorrowful dirge] (*Il.* 23.10;98, cf. *Od.* 11.212) and τοῖσι δὲ πᾶσιν ὑφ' ἵμερον ὦρσε γόοιο [he stirred in them all the passion for mourning] (*Il.* 23.108;153, *Od.* 4.183; cf. *Od.* 4.113, 16.215, 19.249 = 23.231); also the extensive (7X, 14X) formula αὐτὰρ ἐπεὶ πόσιος καὶ ἐδητύος ἐξ ἔρον ἕντο# [But when they had put aside desire for drink and food]. On lamentation and epic poetry, see Nagy 1979:94-117.

43. Pucci 1979, 1987:209-13.

44. On λειριόεσσαν as "lily-like" and thus "delicate," see Kirk 1985:283; and cf. λεπταλέῃ φωνῇ, with reference to the youth who sings the Linos song on the Shield of Akhilleus (*Il.* 18.571).

45. Note that, for Hesiod (*Erga* 582-89), this is always a summer that unfolds under the sign of the Dog-Star, when "wine is sweetest and women most wanton, but men are feeblest, for Sirios parches head and knees and the skin is dried by the heat" (. . . καὶ οἶνος ἄριστος, | μαχλόταται δὲ γυναῖκες, ἀμαυρότατοι δέ τοι ἄνδρες | εἰσίν, ἐπεὶ κεφαλὴν καὶ γούνατα Σείριος ἄζει, | αὐαλέος δέ τε χρὼς ὑπὸ καύματος). It is also (*Aspis* 397-400) the time when "Sirios scorches the flesh . . . and the grapes change color—which Dionysos gives as both a joy and a sorrow to men" (. . . ὅτε τε χρόα Σείριος ἄζει, | . . . ὅτ' ὄμφακες αἰόλλονται, | οἷα Διώνυσος δῶκ' ἀνδράσι χάρμα καὶ

ἄχθος). The cicada thus not only represents sweet clarity of voice, but is also emblematic of male impotence—itself traditionally a concommitant of ageing. See Boedeker 1984:42-43.

46. Segal 1973:205-12, King 1986:15-35Kirk (1985:284) suggests that "the cicadas certainly represent the ceaselessness of these old men's talk."

47. Ferrari 1987:26-30.

48. West 1966:181-83 and Boedeker 1984:88-99

49. Tornow 1893.

50. Plato (*Phil.* 47e) quotes these lines as evidence of the pleasure that often attends even the most painful human passions, which in turn serves as an index of the soul's variance with the body.

51. Formulas for αὐδήν/αὐδῆς# in line-final position most often (7 of 12X) occur as a hemistich stretching back to the B1 or B2 caesura and filled with a noun (usually a proper name) in the Genitive case (expressing source) plus ἔκλυεν αὐδ-# (*Il.* 13.757, 15.270, *Od.* 2.297, 4.831, 10.311;481, 14.89). They are not especially relevant to an analysis of *Il.* 1.249.

52. Pucci 1977:27-29. He comments (28) that "the viscosity of honey represents the thick body of words, the materiality of sound in rhythmic lines, the pleasantness of song and music," and in a footnote (p. 40, note 33) calls attention to the frequency, especially in later poetry, of the metaphor of poetic speech as a flowing of honey; cf. Pindar *Ol.* 6.83;91, 10.10;98, *Pyth.* 4.299, 8.57, 9.103, 10.56, *Nem.* 3.6-7, 4.4, 7.12;62, *Isth.* 6.21, 7.19, 8.65.

53. ἐπέλθοι (*Od.* 5.472), ἱκάνοι (*Il.* 1.610, *Od.* 9.333, 19.49); ἔχε (*Il.* 10.4), ἕλοι (*Od.* 19.511); ὄρουσεν (*Il.* 23.232); ἀνῆκεν (*Il.* 2.71, *Od.* 7.289, 18.199).

54. Compare *Il.* 23.108;153, *Od.* 4.183, 16.215, 19.249, 23.231; cf. *Il.* 24.507, *Od.* 4.113.

55. Detienne 1967:9-27, Pucci 1980.

56. Note Vivante's description (1970:24) of Nestor as "a pathetic witness of past and present, an old man for whom heroic prowess is but a memory or a dream." He remarks later (190) that the old man "speaks about himself *as about another person seen and admired long ago*. There is no link between his youth and old age" [emphasis added]. Despite the first-person structure of his recollections, Nestor indeed speaks of himself

with *authorial* distance, visually, with a storyteller's detachment.

57. Compare Atchity 1978:260: "Though not a singer, Nestor by his frequent storytelling defines the social role of the experienced counselor as being practically synonymous with that of the poet of memory. . . . From Nestor's habit of justifying his advice through recollection, it becomes clear that bard and counselor are just different expressions for a function that is also performed by the prophet." The following chapter will explore this last analogy in some depth.

58. Sachs 1933, Cantieni 1942, Vester 1956, Willcock 1964, Braswell 1971, Andersen 1975, Atchity 1978:260-63, Pedrick 1983, Davies 1986.

2

Nestor as AOIDOS: Narrative Authority

1. INTRODUCTION

The identification of Nestor as a kind of *aoidos* in his own right is clear not only from the traits that formulate his character, but also from both the structure and the function of his actions and words in the poems. This chapter will address some of their structural features, with a view towards strengthening the analogy already proposed between Nestor and the storyteller in archaic Greek *epos*; their function is the subject of Chapters 3 and 4. At the same time, the analysis that follows will also begin to raise the issue of authority in traditional tales, namely the grounds on which Thamyris, Nestor, other singers in the poems and the Homeric narrator too seek to legitimate the truth of what they tell.

Narrative authority is of no small moment in oral tales.[1] Prone to familiar vicissitudes in the course of its transmission—to ordinary forgetfulness, due to the influence of space and time on the limited reach of unlettered memory; to pressures that make themselves felt within the performative situation, where the storyteller must presumably cater in some degree to specific interests expressed by or else tacitly present in his audience; and also to whatever peculiar aims and motives urge the *aoidos* himself to shape his tale in one way or another—oral narratives are eminently fragile things.[2] As represented within Greek epic tradition, they implicitly vacillate between established fact and mere hearsay. This is of course reflected in the polysemy of the term *kleos*, which can mean either authentic *fame* or unsubstantiated *rumor*.[3] To be sure, this is an opposition in meaning encouraged and doubtlessly even exploited by the agonistic structure that governs the performance of narrative—and so much else—in ancient Greece, where truth is usually asserted in terms of a victory over rival claims.[4] This much is implicit in the negative paradigm that

Thamyris embodies in the fragmentary tale embedded in the
Catalogue of Ships (*Il.* 2.594-600), with which the Iliadic
narrator's own relation to the Muses is meant to contrast (484-
92). But such antagonism also owes much to the simple fact that
preliterate cultures recognize the problems involved in insuring
the basic stability of narratives from one telling to the next,
and over the course of generations of tellers.

The need for stability is of course in large part answered by
the formulaic structure of many oral literatures. At the same
time, however, more explicit, self-referential gestures made at
the level of the narrative itself also draw attention to the
problem of authenticity. How storytellers, the act of
storytelling and stories themselves are represented within the
tales addresses, among other issues, the basis on which rests
the narrator's own claim to be believed.[5] The present chapter
will consider a somewhat neglected aspect of this issue, and
will focus on two interrelated questions. How does the problem
of authority figure in the poet's construction of his own voice in
the person of the story's narrator?[6] And how does the narrator's
authority stand related to the authority to which characters
within the story are made to appeal to guarantee the truth of
what they themselves say?

The first appearance of Nestor (*Il.* 1.245-84) in Book 1 of
the *Iliad* is enframed by formulas and scenic idioms that mark
him as a character endowed with a specific function; as the
next chapter will show, he is often cast in the role of an
intercessory figure. In this he plays much the same part—
though of course with quite different results—as Athene (193-
222), Thetis (495-530) and Hephaistos (571-600) in the same
book, and the analogies that link them have been noted
before.[7] To be sure, formal likeness need not imply sameness of
intention or effect. The use of similar formulas, generic
characterizations and scenic types in oral literature can also
provide a vehicle for irony, contravening expectation, and may
often serve more as means to generate contrast than to assert
identity. With reference to the parallel between Nestor and
Hephaistos, for instance, Segal has noted the extent to which
it highlights an implicit and crucial difference, in that it
"dramatizes the gulf between the urgency and finality of
human affairs and the almost comic triviality of the divine."[8]
Hephaistos defuses the tension and successfully mediates what
amounts to a marital spat between Zeus and Hera by an act of

self-deprecatory clownishness. The stakes involved in the intercessions of Athene and Thetis are of course more consequential than this; and it is not long before even the trivial existence of divinity becomes embroiled in the urgent concerns of mortal women and men.

What has escaped attention, however, is the analogy between Nestor and the figure of the prophet Kalkhas some two hundred lines earlier (*Il.* 1.68-100), during the first series of exchanges in the Assembly with which the *Iliad* opens.[9] This oversight is even surprising, given the degree of formulaic echo between these two scenes. Added to this is of course the fact that both Prophet and Elder—unlike their divine counterparts—initially *fail* in their attempts at mediating conflict. Moreover, just as in the case of the parallel between Nestor and Hephaistos noted by Segal, the similarities of formula and narrative structure shared by Nestor and Kalkhas also point up implicit differences that merit consideration, especially as they touch upon the issue of narrative authority.

Let me first briefly address their sameness, deferring a more detailed discussion to a later point. A basic similarity occurs at the level of direct formulaic echoes, which in turn evoke similarities of ethical type and narrative function. To begin with, both characters are introduced during the course of a formal Assembly scene;[10] here their appearance is signalled (with only slight variation) by the usual formula (6X) for Alternation of Speakers: ἤτοι ὅ γ᾽ ὣς εἰπὼν κατ᾽ ἄρ᾽ ἕζετο· τοῖσι δ᾽ ἀνέστη [He spoke thus and sat down again, and among them stood up . . .].[11] This is followed by their identification by name, along with an expanded, "particularizing" description of some three or four lines,[12] and closes with a formulaic line (15X) that expressly refers to the new speaker's goodwill: ὅ σφιν ἐϋφρονέων ἀγορήσατο καὶ μετέειπεν [With kind intention he spoke and addressed them]. Omitting certain unimportant details, the general pattern can be schematized as follows:

§12

(a) X finishes and sits; (Y) stands	*Il.* 1.68 / 1.245-48
(b) Naming of Y	*Il.* 1.69 / 1.248
(c) Expanded description of Y	*Il.* 1.70-72 / 1.249-52
(d) Address-formula (Goodwill)	*Il.* 1.73 = 1.253

Chapter 3 will explore the degree to which the formula at §12(d) marks both Kalkhas and Nestor as types of Mediator. There they will be identified as characters whose function it is to steer the narrative of the tale in one direction or another at moments of crisis. Such a role allows both to serve as cloaked authorial presences in the text of the *Iliad*, surrogate figures of the narrator. This is because not just the content of their words but especially, as I will now argue, the perspective from which they are uttered highlight mutually exclusive trajectories along which the ensuing narrative can proceed. These are paths ostensibly chosen by the characters who either embrace or reject their advice, though of course they always lead towards an end predetermined by the storyteller himself. The different ways in which Kalkhas and Nestor fulfill this same function are the subject of the present chapter. Each embodies a distinct narrative strategy in the text of the *Iliad*, and their difference additionally throws light on the relation between the storyteller and the tradition within whose conventions he shapes his own tale.

2. THE NARRATOR AS PROPHET

The best place to begin is by noting one obvious difference of attribution in the expanded description of these characters in the formulaic slot designated by §12(c). Despite their functional identity in places, the ethical types represented by Kalkhas and Nestor are not strictly isomorphic, and indeed embody unique narrative viewpoints. To borrow a term supplied by narratological theory, these different points of view constitute different *focalizations* of the *Iliad*, namely different ways in which what gets narrated is influenced and shaped by the narrating figure. Bal (1985:100) offers the following concise definition:[13]

> Whenever events are presented, they are always presented from within a certain 'vision.' A point of view is chosen, a certain way of seeing things, a certain angle, whether 'real' historical events are concerned or fictitious events. It is possible to try and give an 'objective' picture of the facts. But what does that involve? An attempt to present only what is seen or is perceived in some other way. All comment is shunned and implicit

interpretation is also avoided. Perception, however, is a psychological process, strongly dependent on the position of the perceiving body. . . . I shall refer to the relations between the elements presented and the vision through which they are presented with the term *focalization*. Focalization is, then, the relation between the vision and that which is 'seen,' perceived.

This relation between *what* is narrated and the perspectival position *from which* the narration occurs can convey a variety of information about the speaker in a text, and it is in fact as a privileged (if indirect, since nuanced) index of that speaker's psychology that the issue of "point of view" or "focus of narration" has been most often explored. Narrative focalization signals narrative bias. It marks the inscription of the speaker himself in what the speaker says, thus in turn tacitly limiting what gets said as provisional, perhaps even distorted and therefore open to suspicion. The extended characterization of Thersites that precedes his speech in the second Akhaian Assembly (*Il.* 2.211-24) is perhaps the most familiar instance in the *Iliad* of this last extreme, and in fact represents the polar opposite of speeches introduced by the "goodwill formula" ὅ σφιν ἐϋφρονέων ἀγορήσατο καὶ μετέειπεν.[14] Thersites' bias is clearly a hostile one.

At the same time, however, emphasis on focalization as a *psychological* marker should not be allowed to obscure the even more basic issue of narrative authority that it raises. Thersites may well be malicious and abusive, a despicable agent of *neikos* (strife) "beyond all others hated by Akhilleus and Odysseus, whom he was forever rebuking" (220-21), but this *in itself* is insufficient ground on which to reject the content of his speech. Even despite its motivation, Thersites' assessment of the situation may well have some merit; it certainly does in the eyes of the Akhaian troops.[15] What more tellingly undermines his credibility is not his *personal* bias but instead those elements in his description that advert to the bias of his *words* (212-14):

§13

Θερσίτης δ' ἔτι μοῦνος ἀμετροεπὴς ἐκολῴα,
ὃς ἔπεα φρεσὶ ᾖσιν ἄκοσμά τε πολλά τε ᾔδη,
μάψ, ἀτὰρ οὐ κατὰ κόσμον . . .

> But one man, Thersites of unmeasured speech, still scolded,
> who knew in his head many words, but disordered,
> vain, and without decency . . .

The description of Thersites' physical flaws in the lines that follow (216-19) is as much an icon of what is skewed and deformed in his perspective as it is an outward mirroring of his nonaristocratic status.[16] His point of view is suspect precisely because he lacks the authoritative vision that would otherwise lend orderliness and propriety to his words; in its absence, what he says is disorganized (ἄκοσμα), at one and the same time random and unseemly (οὐ κατὰ κόσμον), and thus ineffectual (μάψ). As Martin notes (1989:111), it is precisely the lack of a legitimate framework in which to orient his speech that renders his arguments vain: "because Thersites does not have a valid poetic memory for his own career, . . . [his argument] remains 'indeterminate' or 'undiscriminated'." The precise nature of this "valid memory" will be explored in the next section of this chapter, with reference to the perspective that informs Nestor's speeches.

The issue of "viewpoint" or authoritative vision is likewise prominent in the lines (§12c) that identify Kalkhas in his first appearance in the *Iliad*, and the terms of this description contrast—though in radically different ways—with how Nestor is later described (*Il.* 1.247-49) no less than with the representation of Thersites. This is a function of Kalkhas' role in the tale, informed as it is by a unique narrative focus. For like Kassandra in the *Iliad* and Tiresias, Leodes, Theoklymenos, Telemos and the unnamed Phaikaian prophet in the *Odyssey*, Kalkhas is a professional seer, and his characterization explicitly appeals to the special powers he enjoys (*Il.* 1.68-73):

§14

Ἤτοι ὅ γ' ὣς εἰπὼν κατ' ἄρ' ἕζετο· τοῖσι δ' ἀνέστη
Κάλχας Θεστορίδης, οἰωνοπόλων ὄχ' ἄριστος,
ὃς ᾔδη τά τ' ἐόντα τά τ' ἐσσόμενα πρό τ' ἐόντα,
καὶ νήεσσ' ἡγήσατ' Ἀχαιῶν Ἴλιον εἴσω
ἣν διὰ μαντοσύνην, τήν οἱ πόρε Φοῖβος Ἀπόλλων.
ὅ σφιν ἐϋφρονέων ἀγορήσατο καὶ μετέειπεν·

Thus he spoke, and sat down again, and among them stood up
Kalkhas, Thestor's son, by far the best of bird interpreters,
who knew the things that were, the things to come and the things
past, who guided into the land of Ilion the ships of the Akhaians
through his seercraft, which Phoibos Apollo gave him.
With kind intention he spoke and addressed them.

These are impressive credentials. In brief compass, these
lines advance three claims that expressly confirm the
authority of Kalkhas' vision; in so doing, they also
proleptically discredit the accusations Agamemnon will level
against him (*Il.* 1.101-08).[17] Once again, it is the nature of the
perspective *from which* he speaks that receives emphasis,
rather than the psychological quality of his motivation
(Goodwill). Taking them in order, the terms of his
characterization move backwards from the powers he possesses
to Apollo himself as their donor, namely from gift to its
unimpeachable source in deity. The formula identifying him as
"by far the best of interpreters" (οἰωνοπόλων ὄχ'
ἄριστος#) appears elsewhere only once (*Il.* 6.76), in the
functionally identical but abbreviated description of the Trojan
seer Helenos (cf. *Il.* 7.44-45). Next, the line (70) that mentions
the range of his vision is tellingly echoed in the later and
famous description of the Muses themselves at *Iliad* 2.485:
ὑμεῖς γὰρ θεαί ἐστε, πάρεστέ τε, ἴστέ τε πάντα [For
you are goddesses, you are present, and you know all things].[18]
It will be remembered that the Muses also look to Apollo as the
guarantor of their vision; this evokes a kind of symmetry, to
which I will return in a moment. Finally (71-72) comes the
mention of his earlier success in guiding the expedition to Troy,
by way of practical confirmation of his gifts; this point is in
fact recalled and expanded upon in somewhat greater detail in
Odysseus' recounting of the prophecy delivered by Kalkhas
when the troops were assembled at Aulis (*Il.* 2.299-330).

Above and beyond these explicit appeals to authority,
however, the scene incorporates certain tacit narrative
strategies that also lend Kalkhas further credibility. Most
conspicuous is the fact that the very content of his ensuing
speech neatly corroborates the scope of his prophetic vision (*Il.*
1.93-100):

§15

οὔτ' ἄρ' ὅ γ' εὐχωλῆς ἐπιμέμφεται οὔθ' ἑκατόμβης,
ἀλλ' ἕνεκ' ἀρητῆρος, ὃν ἠτίμησ' Ἀγαμέμνων
οὐδ' ἀπέλυσε θύγατρα καὶ οὐκ ἀπεδέξατ' ἄποινα,
τοὔνεκ' ἄρ' ἄλγε' ἔδωκεν ἑκηβόλος ἠδ' ἔτι δώσει·
οὐδ' ὅ γε πρὶν Δαναοῖσιν ἀεικέα λοιγὸν ἀπώσει,
πρίν γ' ἀπὸ πατρὶ φίλῳ δόμεναι ἑλικώπιδα κούρην
ἀπριάτην ἀνάποινον, ἄγειν θ' ἱερὴν ἑκατόμβην
ἐς Χρύσην· τότε κέν μιν ἱλασσάμενοι πεπίθοιμεν.

Not for the sake of a vow or hecatomb does he blame us,
but because of the priest Agamemnon dishonored
and would not return his daughter nor accept the ransom.
For this the Archer sent us pain and will continue to send it,
nor will he ward off shameful plague from the Danaans
until we return the glancing-eyed girl to her father
without payment or ransom, and also lead a sacred hecatomb
to Khryse; then we might propitiate and persuade him.

Roughly symmetrical with the claim in line 70 to know past, future and present, his interpretation at one and the same time comprises both aetiology and projection, along with an assessment of the predicament in which the Greeks now find themselves as the objects of Apollo's blame. That is, his account ranges over (a) the genuine causes of the plague (93-95), (b) the fact of the god's present and persistent anger (96), and (c) the anticipated outcome of the Greek's success or failure in propitiating deity (97-100). Even more important than this internal match, however, is the fact that the aetiological part of his speech (=a)—and, *a fortiori*, his reading of the current situation (=b)—together correspond, albeit in abbreviated form, with the account given in the opening scenes of the *Iliad* itself (*Il.* 1.8-52). That is to say, Kalkhas' speech in substance recapitulates the very narrative that frames it, and to this extent his viewpoint or focalization coincides with that of the narrator of the tale.[19] His vision and that of the storyteller merge in these lines, and the rhetorical effect of this merger should be immediately clear. For just as there is no reason (or even any means) to doubt the veracity of the narrator's account—which in turn appeals to the Muses themselves for its own authority—what Kalkhas says must likewise be accepted as true.

The shape of this narrative convergence is worth a somewhat closer look. It exhibits a hierarchical structure in which the vertical relations between Narrator and Muse on the one hand and Kalkhas and Apollo on the other form mirror-images. Just as the Muse allegedly underwrites Homer's account, so the seer refers to Apollo as the source and ground of his own inspiration. At first glance, these two relations may well appear to be independent of each other, paired yet actually parallel. Moreover, they may even seem to be details that are supplied not by the story but instead by the cultural tradition in which the story itself is nested, and whose framework implicitly supports the telling of this and every other story within the same group of singers and listeners. This tradition is of course in a sense something external to the narrative itself, and in fact apparently serves as one of the very conditions of its possibility. After all, within the horizon of practices and institutions endorsed by the community in which poems like the *Iliad* are sung, the authority of prophets is believed to derive from the mantic gift of Apollo, and that of poets from the Muses' divine intercession. These and other cultural details indeed altogether help to dictate the terms of a given tale's verisimilitude, thus mapping out patterns and contours of its very intelligibility. Without their implicit framework, it might be argued, the tale would lose all possibility of being understood.[20]

This first glance, however, in fact overlooks the actual place that Apollo himself occupies in the narrative. The truth is that the god's status far more closely resembles that of Kalkhas than it does that of either the narrator or his Muse, who both belong to the tale's *outer* frame. This affords them a distance to which neither the prophet nor his god can lay claim, and at the same time bestows on them a relatively higher narrative authority. For like all the Greek and Trojan characters—like all the other gods themselves, for that matter—this Apollo is just one among many figures *within* a narrative that is presented by a storyteller who claims to base the truth of his tale on the Muse's splendid inspiration.[21] One symmetrical relation (Apollo→Kalkhas) is thus actually subordinate to the other (Muse→Narrator), as the following schema illustrates:

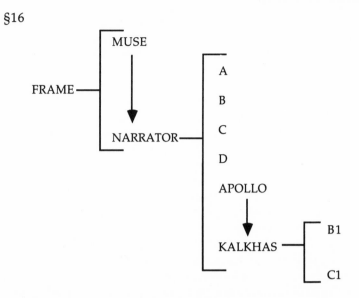

The letters A-D arbitrarily designate events (the appeal
and rejection of Khryses, the onslaught of the plague, the
Akhaian Assembly, etc.) recounted by the narrator prior to his
introduction of Kalkhas as Apollo's prophet; B1-C1 designate
those elements in Kalkhas' own narrative that recapitulate
events told at the next higher level. Whatever the drawbacks
of such an attempt at visualizing these relations, this schema
at least points first to the fact that the line of authority
(Apollo→Kalkhas) that ostensibly guarantees the seer's vision
of the cause of the plague is actually *embedded* in the
narrative, for whose veracity the authoritative link between
Narrator and Muse must stand surety. Thus it depends for its
own truth on the strength of that prior hierarchical relation,
and is in fact largely conditioned by it. In this sense, the
authority Kalkhas enjoys derives from a link not *external* to but
instead *within* the narrative. Although in terms of cultural
tradition and verisimilitude it would be scandalous indeed to
imagine a false Apollo or one who deceives his prophets,[22] it is
the degree to which the seer's aetiology matches the reasons
for the plague presented in the frame-narrative that in fact
confirms its credibility for the audience to whom the poem is
addressed. *It is the narrative that finally determines the
representation of cultural norms, not the other way around.*

To be sure, this needs some qualification. There is certainly a sense in which this strategy of authorization works *in both directions* at once; and this is what makes the schema at §16 a less than perfect way of visualizing these relations. For Apollo is of course no sheer invention of the storyteller; his role as the divine guarantor of prophecy is also a tenet firmly held by the audience for whom the tale is performed. The fact that Kalkhas' aetiology of the plague coincides with what was earlier said by the narrator thus has the effect of corroborating the latter's account as well, retrospectively endorsing it through an appeal to the audience's willingness to believe in a god who inspires true seercraft—and who, by convention, also embodies the source of the Muses' own truthfulness. Mantic authority thus also underwrites the poetic claims made at the opening of the tale (*Il.* 1.8-52), despite the fact that this relation is reversed within the framework that the tale itself constructs. The result is a kind of double vision, in which the schema at §16 competes with a schema of the following shape:

§17

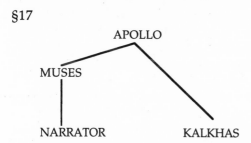

For that matter, it should not be overlooked that there is even a sense in which the figures of Muses themselves are no less narrative constructs than Kalkhas and Apollo, even though they belong to a higher level of the tale. The fact is that the authority of final appeal always remains the author himself, who is also responsible for the construction of the narrator—his "fictional delegate in the text" (de Jong 1987:29)—as a speaker inspired by a Muse.[23] This point will occupy us later. What the initial schema (§16) therefore fails to represent accurately is the degree to which social and cultural institutions interact with narrative strategies, namely how claims made *within* the text can refer back to other narrative claims *and also* simultaneously *outside* the text, to extranarrative realities, for their confirmation. The two frameworks, textual (§16) and cultural (§17), therefore in fact interpenetrate. If nothing else, this explodes the notion of the tale as a hermetically sealed entity understandable solely on its "own" terms. Its narrative horizon always merges with the social and cultural horizon of beliefs, practices and institutions that serve to define the community that makes up the tale's audience. Notwithstanding all this, it is clear that the description (§12c) linking Kalkhas to Apollo in the first place—and possibly also the invocation of the Muse in the tale's opening—embodies a choice made *at the level of the narrative*. Although he is more than likely restrained by traditional beliefs from representing a false or deceptive Apollo, the narrator is presumably under no compulsion to mention him here at all.[24] To this extent, at least, certain constraints of tradition appear to be constraints *freely chosen* by the teller of the tale.

Whatever the force of implicit appeals to *tradition*, the link between prophet and storyteller is directly confirmed by a *narrative* strategy ("embedded analepsis"). What is the nature of this link? In what senses do poet and seer speak univocally? What Kalkhas tells the Akhaians at Troy (*Il*. 1.93-100) is in substance identical to what the narrator has already told his eighth-century audience (8-52). Since his account recapitulates the narrator's and thus amounts to a *mise en abyme* or "mirror story" of the story that enframes it, it may profit to think of Kalkhas himself as a mirror of the storyteller, a cloaked authorial presence in the text.

What makes them similar is that both figures enjoy the same *mode of vision*. That is, the relation between Kalkhas and the future he envisions in some respects resembles the one that obtains between the narrator himself and the events in his own tale. With reference to what he recounts, the narrator (thanks to the Muse) can range with equal facility as does the seer (thanks to Apollo) over things past, present and future.[25] The echo between the description of Kalkhas in §13 and the narrator's own invocation of the Muses prior to the *Catalogue of Ships* (*Il*. 2.485) already suggests this identity. The quality of their vision is at one and the same time synoptic and immediate. This seems obvious in the case of Kalkhas; the formula itself (*Il*. 1.70) explicitly says as much. As for the narrator, his power to anticipate events attests to the comprehensive scope of his inspired vision. By this I mean that the Muses do not seem to feed him one line at a time, as it were, keeping him ignorant of the prior history and eventual outcome of each particular action he narrates. He does not remain blind to the past course and future possibilities of each event as he tells it. This is clear in the text from the frequency with which he resorts to the tropes of analepsis and prolepsis,[26] as well as to contrafactual assertions of what *would have* ensued *had not* something else happened instead.

His use of the contrafactual trope is worth considering more closely.[27] Its structure in the poems is rigorously formulaic (38X), and generally takes the form of #καί νυ κε{ν} or #ἔνθά κε{ν} + Aorist or Imperfect Indicative [And then X would have . . .] followed immediately by a line beginning #εἰ μὴ + Aorist Indicative [. . . if Y had not . . .]. A single example will serve here to illustrate the overall pattern; it comes from the failed *aristeia* of Nestor (*Il.* 8.90-91):

§18

. . . καί νύ κεν ἔνθ’ ὁ γέρων ἀπὸ θυμὸν ὄλεσσεν,
εἰ μὴ ἄρ’ ὀξὺ νόησε βοὴν ἀγαθὸς Διομήδης.

. . . now the old man *would have* lost his life there, *had not* indeed Diomedes of the great war-cry sharply perceived him.

De Jong and others are correct in noting that this device is essentially a means by which the narrator indirectly engages his audience in the unfolding of the narrative by addressing expectations raised by events that have just been described.[28] The tide of battle suddenly turns in favor of the Trojans, stranding Nestor—one of whose horses has been killed, tangling the reins—in a vulnerable position, as Hektor bears down menacingly. Diomedes alone comes to the rescue. Along with heightening suspense or inciting *pathos*, however, the trope also and more significantly reveals the framework that underpins the narrative: forking vectors implicitly structure this and *a fortiori* every point in the course of the tale. Along with revealing that framework, contrafactual claims also reveal the storyteller's control over the paths along which his narrative will actually proceed.[29] He of course knows in advance that Nestor will not die by Hektor's hand, but chooses to present that outcome as one of a mutually exclusive pair of possibilities, an option present at this juncture in the tale—albeit one denied as soon as it is posited, namely by Diomedes' arrival.

There is at least a superficial resemblance between this strategy—or rather, between the branching structure of alternatives that it reveals—and the way in which prophecies are generally cast in the poems. Both exhibit an *if-then* pattern that calls attention to the distinct and competing possibilities inherent in any given narrative situation. While Kalkhas' prophecy in *Iliad* 1 may not be the most overt example of this pattern, it is still worth considering before adducing other instances. The entire passage has already been quoted above (§15); I cite here only those lines that bear on the future open to the Akhaians at this point in their story (*Il.* 1.97-100):

§19

οὐδ' ὅ γε πρὶν Δαναοῖσιν ἀεικέα λοιγὸν ἀπώσει,
πρὶν γ' ἀπὸ πατρὶ φίλῳ δόμεναι ἑλικώπιδα κούρην
ἀπριάτην ἀνάποινον, ἄγειν θ' ἱερὴν ἑκατόμβην
ἐς Χρύσην· τότε κέν μιν ἱλασσάμενοι πεπίθοιμεν.

Nor will [Apollo] ward off shameful plague from the Danaans
until we return the glancing-eyed girl to her father
without payment, without ransom, and also lead a sacred
    hecatomb
to Khryse; then we might propitiate and persuade him.

The statement that something *will not* happen *unless* or *until* (πρίν) something else is done amounts to a projection into future time of the *would have . . . if not* structure of contrafactual assertions. Kalkhas' prediction tacitly offers the Akhaians a choice, and so raises two mutually exclusive possibilities for how events can proceed from this point on. *If* they return the girl and offer sacrifice to Apollo, *then* the plague might be lifted; but *if* they do neither—or one but not the other—*then* all the Greeks will presumably die as a result of the affliction called down on them by Agamemnon's rejection of Khryses. Moreover, the degree to which this forecast in particular has a reach that encompasses the very tale that enframes it only strengthens the link between seer and storyteller. The alternative engaged by failure to heed Kalkhas' advice is of course final for the narrative no less than for the fate of its characters, for the story of the *Iliad* no less than for the agents whose story it purports to be; for with the death of the Akhaians by plague, the poem too will reach an untimely end.

Other instances of prediction in the poems use this conditional structure more overtly. The Tiresian prophecy in *Odyssey* 11 offers the most noteworthy example, and has already been the subject of extensive analysis.[30] Here the forecast of Odysseus' return home, slaying of the suitors, inland journey and gentle death is projected over no less than four paired sequential alternatives, each of which holds out the possibility of either success or else nonfulfillment and failure— and with the latter, of the abrupt termination of all subsequent alternatives, the death of the hero and the dead end and closure of the narrative itself. The same *if-then* structure also informs the prophecy given by Proteus to Menelaos (*Od.* 4.546- 47), in which the Spartan's return to a funeral at Mykenai is represented as contingent on whether Orestes will already have killed Aigisthos. Likewise, Nausithoos' forecast of the wrath of Poseidon as a result of safe passage granted an enemy of the god (*Od.* 8.564-71, 13.172-78) clearly leaves Alkinoos with a choice in the matter.[31]

On the overall relation between prophecy and the structure of Homeric narrative, Peradotto (1990:67-68) observes:

> What the prophet is represented as knowing is not so much the future as the fact that there is a measure of order and regularity in events, that characters and actions issue in definite or usual—and therefore predictable—results. He does not *see* future events; he reads their seeds or sign. It is not a matter of revealing a mystery, but of stating conditioned probabilities. It is not a matter of constricting the field of decision, but of clarifying the framework within which it operates. . . . The prophecy [of Teiresias in *Odyssey* 11] could be conceived of as a narrator's grid of possibilities. Placed at the turning-point of the poem it both summarizes the turns of plot that have kept the story going so far, and anticipates the possibilities of the tale's future. It is both review and preview from the still, timeless perspective of death, *outside the plot*, as it were.

As "a narrator's grid of possibilities," a projection of "the possibilities of the tale's future," prophecy offers a viewpoint that is essentially *external* to the text. To this extent, it coincides with the vision enjoyed by the storyteller himself, who controls the development of the narrative from a position

somewhere "outside the plot." It is tempting to see in the figure
of Kalkhas an embodiment of precisely this detached
perspective. Despite the suspicions Agamemnon entertains (*Il.*
1.101-08)—and Kalkhas himself has the wits to anticipate
(76-83)—the seer's viewpoint is a *disembodied* one, atemporal
and ostensibly free from bias and any ulterior motivation. His
is an authoritative voice that speaks from *outside* the
parameters of his own historical—and textual—situation.
Before he agrees to prophesy, Kalkhas in fact insists (74-83)
that Akhilleus promise to protect him from whatever ill will
his interpretation will provoke. This request is unique; nowhere
else in Homer are participants in Assembly scenes immune from
the give-and-take of their agonistic structure.[32] Akhilleus
takes up the challenge that Agamemnon throws in Kalkhas'
face (106-15), and the seer himself disappears from the scene—
making his only other appearance some twelve books later (*Il.*
13.43-65), in an unrelated scene in which Poseidon assumes his
persona to encourage the Aiantes to hold their own against
Hektor. However it is motivated in the tale, this request for
protection in fact functions as the door through which
Akhilleus now enters the conflict.[33] The seer's demand that
another act as surrogate, to defend his truth against the
hostility he foresees it will cause, thus highlights his own
privileged and also necessarily liminal status within the
society of warrior elite at Troy. This marginality mirrors the
viewpoint from which he observes events.

Such a viewpoint could be called *synchronic*, as long as it is
understood that by this term is meant a vision that
comprehends the delicate web of events—*woven from strands
both of necessity and choice*—that delineates the likely or
perhaps even determined consequences of unique acts of
ostensibly free will. As Peradotto (1990:67) notes, "the seer is
less inclined to present a simple and absolute vision of future
events that to illuminate what philosophers would later call
certain necessary or probable causal relationships." Ehnmark
(1935:75; quoted by Peradotto), on the subject of "conditional
prediction" in Greek seercraft, observes that "the oracle
foretells the future subject to certain conditions; it can predict
the consequences of a certain course of action" that is itself
subject to choice. Let me translate these claims into
narratological terms, on the assumption that Kalkhas indeed
embodies a cloaked authorial presence. What both storyteller

and prophet "see" are the concatenations of events that follow necessarily from any given decision—whether that decision belongs (from Kalkhas' viewpoint) to peer individuals enmeshed in the sack of Troy, or else (from the narrator's viewpoint) to characters (including Kalkhas himself) in the song of that siege. Both viewpoints implicitly embody a range of vision and also a strategy of control over the progress of the narrative that none of the other characters can enjoy. Where their vision differs is in the narrator's privileged access to how the enframing story in fact will end, while for the prophet that end is represented as a matter of pure contingency, a statement of little more than "conditioned probabilities." *If* the Greeks return the girl to her father *and* propitiate Apollo with a hecatomb, *then* the god *might* lift the plague from them. For the storyteller, on the other hand, this contingency is a feigned one, merely a narrative ploy. It is in fact just another instance of the contrafactual trope of what *would have* happened *if . . .* His characters choose to act as he alone—or in conformity with his narrative tradition—chooses for them.

What this suggests is that the range of Kalkhas' vision is itself a trope for the storyteller's control over the temporal dimensions and the competing narrative vectors of his tale. The synchronic nature of this character's viewpoint marks one strategy engaged by the storyteller for representing himself and his relation to the narrative he tells. Kalkhas offers a perspective implicitly external to the context in which he speaks, thanks to his association with an authority that lends him credibility either "directly"—by appeal to the belief-systems of a community in which prophetic vision is thought to be divinely inspired—or else through reference to lines of authority drawn within the text itself, by mirroring the relation within the frame-narrative between Muse and storyteller. Whichever perspective we ourselves adopt, the final result is one and the same. For from either viewpoint, the tale takes the form of a linear course punctuated by moments of ostensible choice at which alternative paths for the narrative fork and fork again until some closure is finally reached and the tale comes to its end.[34] From either viewpoint, moreover, and notwithstanding all appearances, the rhetorical device that structures how this vision operates is that of *projection*. Despite the fact that what seemed first to legitimate Kalkhas' vision is his *reprise*—in an *analepsis* or "flashback"—of prior events in the story, his vision and that of the narrator ultimately both coincide in a "still, timeless perspective...*outside the plot*" (Peradotto 1990:68) that is dominated by the strategy of *prolepsis*. Their vision is gridlike and schematic. Like all seers, Kalkhas recounts prior events only in order to lay bare their abstract causal nexus and to project their future narrative contingencies, all the better to clarify "the framework within which [decision] operates." The poet's mirroring of his own control over the tale in the figure of the prophet as an *embedded* narrator thus paradoxically draws attention to how *disengaged* and *extratextual* this position truly is.

3. THE MUSE AT PYLOS

Although he shares with Kalkhas the same formulaic introduction in *Iliad* 1—at least at the structural level of the type-scene (§12)—and functions equally in an intercessory role, the figure of Nestor embodies a radically different focalization. The contrast is already implicit in the terms of the expanded description (§12c) used in his case. The full passage (*Il.* 1.247-52) has been quoted and discussed earlier (§7); there the opening lines (247-49) received primary emphasis, and led to the conclusion that his characterization draws on traits that identify him as a bard in his own right, a kind of "self-singer." The closing lines, which advert to Nestor's remarkable age, also demand consideration in terms of how authority is structured in the narrative (250-52):

§20

τῷ δ᾽ ἤδη δύο μὲν γενεαὶ μερόπων ἀνθρώπων
ἐφθίαθ᾽, οἵ οἱ πρόσθεν ἅμα τράφεν ἠδ᾽ ἐγένοντο
ἐν Πύλῳ ἠγαθέῃ, μετὰ δὲ τριτάτοισιν ἄνασσεν.

In his time two generations of mortals had already died—
those who had before grown up with him, and the ones born
    to them
in sacred Pylos—and he was ruling among the third.

What is most striking here is the degree to which these lines dwell on Nestor's relation to his community—or better, communities, given the fact that his life to date has already spanned two generations.[35] This contrasts sharply with the marginal status of Kalkhas among the Akhaians, where the seer's connection with his community is minimized in favor of the vertical line of authority that binds him with Apollo, thus ensuring his detachment from his peers (§§15-16). Though identified by the patronymic Thestorides (*Il.* 1.69), Kalkhas in fact has a relatively unknown and perhaps even suspect genealogy; his father indeed "looks fictitious" and— considering the fact that the same name is given to two different individuals later in the poem (*Il.* 12.394, 16.401)— "Thestor" may well be "for Homer . . . a general-purpose name devoid of very specific associations" (Kirk 1985:60). Nestor, on the other hand, is directly engaged in the history of his group. As leader of troops, participant in battle—albeit to a limited extent—and chief counselor to the Akhaian kings, his involvement in the life of his community is immediate and full. Moreover, the range of experience he enjoys as a result of his extraordinary years gives him a privileged perspective on the events that unfold around him. I will return to this issue shortly. At the same time, his viewpoint also has bearing on the analogy between Nestor the *aoidos* and the narrator himself, which must now be examined.

Above and beyond the specific attributes they have in common—fluency, sweetness, clarity, honeylike allure—the *mode of narration* both Elder and Bard use strengthens their likeness. Here a distinction drawn initially by Plato, transformed by Aristotle (*Poetics* 1448a19-28, 1460a5-11) and most recently reworked by narratologists offers a useful framework for analysis.[36] In a famous passage in the *Republic* (Book 3, 392c-395d), Plato identifies two different "styles of speaking" (λέξεις) in literature. On the one hand, there are those parts of a narrative in which the narrator simply describes events and agents "in his own person," with no attempt "to persuade us that the speaker is anyone but himself" (393a); this Plato calls διήγησις (*diêgêsis*).[37] It must be distinguished, on the other hand, from those parts in which—as if through a kind of impersonation[38]—he speaks "as if he were someone else" (ὥς τις ἄλλος ὤν), representing the direct speech of his characters by "assimilating his manner of speech as nearly as he can to that of the character concerned" (393c), and thus through μίμησις (*mimêsis*). The Homeric epics, along with such genres as the dithyramb, obviously embody a mixture of both styles (cf. 394c: δι' ἀμφοτέρων), a blend of "simple narrative" or "*narratized* discourse" (Genette 1980:170) and "reported" or "imitated" speech.

So-called "direct," mimetic discourse may of course also incorporate a diegetic mode. That is, a fictional character can be represented by the storyteller not only as *speaking* his own words, but also in the act of *narrating* events, namely as what can be called a "secondary narrator," as distinct from the principal narrator of the frame-story. For example, the narrative structure underlying the passage in Book 7 of the *Iliad* in which the storyteller, speaking in the *persona* of Nestor, has the old man relate the tale of his single combat against the Arkadian Ereuthalion (*Il.* 7.132-56), would take the following form. Here the letters A-C and D-F once again arbitrarily designate events narrated at each level of the discourse:

§21

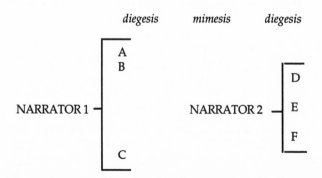

In addition to sketching the lines of authority that structure embedded narration, what this schema also suggests is that the diegetic activity of the narrating character may serve as an analogue of that of the main narrator himself. Figures within the story can themselves function as storytellers in their own right. This raises the possibility of mirroring at the level of both the narrative *content* and also the *act* of narration, both the tale and the mode of its telling. To a certain degree, this applies in the case of Kalkhas (§§14-15). The content of his account of the plague duplicates, albeit in the bare form of a synoptic aetiology and projection, the fuller narrative of events already told and yet to be recounted by the principal narrator.

This kind of "secondary" *diegesis* or embedded narration is far more characteristic of the speeches of Nestor, however. Here the *mimesis* of his words more often than not takes the form of his reminiscence of stories that closely resemble the principal narrator's discourse. The tales the old man tells are in substance the same as the singer's longer tale of the Akhaians at Troy, with which they incidentally also share the same moral horizon, both shaped by the values of a warrior elite. While the trope of embedded *diegesis* is exploited to its fullest in the *Odyssey*, especially but not exclusively in Odysseus' tale to the Phaiakians, the major instances in the *Iliad* are Glaukos' account of Bellerophontes in Book 6 (*Il.* 6.155-95); the autobiography of aged Phoinix in the *Embassy* scene (*Il.* 9.438-95), along with his tale of Meleager (*Il.* 9.527-99); and the fable of Niobe, recounted by Akhilleus in Book 24 (*Il.* 24.602-17).[39] Only the second of these is an example of the first-person *diegesis* so characteristic of Nestor's tales; the others are examples of "simple" (ἁπλῆ)—albeit embedded—narrative. It is worth noting that the Meleager story is prefaced by the statement (*Il.* 9.524-27) that it is a recollection (μέμνημαι) of what "we have heard" (ἐπευθόμεθα) about "the ancient (πάλαι) glory of heroes" (κλέα ἀνδρῶν | ἡρώων), whereas Phoinix's account of his own life obviously draws on his own experience. The status of memory as the source of his tales—and of Nestor's as well—will concern us shortly.

Nestor's stories differ from those of the main narrator in two important respects. First, and like the tale Phoinix tells about himself, they are generally autobiographical,[40] and thus embody an explicit first-person perspective that, except in invocation of the Muses and occasional apostrophes in the frame-narrative,[41] is absent from the tale told by the principal storyteller. The high frequency of autocitation in his speeches, as we saw, is what makes Nestor the bard of his *own* story. The fact that he is the protagonist of most of his tales has the effect of minimizing the narrative distance between himself and what he tells, while for the singer of the frame-story that

distance is usually kept at a maximum.[42] The extent to which
the latter, prophetlike, assimilates his perspective to that of
the Muse who inspires him from "outside the plot" contributes
to the illusion that his viewpoint, strictly speaking, has no
bias at all—that it is less one perspective among many than a
kind of clear, objective light in which the truth of the events
narrated can stand forth in and of itself.[43] Nestor's
personality, by contrast, is an integral part of his focalization.
Not only is the old man directly engaged (even intrusive) in the
life of his community, but his involvement more often than not
takes the form of self-promotion—or better, in a sense that will
soon be explored in more detail, of promoting the unique
perspective that he brings to events, a perspective informed by
the long reach of memory to which his great age gives him
access.

Second, and closely related to this first point, is the fact
that the *mimesis* of his words is generally restricted to
embedded *diegesis*. Unlike the principal narrator, Nestor
recounts events "purely" and only rarely incorporates direct
speech (*mimesis*) in his tales, whereas *mimesis* amounts to some
45% of the "mixed" text of the *Iliad* itself.[44] That is to say, his
own viewpoint is hardly ever effaced by that of any other. A
single, notable exception would seem to be the old man's
"impersonation" of the speech of Menoitios to Patroklos during
his account of his visit to the house of Peleus in order to recruit
Akhilleus for the war (*Il.* 11.783-91):

§22

Πηλεὺς μὲν ᾧ παιδὶ γέρων ἐπέτελλ᾽ Ἀχιλῆϊ
αἰὲν ἀριστεύειν καὶ ὑπείροχον ἔμμεναι ἄλλων·
σοὶ δ᾽ αὖθ᾽ ὧδ᾽ ἐπέτελλε Μενοίτιος, Ἄκτορος υἱός·
Ἀτέκνον ἐμόν, γενεῇ μὲν ὑπέρτερός ἐστιν
    Ἀχιλλεύς,
πρεσβύτερος δὲ σύ ἐσσι· βίῃ δ᾽ ὅ γε πολλὸν
    ἀμείνων.
ἀλλ᾽ εὖ οἱ φάσθαι πυκινὸν ἔπος ἠδ᾽ ὑποθέσθαι
καὶ οἱ σημαίνειν· ὁ δὲ πείσεται εἰς ἀγαθόν περ.᾽
ὣς ἐπέτελλ᾽ ὁ γέρων, σὺ δὲ λήθεαι· ἀλλ᾽ ἔτι καὶ
    νῦν
ταῦτ᾽ εἴποις Ἀχιλῆϊ δαΐφρονι, αἴ κε πίθηται.

And old Peleus was telling his own son, Akhilleus,
to be always best and preeminent beyond all others,
but Menoitios, Aktor's son, spoke to you in turn as follows:
'My child, by right of blood Akhilleus is higher than you,
though you are elder; but he is greater by far in strength.
Speak sound words to him, and give him good counsel,
and show him the way. If he listens it will be for his good.'
This is what the old man said, but you have forgotten. But
     even now
you might say this to wise Akhilleus, and he might be
     persuaded.

Direct quotation in a text is conventionally read as an index of objectivity, a sign that the speaker is "assimilating his manner of speech . . . to that of the character concerned" (*Rep.* 393c), thereby faithfully representing that other's perspective.[45] But this should not be allowed to obscure the fact that this trope is always controlled by the perspective of the speaker who chooses to nest the direct statement in his own speech.[46] Nestor cites Peleus' admonition to Akhilleus (783-84) indirectly, with the infinitive construction favored by *oratio obliqua*, whereas Menoitios' words to Patroklos (786-89)—who is himself the addressee of the speech in which Nestor embeds them—are directly quoted here.[47] This *mimesis* may briefly hide his face, but it cannot mask his motive. His use of mimetic, embedded speech aims at "strengthening the hortatory effect of his own speech" (de Jong 1987:174), whose goal is to convince Patroklos to prevail upon Akhilleus to return to battle. This serves implicitly to establish the dominance of his own perspective; even when he "impersonates" another speaker, his quotation is selective, governed not only by a certain viewpoint but also a definite rhetorical aim. There is of course a sense in which the same might be said in general of the principal storyteller's own "impersonation" of characters such as Nestor.

Let me first address the issue of viewpoint, resuming the contrast between Nestor and Kalkhas. At the level of their content, it is obvious that Nestor's speeches incorporate appeals to tradition to a far greater extent than does the speech of Kalkhas. My point here is not that prophets are somehow "untraditional" figures. It is true that the nature of their type may well give them far more leeway for riddling or unconventional statements than does that of other characters, but this is itself of course very conventional indeed, and in fact to be expected whenever they appear on the scene.[48] It is instead that *explicit* references to tradition—to the way things were before and so, *a fortiori*, to how they always are or should be—more often characterize the speech of other figures, and that of Nestor in particular. The preceding chapter argued that the emphasis placed on his remarkable longevity in the second half of his description (§20) serves to formulate his *ethos* in terms of the generic type of the Elder. Both textually and by convention, the aged are ever long-winded and prone to talk about the past.[49] Thanks to their vast experiential breadth, they can see circumspectually "both before and behind" (ἄμα πρόσσω καὶ ὀπίσσω#), since they "know many ancient things" (παλαιά τε πολλά τε εἰδώς#), and their vision is informed by an unerring sense of propriety, namely by what their moral tradition deems "right and fitting" (κατὰ μοῖραν). Of course, a similar match between verisimilitude and characterization can be found in the case of *all* generic figures properly so-called.[50] The impulsive behavior of Iliadic warriors, for instance, draws no less on the terms in which male youth is habitually understood by the community that receives the tale of their exploits. So too in the case of the elderly, for whom heroic restlessness has "naturally" yielded to prudent loquacity. What is special about the conventions that motivate the behavior of figures like Nestor, however, is how the cultural constraints that help shape their representation in narratives also involve conventions that govern the production of those narratives themselves. Young men are expected to *act* rather than *talk*, but the talk traditionally associated with the elderly engages issues that bear directly on how—and when, and for whom, and under what circumstances—the past gets remembered and passed on to subsequent generations. Such memorialization and transmission are central to epic in a way that the specific acts recalled and retold perhaps are not.

Chief among the traits Nestor shares with the storyteller of the frame-narrative are those that involve the *activity* of memory.[51] For however privileged the narrator's position may be with respect to the outcome of the events he recounts, and to whatever degree (thanks to the Muses) he can scan their contingencies with the detached and proleptic view of a seer, the mode of presentation that dominates his own work *as a narrator* is actually that of *analepsis*. He is as much the conduit of a relatively fixed though still flexible tradition of

tales—the sung "glory of men" (κλέα ἀνδρῶν)—as is Nestor
of the glories of his own lost youth. The singer's invocation of
the Muses at the opening of the *Catalogue of Ships* (*Il.* 2.484-
93), as Pucci has argued,[52] in fact embodies *both* these
viewpoints simultaneously. At the same time as he appeals to
the eternal (non-repetitive) presence of divinity to guarantee
the truth of his account (485), the act by which they reveal
that truth to him, and he to his audience, always remains one
of *recollection* (492: μνησαίαθ'). This speaks to the unique
poetic and social dynamics of oral performance. Beneath the
narrative fiction of direct inspiration by gods, this reference to
memory implicitly adverts to the oral transmission of tales—
namely, to the extensive tradition of narratives to which the
storyteller himself is heir and by which he is to some extent
constrained. The proleptic or "prophetic" influence he may
exercise over his narrative is limited by the very form and
content of the stories told by other narrators over the long course
of narratives performed on countless other occasions before
countless other audiences. His "prophetic" vision and control
are thus in turn subject to control by the activity of memory, by
the shape of the tale he has inherited from that tradition, and
no less from the expectations and interests of the audience
before whom his tale is sung.

In this light, the degree to which Nestor's speeches so often
open out on the antiquity of pre-Iliadic narratives is
significant. Once the analogy between Elder and Bard has been
asserted in the opening lines (*Il.* 1.247-49), the second half of
Nestor's description (§20) cites his remarkable age. His
longevity determines his focalization and also the specific
direction of his view. His vision is informed by the vanishing
world of the past, the lost glory of his own *aristeia* some two
generations prior to the war at Troy. More than any other figure
in the *Iliad*, Nestor embodies the activity of recollection, the
ambiguous sweet grief of *mnêmosynê* so central to oral
traditions. His direct, experiential access to the past contrasts
sharply with the mediated access most others enjoy, for whom
it is largely a matter of fabled song, of *kleos* in the sense of
"hearsay" or "rumor." Agamemnon qualifies his mention of the
hero Tydeus with the words ὣς φάσαν οἵ μιν ἴδοντο
πονεύμενον· οὐ γὰρ ἔγωγε | ἤντησ' οὐδὲ ἴδον· περὶ
δ' ἄλλων φασὶ γενέσθαι [*So they say* who had seen him in

action, since I myself neither encountered or saw him; but *they say* he surpassed all others.] (*Il.* 4.274-75). And even for old Phoinix in the *Embassy* scene, the heroic past is represented as something indirectly transmitted, a matter of fables *heard* from others—οὕτω καὶ τῶν πρόσθεν ἐπευθόμεθα κλέα ἀνδρῶν | ἡρώων [So it was in the old days too, the glory of men we *heard about*, of heroes] (*Il.* 9.524-25)—although he characterizes his tale of Meleager as an "event" (ἔργον) that he himself remembers, as a contemporary if not as an eyewitness (527).[53] Nestor, on the other hand, is quite literally the encyclopedic memory of his group, the keeper of its narrative bloodlines. He alone in fact has access to the genealogical inventory of *all* the Greeks who came in ships to Troy, which he relates for Peleus at Phthia when the troops are first being recruited for the expedition (*Il.* 7.125-28):

§23

ἦ κε μέγ' οἰμώξειε γέρων ἱππηλάτα Πηλεύς,
ἐσθλὸς Μυρμιδόνων βουληφόρος ἠδ' ἀγορητής,
ὅς ποτέ μ' εἰρόμενος μέγ' ἐγήθεεν ᾧ ἐνὶ οἴκῳ,
πάντων 'Αργείων ἐρέων γενεήν τε τόκον τε.

Surely Peleus, aged horseman, would groan greatly,
best counselor of the Myrmidons, and their speaker.
Once, questioning me in his house, he greatly rejoiced
to hear the generation and parentage of all the Argives.

This statement deserves consideration. Embedded in an analepsis (cf. ποτε) that extends back behind the *Iliad* tale to events near its very origin, Nestor's reference to his enumeration of the troops man by man is at the same time also anticipatory of events within the poem itself. It reaches back only to point *forward* to the narrator's own catalogue five books "earlier" (*Il.* 2.493-760). The speech the old man gives in Peleus' house and subsequently recalls some ten years later in substance recapitulates the storyteller's feat in Book 2. More properly, however—within the story's absolute chronology— that catalogue is in some sense a reprise of what Nestor has *already* recounted at Phthia. Much like Kalkhas' account of the events leading up to the Plague (§15), the present passage assimilates Nestor's act of recollection to that of the principal narrator and thereby marks the point at which their focalizations converge. But here the convergence is in one crucial respect even closer, since *the old man's inventory is the authoritative one.* Nestor's is the *original* list against which the narrator's *Catalogue* should be checked—if only it were possible—for its accuracy. The relation between them is thus much harder to schematize than in Kalkhas' case (§§16-17), and the following is only a partial representation of its complexity:

§24

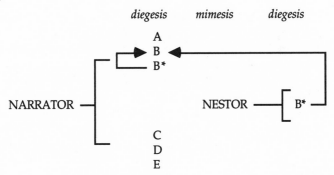

Here the unbracketed letters A, B, D and E designate events—the abduction of Helen, the recruitment and mustering of the troops; the death of Akhilleus, the fall of the city—that belong to the story of the sack of Troy but which are not explicitly told within the *Iliad* itself. In strict narratological terms, they are *extradiegetic,* in the sense that their referents fall outside the temporal scope of our poem.[54] An asterisk indicates analepsis, marking the fact that an event cited within the tale (B*) refers back to one of those external events (B); and the lines terminating in arrows trace the direction of backward reference in the *Catalogue of Ships* as well as in Nestor's reprise of his conversation with Peleus. What complicates the latter and makes visual representation difficult is the fact that the old man's recollection in Book 7 is simultaneously flashback *and* foreshadowing, analepsis *and* prolepsis. A second line might be drawn between the two events designated by B*, to indicate that Nestor and the Narrator are performing essentially identical catalogues at two different points in the chronology of the *Iliad* story; but this would make the diagram more intricate than useful.

This abbreviated mention of the scene at Phthia is itself of course but a fragment of a larger embedded tale whose narration is resumed and developed more fully at a later point (*Il.* 11.765-803), when Nestor reminds Patroklos of his visit (along with Odysseus) to Peleus' house (cf. §22); both will shortly be considered in greater detail. The only other significant examples of "extradiegetic analepsis" in the *Iliad* that are in any way similar to Nestor's here—namely, which evoke prior events within whose framework the *Iliad* itself is situated—are Odysseus' recollection of the prophecy at Aulis (*Il.* 2.299-30) and Antenor's (*Il.* 3.203-24) of the original embassy of Odysseus and Menelaos to the Trojans. Neither, however, enjoys additional reference "forward" to a flashback by the narrator himself.

Another and even more significant aspect of Nestor's analepsis directly touches on this central issue of narrative authority. For what the singer of the *Catalogue* claims (*Il.* 2.484-92) cannot be done unless he is somehow aided by divine inspiration—

§25

ἔσπετε νῦν μοι, Μοῦσαι Ὀλύμπια δώματ' ἔχουσαι—
ὑμεῖς γὰρ θεαί ἐστε, πάρεστέ τε, ἴστέ τε πάντα,
ἡμεῖς δὲ κλέος οἶον ἀκούομεν οὐδέ τι ἴδμεν—
οἵ τινες ἡγεμόνες Δαναῶν καὶ κοίρανοι ἦσαν·
πληθὺν δ' οὐκ ἂν ἐγὼ μυθήσομαι οὐδ' ὀνομήνω,
οὐδ' εἴ μοι δέκα μὲν γλῶσσαι, δέκα δὲ στόματ'
        εἶεν,
φωνὴ δ' ἄρρηκτος, χάλκεον δέ μοι ἦτορ ἐνείη,
εἰ μὴ Ὀλυμπιάδες Μοῦσαι, Διὸς αἰγιόχοιο
θυγατέρες, μνησαίαθ' ὅσοι ὑπὸ Ἴλιον ἦλθον.

Tell me now, Muses who have your homes on Olympos—
for you are goddesses, you are present, and you know all
        things,
whereas we only hear what is said, and know nothing at all—
who were the leaders and chief men of the Danaans.
I could not tell or name the multitude [of troops],
not even if I had ten tongues and ten mouths,
an unbreakeable voice and a heart of bronze within me,
unless the Olympian Muses, daughters of Zeus

who wields the *aigis*, remembered all those who came
beneath Ilion.

—is a feat that Nestor himself ostensibly accomplishes relying
only on his powers of recollection. Moreover, his single voice—
clear, honeyed and fluent—apparently enjoys strength enough
to name *all the Greeks* and their parentage (*Il.* 7.128: πάντων
'Αργείων), namely to perform what the storyteller would
need "an unbreakable voice and a heart of bronze" to narrate
fully.[55] Whereas the principal narrator, with seerlike
detachment, appeals to his link with the Muses who "know all
things" for the source of his knowledge (cf. *Il.* 11.218, 14.508,
16.112), the old man draws on no source other than that of his
own vast personal memory. He therefore replicates the
Catalogue from a point of view *within the plot*, not from some
aloof and timeless perspective *outside* it; and his authority for
what he says is grounded in what he himself has *seen*, not in
some mediated access—e.g. hearsay—to the events in question.
I will return to these issues.

A passage from the *Odyssey* implicitly raises many of the
same issues in substantially the same way. On the beach at
Pylos, Nestor begins his reply to Telemakhos' request for news
about Odysseus with a speech that in significant respects
resembles the prologue to an epic narrative (*Od.* 3.103-19):

§26
Ὦ φίλ', ἐπεί μ' ἔμνησας ὀϊζύος, ἥν ἐν ἐκείνῳ
δήμῳ ἀνέτλημεν μένος ἄσχετοι υἷες 'Αχαιῶν,
ἠμὲν ὅσα ξὺν νηυσὶν ἐπ' ἠεροειδέα πόντον
πλαζόμενοι κατὰ ληῖδ', ὅπῃ ἄρξειεν 'Αχιλλεύς,
ἠδ' ὅσα καὶ περὶ ἄστυ μέγα Πριάμοιο ἄνακτος
μαρνάμεθ'· ἔνθα δ' ἔπειτα κατέκταθεν ὅσσοι
    ἄριστοι.
ἔνθα μὲν Αἴας κεῖται ἀρήϊος, ἔνθα δ' 'Αχιλλεύς,
ἔνθα δὲ Πάτροκλος θεόφιν μήστωρ ἀτάλαντος,
ἔνθα δ' ἐμὸς φίλος υἱός, ἄμα κρατερὸς καὶ
    ἀμύμων,
'Αντίλοχος, πέρι μὲν θείειν ταχὺς ἠδὲ μαχητής.
ἄλλα τε πόλλ' ἐπὶ τοῖς πάθομεν κακά· τίς κεν
    ἐκεῖνα

πάντα γε μυθήσαιτο καταθνητῶν ἀνθρώπων;
οὐδ' εἰ πεντάετές γε καὶ ἑξάετες παραμίμνων
ἐξερέοις ὅσα κεῖθι πάθον κακὰ δῖοι Ἀχαιοί·
πρίν κεν ἀνιηθεὶς σὴν πατρίδα γαῖαν ἵκοιο.
εἰνάετες γάρ σφιν κακὰ ῥάπτομεν ἀμφιέποντες
παντοίοισι δόλοισι, μόγις δ' ἐτέλεσσε Κρονίων.

Friend, since you have reminded me of the grief in that land
we sons of Akhaians suffered, unrelenting in our strength—
whether how much in ships on the misty ocean
as we wandered for plunder wherever Akhilleus led,
or how much around the huge city of lord Priam
we fought, where those who were the best among us were
    killed:
there lies Aias the warlike, and there Akhilleus,
there Patroklos, equal to a god in council,
there my beloved son, both strong and blameless,
Antilokhos, who excelled as a runner and a fighter
—and we suffered many other evils in addition to these.
Who among mortal men could recount them all?
Not even if you stayed here five years or six
could you ask about as many evils as the bright Akhaians
    suffered there;
you would return home, worn out, before then.
For we contrived against them intently for nine years
with all kinds of strategems, and finally Kronos' son brought it
    to pass.

The similarities these lines bear to formal epic proems, if
not exact, are nonetheless noteworthy. The traditional prologue
generally includes the following elements, in somewhat
variable order but still with a very high degree of consistency.
In keeping with my limited purpose, I offer only the barest
summary here, much simplified, and refer to other scholarship
for fuller discussion, analysis and examples:[56]

§27
    (a) INVOCATION
    A divinity (or divinities) is invoked to sing, inspire or call to
mind a certain narrative of events.

    (b) THEME
    A noun, generally specified by a short qualifier, identifies
the theme and so functions as a title—e.g. *The Wrath of
Akhilleus, The Building of the Wooden Horse* (cf. *Od.* 8.492-
93)—for the narrative that follows.

    (c) ELABORATION
    A series of relative clauses fleshes the title out, sometimes
taking the form of a *de facto* Table of Contents for the tale, but

more often with more general purpose, "to refer to the great scope of the action, its pathetic quality, the nations involved, and the role of the gods in all of it" (Ford 1992:20).

(d) POINT OF DEPARTURE

An episode within the overall narrative account is specified—or the divinity is given leave to pick any episode (*Od.* 1.10: ἐξ ἀμόθεν γε)—as the point at which the present narration will begin.

It is clear that Nestor's reply to Telemakhos roughly conforms to this basic pattern. To be sure, a formal Invocation is lacking. Nestor's account is inspired by no Muse, but instead occasioned by a request that he recall (101: μνῆσαι) the death of Odysseus; the verb is repeated at the opening of his response (103: ἔμνησας). Still, this emphasis on memory in the context of formal narrative in itself serves as a kind of "secular" invocation.[57] Though Telemakhos offers him the (formulaic) alternative of speaking either on the basis of what he has *seen* with his own eyes or else what he has *heard* from another—εἴ που ὄπωπας | ὀφθαλμοῖσι τεοῖσιν ἢ ἄλλου μῦθον ἄκουσας (93-94; cf. *Od.* 8.491)—the basis for Nestor's tale is, once more, not "rumor" but his own direct eyewitnessing of the events.

Its Theme is extremely broad. With "titling syntax" (Ford 1992:20), Nestor begins as if he has been asked to recollect what could be called *The Grief the Akhaians Suffered Abroad* (ὀϊζύος, ἣν ἐν ἐκείνῳ | δήμῳ ἀνέτλημεν...υἷες Ἀχαιῶν)—and it is at this early point, as Ford (1992:74-75) notes, that his proem modulates into a traditional *recusatio*, to the effect that no mortal could give a full account of such a topic. Other characters who also act as narrators in the *Odyssey*—Helen (*Od.* 4.240-43), Odysseus (*Od.* 7.241-43, 11.328-31)—make similar apologies before speaking. More important, however, is the fact that this trope of refusal is central to oral poetry, marking the singer's dilemma in the face of the vast and unwieldy narrative tradition from which he must select the material for the performance of his present (and always incomplete) tale.[58] The touchstone for this dilemma is of course the *Iliad* narrator's claim (*Il.* 2.484-93 = §25) to be unable to "tell or name the multitude" (πληθὺν δ' οὐκ ἂν ἐγὼ μυθήσομαι οὐδ' ὀνομήνω) of troops who came to Troy unless the Muses called them to mind (μνησαίαθ᾽) for him. Much the same need expressly motivates their invocation on other occasions—before the list of men slain by Agamemnon (*Il.* 11.218) and by the Akhaians as a group (*Il.* 14.508), as well as prior to the description of the burning of the Greek ships (*Il.* 16.112).[59] It is also implicit in the emphasis laid in the prologues to both poems on the great quantity of material at hand, which in turn generates countless narrative possibilities. This is the case whether it be a question of the "myriad pains" (μύρι᾽. . .ἄλγεα) and loss of "many lives" (#πολλὰς. . . ψυχάς) caused by Akhilleus (*Il.* 1.2-3); or else the "very much" (μάλα πολλά#) wandering done, "many people" (#πολλῶν. . .ἀνθρώπων) seen and "many pains" (#πολλὰ. . . ἄλγεα) suffered by Odysseus (*Od.* 1.1-4).

Nestor's Elaboration, with its rhetorically balanced #ἠμὲν ὄσα / #ἠδ᾽ ὄσα clauses (*Od.* 3.105/107), is perfectly consonant with this pattern, as is his reference to the "many other evils" (#ἄλλα τε πόλλ᾽. . .κακά) the Akhaians endured (113). What is most remarkable here, though, is the sheer breadth of the expansion, for despite the *recusatio* that is attached to it, his Theme looks to be all-inclusive. Far more comprehensively than any other reference in either poem to the subject matter on which both draw for their content, Nestor's remarks range from (a) events *prior* and tangential to the actual siege, namely the Akhaian raids (106: πλαζόμενοι κατὰ ληΐδ᾽) alluded to on occasion in the *Iliad* (cf. *Il.* 1.163ff., 9.328ff.); through (b) events *during* the siege itself (107: περὶ ἄστυ μέγα); right up to (c) its *conclusion* in the sacking of the city (cf. 130) and its aftermath, culminating in a Catalogue of Fallen Heroes (108-12). The sweep of his proposed tale of *The Grief Abroad* would thus encompass the whole narrative tradition of the *Iliad* story—as distinct from our *tale* of the *Iliad*, whose scope is far narrower. In this respect, it intriguingly seems to match the range of what the Sirens themselves later promise to recount for Odysseus, namely πάνθ᾽ ὄσ᾽ ἐνὶ Τροίῃ εὐρείῃ | ᾿Αργεῖοι Τρῶές τε θεῶν ἰότητι μόγησαν [everything that in wide Troy the Argives and Trojans suffered by the will of the gods] (*Od.* 12.189-90).

Nestor's first appearance in the *Odyssey*, then, coincides with a sweeping synopsis of the *Iliad*, even if this is cast in the form—itself conventional and highly "poetic"—of a refusal to fulfill the promise of such a tale. Similar to the passage from *Iliad* 7 just examined (§§23-24) is the wide, "extradiegetic" reach of his reference here. It moves outside the poem in which it is embedded to incorporate that poem's narrative basis, evoking its context and—given the story's chronology—its *pretext* as well. Implicitly, it recapitulates what has transpired from the beginning of the prior tale right up to the threshold of the present one, concerned as it is with the issue of tales of Return. Moreover, these two passages (§§23/26), one from each poem, are linked to each other by a striking symmetry. The Catalogue of Fallen Heroes to which Nestor briefly alludes in the *Odyssey* (*Od.* 3.108-12) to summarize *The Grief Abroad* echoes the Catalogue of Troops he delivered nearly twenty years earlier at Phthia (*Il.* 7.127-28) at the very outset of the campaign. The old man is their living memory and everliving witness; he chronicles them first and last, both quick and dead. His honeyed voice sings the history of their grief through from beginning to end.

This is because his *recusatio* in the *Odyssey* is of course merely prologue to yet another comprehensive tale. Its reference (*Od.* 3.119) to god's will—μόγις δ' ἐτέλεσσε Κρονίων# [and finally Kronos' son brought it to pass]—not only marks the formulaic end of the proem (§22[c]), but also the introduction of a new song to be sung.[60] For after a short digression on how much Telemakhos resembles his father, Nestor launches next into a narrative of what can be titled *The Akhaian Nostoi* (130-200; 253-316). It begins from a specific point in time (130 = §27[d])—αὐτὰρ ἐπεὶ Πριάμοιο πόλιν διεπέρσαμεν αἰπήν [But when we had sacked the steep city of Priam . . .]—to recount the quarrel between the Atreidai (131-50), the departure of half the divided army (151-64) and the successful returns of Diomedes, Menelaos and Nestor himself (165-83). That is to say, it lays out the narrative ground for the tradition of homecoming tales of which the *Odyssey* is itself a part.

What is more, and despite its abbreviation, the very form his *Akhaian Nostoi* takes mirrors authorial structures, tropes and techniques familiar from the enframing tale. It opens (132-

50), as does the *Iliad* itself, with polarization and dispute—
ἔριν (136); cf. *Il.* 1.6 and the same trope employed in the scene
at Tenedos (*Od.* 3.161)—behind which lurks divine influence
(131-34), the grand mover of all plots, and specifically the
wrath (μῆνις) of Athene (135-36).[61] Once again, an Assembly
is convened to attempt resolution of the dispute; once again, it is
predictably unsuccessful. Its failure is in fact signalled
proleptically by reference to conspicuous violations of
convention and propriety that occur—the Assembly takes place
οὐ κατὰ κόσμον (138)—since the Akhaians meet towards
nightfall, and when they have all been drinking (138-39).
Further, Nestor's characterization of Agamemnon's plan to
placate Athene has recourse to the editorial νήπιος (146-
47)—as the device that both ironically foreshadows the
disastrous outcome of a narrated event and also expressly
asserts the narrator's foresighted control over the course of its
development.[62]

The simple structure of Nestor's tale, moreover, exhibits
precisely the pattern of branching alternatives we have just
examined, along which the narrator maps out the direction and
progress of his story. Specifically, the account takes the form of
a travelogue, in which the characters traverse three sites on
three successive days, at each one encountering mutually
exclusive alternatives for how and even whether their journey
will proceed. The tale ostensibly follows—though in fact
directs—them along a series of bifurcating decisions and
paths:[63]

§28
   (a) **Troy (130-58)**
      Delay (Agamemnon) vs. Departure (Menelaos)
   (b) **Tenedos (159-67)**
      Return to Troy (Odysseus) vs. Perseverance homeward
      (Diomedes, Nestor & Menelaos)
   (c) **Lesbos (168-75)**
      Long, safer route "inside" Khios vs. Short, more dangerous
      route "above" Khios (= 169: δολιχὸς πλόος)

At each of these sites, moreover, the influence of divinity is
invoked—Zeus (152 and 160-61), an unnamed δαίμων (166), a
divine sign (173-75), the "god" (183)—as the deep mechanism
that steers the homebound Akhaians and *a fortiori* the tale

itself along one of the two competing tracks. These sites are of course no less textual than spatial, opening out upon paths (οἶμαι) of song as much as paths through the Aegean.[64] They represent junctures in the narrative, nodes from which different trajectories for the tale can veer off towards different destinations, and upon whose "grid" the singer maps his story out. Nestor demonstrates precisely the same "navigational" control over these paths as does the narrator of the larger tale in which his is embedded. For the storyteller no less than his characters, these sites are the μέτρα κελεύθου (cf. *Od.* 4.389, 10.539), the marked stages along the way; and it is in their terms that the tale itself may well be stored mnemonically.[65]

To be sure, his tale is not, strictly speaking, the first in the poem to have *nostos* as a subject for narrative, hence the first to bridge the *Iliad* and the *Odyssey*; the allusion (*Od.* 1.325-27) to Phemios' story of *The Bitter Homecoming of the Akhaians* precedes it by several books. The latter is merely related as an event, however, diegetically and not through *mimesis*. Homer's audience hears this song only obliquely, as background music for the conversation between Athene and Telemakhos, and also through Penelope's aggrieved response (328-64); it is never sung within their own earshot, thus incidentally preserving their distance from the audience of suitors who actually hear the bard. Nestor's tale in Book 3, on the other hand, is produced directly, as the old man again assumes the role of an embedded narrator. His voice merges with that of the principal storyteller, and the latter's audience in turn rhetorically merges with Telemakhos.

The prophet-narrator's "synchronous" viewpoint thus finds its counterpart in the essentially *diachronic* vision that Nestor represents. The range of its diachrony is clear from the fact that his long speeches are always characterized by analepses that stretch back to events that lie well outside the text of both poems are *external* to the frame-narrative, as in the cases just cited.[66] To borrow Genette's terminology (1980:50), they for the most part amount to *heterodiegetic* analepses, defined as "analepses dealing with a story line (and thus with a diegetic content) different from the content (or contents) of the first [sc. the frame-] narrative." They touch on the vast antiquity of stories belonging to the otherwise unrecorded tradition of

narratives from which poems like the *Iliad* and *Odyssey*
emerge. To this extent, they mirror the larger epic tales that
enframe them, at the same time as they contextualize (or
"temporalize") that frame by appealing to the still greater
range of "absent" narratives that support and orient those tales
themselves. The events told in both poems, and represented as
already on the verge of cultural memory for Homer and his
eighth-century audience—who have only "hearsay" (κλέος)
to rely on in the absence of the Muse (*Il.* 2.486)—are themselves
just episodes in the broader temporal range of events spanned by
Nestor's own memory. By invoking the heritage of stories on
which the narrator also implicitly depends, the old man opens
the *Iliad* and *Odyssey* out towards their fabled past and
towards all other occasions on which their stories—or stories
like or unlike them—have been told, thus helping to situate
both within the long tradition of storytelling of which they
are only a small part.

It is indeed the temporality and direction of his viewpoint
that most immediately distinguish it from that of Kalkhas
and the narrator in his role as an inspired, "omniscient" singer.
If the link that authorizes the truth of Kalkhas' statements
and those of the principal narrator is a *vertical* one, binding
them—directly or otherwise—to Apollo and the Muse above,
Nestor's is *horizontal*. The old man is thoroughly embedded
within Akhaian society as the spokesman of its heritage, and
the specific kind of vision he enjoys is entirely conditioned by a
historical perspective.

Moreover, its historicity is not limited simply to what
could be called "hard" cultural data—ancient chronicles, lists
of men and genealogical inventories—but instead represents a
focus wider than that of merely individual experience. Nestor's
awareness, like that of the elderly in general (cf. *Il.* 3.108-10 =
§3), of what has already transpired on other occasions lends
him a vision that comprehends the pattern under which any
given situation is subsumed, and thus guarantees the quality of
his advice. To this extent, his viewpoint tends to embody that
of his community's moral traditions, and is therefore
paradigmatic, not simply personal. Segal remarks (1971:93)
that Nestor, "the repository of the lore of the past, comes as
close as possible to being the voice of social expectation and
approval"—an approval reflected in the frequency with which

his advice is styled "best" (ἀρίστη) and "right and fitting" (κατὰ μοῖραν) by his peers.[67] He represents the bond between his present community and its cultural heritage. Moreover, this bond is essentially a *narrative* one, a bridge made of stories. For it is through his recollection and telling of events some two generations prior to Troy, or some ten years prior to the time at which the *Odyssey* begins, that Nestor closes the distance separating his younger peers from their heroic ancestry, by conveying in narrative form the values that define that heroism. Rather than typifying a focus that lies "outside the plot," Nestor speaks with *and from within* the voice of the tradition from which the poems issue.

This makes Nestor no less an analogue of the narrator than Kalkhas is, what I have called a "cloaked authorial presence" in the text, even despite these divergent points of view. The portrayal of Nestor as a storyteller in his own right lets the narrator implicitly ground his own narrative activity in the diachronic reach of the old man's tales—just as with Kalkhas (§16) that grounding was sought in the timeless link between Prophet and Apollo, Singer and Muse. The narrator sings "the glory of men" just as Nestor sings his own *kleos* and also— because he represents himself as a model of heroism—the glory to which all warriors should aspire. In turn, the figure of an aged singer whose memory effectively bridges past and present calls attention to the narrator's own dependence on the memory of cultural values preserved through the oral transmission of narratives like those Nestor himself is depicted as telling. Moreover, since Nestor's tales are represented *in the ongoing act of their narration*—namely, as tales performed orally and in keeping with definite narrative conventions, cued by specific exigencies within a specific community of listeners for a relatively specific purpose[68]—his performance also reflects the activity of the speaker of the frame-narrative. The occasions on which he speaks mirror some of the dynamics of traditional oral narration.

The suasive, parainetic and aetiological (or "hypomnetic") functions of his tales come to mind here, since these have received the most attention in recent scholarship.[69] Detailed studies of Nestor's long speeches in the *Iliad* have shown that, however "digressive" they initially seem, they always serve a specific rhetorical aim. On the one hand, they offer themselves as *exempla* designed to illustrate the praiseworthiness and validity of the specific pieces of advice they preface, and thus as both paradigmatic and hortatory. His reference to the likes of Perithoös, Dryas and Theseus (*Il.* 1.262-72) asserts his long-established role as a mediator at the point at which the quarrel between Akhilleus and Agamemnon has reached a dangerous impasse. In turn, the tale of Ereuthalion in Book 7 (*Il.* 7.132-56) calls to mind an occasion that precisely matches the one in which the Akhaians now find themselves, as the objects of Hektor's challenge to single combat. And his extended narrative (*Il.* 11.672-72;765-90) of his own glory in battle against the Eleians is obviously meant to inspire his addressee with a similar sense of heroism.[70] On the other hand, other tales present proofs of the antiquity of customs whose occasions of renewal prompt his speeches, along with confirmation and endorsement of the values these customs embody. A notable example is his story of the funeral games of Amarynkeus at the close of the contests in Patroklos' honor (*Il.* 23.629-43), on which it directly puts the *imprimatur* of tradition for the audience within the narrative as well as for the eighth-century audience to whom it is indirectly addressed by the storyteller, and for whom the remembrance and celebration of the heroic dead is an issue of great moment.[71]

The degree to which Nestor's speeches take their immediate performative context into account is especially clear from those instances in which they seem to exhibit "innovations" on traditional material, "variations" expressly adapted to their situations and the character of their recipients.[72] What this "innovation" above all else suggests is the flexibility of oral narrative traditions, in which preservation of the past is not simply a matter of transmitting fixed content from one generation to the next, but instead an interactive, "homeostatic" process. Meaning in oral narratives arises partly as a function of tradition, but partly also under the influence of the immediate context of performance, thus through an interchange between broadly institutionalized expectations and factional or even strictly personal motives.[73] However much conventional rules may prescribe the form of expression and even (to a greater or lesser degree) the content of what gets expressed, the shape of the past is always a function of the present concerns of the community in which it is remembered.

No less than the viewpoint represented by Kalkhas, Nestor's perspective therefore also implies a certain freedom— at very least, the freedom for omission ("forgetting"), adaptation, amplification and rhetorical emphasis—with respect to his tales. Although subtler, perhaps, his focus too likewise marks a position of authorial control; and it additionally raises the larger issue of the storyteller's own sensitivity to his performative context. The sensitivity alluded to here of course radically differs from the kind exhibited by Kalkhas when he anticipates Agamemnon's anger and insists on Akhilleus' assurance of protection before he agrees to speak (*Il.* 1.76-83). The prophetic message Kalkhas imparts is meant as an objective one, a "divine truth" strictly impartial to the character of its recipients; and it is in fact to insure that its impartiality will be respected that he first calls on Akhilleus for help. Nestor's tales, on the other hand, demonstrate a marked awareness of and adaptability to their audience. Each of his narratives is implicitly tailored—and sometimes even expressly, as in his allusion in *Iliad* 1—to fit the *ethos* of its addressee and the specific nature of the circumstances. As such, performative context appears to play a larger role in determining what shape his tales take. Unlike Kalkhas' "timeless," objective speech, the motivation for Nestor's stories is to a large extent situationally dependent.

4. A FUSION OF VISIONS

The figures of Kalkhas and Nestor exhibit different narrative strategies and delineate distinct narrative focalizations in the *Iliad*. It is tempting to entertain the possibility that together they trace the contours of the position occupied by the principal storyteller himself, and in so doing manifest some of its own inherent tensions.

On the one hand, the seer's view is *detached*, synchronic or atemporal and, from a standpoint external to the plot, proleptically scans the abstract "grid of possibilities" by which the course of events in the tale is structured, the narrative paths that continue to fork until some final closure is reached. It is a point from which even the constraints of the

traditional story seem, at least hypothetically, to be
constraints freely chosen by the narrator whom Kalkhas
represents.[74] On the other, the perspective embodied by Nestor
is an essentially *engaged* one, diachronic and temporal,
enmeshed in the story of the *Iliad* as well as in its telling—
namely, in the long history of narration from which the *Iliad*
emerges in the course of performance as a specific tale. As such,
its relation to the inherited tradition of tales has all the
appearance of being *internal*, as it were. Nestor speaks in the
same diegetic mode as the storyteller and with the same
honeylike voice, implicitly assuming the posture of a bard,
transmitting the κλέα ἀνδρῶν to his audience on well-
defined occasions, within certain situational constraints and
with certain identifiable aims. Moreover, in terms of their
content, his tales always operate within the parameters of
traditional wisdom, to persuade and justify, to offer paradigms
for behavior appropriate to heroes in specific situations, to
praise or blame with reference to values established by the
moral conventions of his community. All the same, of course, he
is not simply an apologist for the settled order of things, no
mere mouthpiece for tradition.[75] The more explicit dependence
on tradition—both epic and ethical—exhibited by his tales
does not make them in their way any less manipulative (or
"innovative"); it is just that the strategies they involve differ
fundamentally from those represented by Kalkhas.

This difference is worth exploring. It will be convenient
here to discard the cloak of fictional characters and address
the issue in terms of the relation between the storyteller and
his inherited tales. The figures of Kalkhas and Nestor
respectively embody positions of seemingly lesser and greater
dependence, focalizations respectively external and internal to
the traditional narrative. How do these two different points of
view match the perspective—or perspectives—of the narrator
of the *Iliad*?

On the one hand, and on those few occasions when the
narrator speaks *in propria persona* to address his own relation
to the tale he tells,[76] the "prophetic" model represented by
Kalkhas is the privileged one, and Nestor's diachronic
perspective seems denigrated and even suppressed. I have
already had occasion to mention this, with reference to the
celebrated invocation that precedes the *Catalogue of Ships* in

the second book (*Il.* 2.484-93). There (§25) the vertical link between Poet and Muse is at first explicitly emphasized at the expense of the narrative model that Nestor embodies. As goddesses, the Muses alone "know everything" (ἴστέ τε πάντα#) by virtue of their eternal presence (πάρεστε) to the events now being told after the fact, whereas mortals (including the narrator himself) have only heard "what is said" and indeed "know nothing at all" (486: ἡμεῖς δὲ κλέος οἶον ἀκούομεν οὐδέ τι ἴδμεν).[77] The ambivalence in the term *kleos*—denoting either unreliable "rumor" or else undeniable "glory," mere "hearsay" or the genuine "fame" that epic narratives claim to preserve—has been addressed by Pucci in a well-known study. There he draws attention to how the invocation strives to exclude the former sense of *kleos* by insisting on the timeless truth of the Muses' vision and the immediacy with which it is imparted to the narrator (1980:174-75):

> As the Muses tell the poet the names and the stories of the heroes, i.e., their *kleos*, he will not repeat a human rumor (*kleos*), a traditional story whose truth remains suspicious . . . but he will repeat the unique vision that the Muses have of the events. Moreover, the direct assistance by the Muses implies that the poet repeats their words directly and immediately; his song should not be like an echo that becomes more and more indistinguishable as it travels. . . . Only in this way will his song be free of those qualities that mark *kleos* as an unverifiable, irresponsible rumor. . . . The poet attempts to minimize and almost to eliminate temporal and spatial dimensions; his rendition of the Muses' tale . . . would in fact eliminate, were it possible, temporality, deferral—the condition of repetition—and the distance which marks the territory of difference.

On this account, it is the poet's desire to forestall suspicion that his tale is only "rumor" (*kleos*)—a doubt encouraged by the well-known risks of loss and adulteration undergone by stories handed down orally, "like an echo," over the long course of time—that motivates his embrace of a "prophetic" perspective for his narrator. This strategy seeks to guarantee the truth of his tale by recourse to an unchanging, atemporal source external to the narrative itself and so untouched by the uncertain vicissitudes of its transmission.[78] It assimilates his viewpoint to that of a seer, a perspective divinely underwritten by the Muses and Apollo, instead of representing him as just one link in a fragile chain of "what others have said." What thus authenticates his story is his claim that deities eternally present to the events themselves impart their own timeless vision to the narrator and inspire him to sing. The frailty of human knowledge of the past is thereby remedied and strengthened by the direct, unerring vision of the gods.[79]

The adoption of a "prophetic" viewpoint therefore allows the storyteller far greater freedom from that tradition than if he portrayed himself as simply the mouthpiece of a history of stories transmitted orally. As a mere conduit for "what others have said"—a purveyor of the κλέα ἀνδρῶν, understood as what has been *rumored* about the heroic dead—he can only repeat their hearsay, and the truth of his narrative can be judged only in terms of a wavering and dubious criterion. At first glance, the inherent instability of oral narration, unaided by the Muse, might seem to favor more latitude for innovation in the story he tells—and thus greater freedom in one sense. In the face of divergent or even contradictory accounts of the same event, the narrator would be less constrained to introduce variations without endangering his own trustworthiness. But this freedom would be bought at the price of acknowledging that his own tale, like every other, is itself subject to question: if its source is mere "rumor" (*kleos*), and in the absence of some warranty external to the oral course of its transmission, the same predicate can be attached to whatever he says, and his own version thus falls under the same suspicion. Implicit reliance on "what others say," like too strenuous an assertion of unique authorial control—a fatal gesture canonized some one hundred lines later in the punishment of Thamyris (*Il.* 2.594-600)—would only undermine his credibility. Hence the Muses. As guarantors of the κλέα ἀνδρῶν—in the positive sense of the true account of deeds performed in the heroic past—they put the seal of unassailable, eyewitness testimony on what the narrator relates. To this extent, the suspicion that clings to the veracity of tales transmitted by so unstable a medium as word of mouth can be safely laid to rest, since through the Muses the inspired storyteller appropriates their power of divine autopsy.[80]

At the same time, however, the vision they lend him does not entirely contravene the narrative tradition within which he operates. Pucci's insistence on a stark opposition between the terms in which the invocation is cast—between immediacy and deferral, atemporality and history, synchrony and diachrony, *kleos* as "truth" and *kleos* as "rumor"—obscures the fact that the appeal to the Muses elegantly engages *both* viewpoints simultaneously. For the narrator's recourse to the timeless vision of the gods does not supplant "what others have said," denying or eliminating the historicity of orally transmitted accounts, but paradoxically serves to confirm it. Earlier comments drew attention to the eminently pliable nature of memory in so-called traditional communities. Without written documentation to fix it permanently, the content of the distant past—and, along with it, the values such content embodies—always remain a freely floating entity, a polymorph continually refashioned, and one whose form on each occasion is ultimately subject to endorsement or rejection by its present audience. Its approval insures that throughout all permutations of the tale, and even despite them, what emerges is always "a perpetually recreated song of truth" (Zumthor 190:84). Within such contours, the Muses themselves—as guarantors of that ever-changing but still always self-consistent truth—come to represent the community's consensus about its own tradition, embodying what Svenbro has called the "contrôle social" exercised over oral narrative performance.[81] The Daughters of Memory are mirrors of verisimilitude, tacitly shaping and reshaping each new tale in terms of the audience's own immediate, shifting interests, and at the same time celebrating those interests as unchanging, timeless and permanent.

Much like Nestor himself, then, the narrator speaks as bards *always* have. The form of his speech—the fixed cola, lines and type-scenes, and even the broad narrative structures or motifs—remains thoroughly traditional, and so too the very content of his tale. His *diegesis* of the κλέα ἀνδρῶν—of events now lost to human sight but recoverable through narratives performed on specific occasions under the Muses' unswerving direction—evokes the *same* conventional patterns in the *same* language, reconstructing a past informed by the "same" values that "tradition" never ceases to endorse. The "prophetic" option embodied in Kalkhas, then, is not chosen at the expense of breaking the chain of inherited stories, erasing the lines of their diachrony, severing the continuous link with the past represented by the figure of Nestor. The narrator's appeal to the Muses, despite its recourse to a vertical, "extratextual" link—in which the outlines of authorial control can be discerned—does not signal his disavowal of oral tradition in the interest of insuring the truth of what he sings. To be sure, by exploiting the ambiguity inherent in *kleos*, his appeal explicitly calls that tradition into question—thus letting us glimpse "the storyteller tipping his hand" (Peradotto 1990:67)—but it never goes so far as to deny it. The work of time intervening between the events themselves and his own performative situation is in one sense undone by his appropriation of the "achronic" perspective of the Muses, but this itself is done in the interest of representing the traditional account in its timeless purity, as is "right and fitting" (κατὰ μοῖραν).

The same strategy is also at work in the case of Nestor's diachronic point of view. While his activity as a storyteller without recourse to divine inspiration might well serve an analogue for the "unregulated" oral transmission of stories—thereby verging dangerously on the condition represented by Thamyris, who would challenge the Muses themselves—the *autobiographical* nature of his tales is a device that implicitly seeks to insure their truthfulness. However much their perspective is historical and linear, and thus implicitly raises suspicions of adulteration and bias, they too claim to embody an immediate, eyewitness account of the events they relate. Unlike deeds that have only been *heard of* but never actually *seen* by their narrators (cf. *Il.* 9.524-27, 20.203-06)—for which "hearsay" (ἐπευθόμεθα, ἀκούοντες) is admittedly the only available source—what Nestor tells is confirmed by his own presence at the scene and his role as an agent.[82] Recourse to immediate experience therefore guarantees his credibility. To this extent, the old man is not only a "self-singer," but also in a sense his own Muse as well. In narratological terms, this is a function of the first-person *diegesis* that characterizes his tales. By grounding Nestor's stories in direct *autopsis*, namely in the memory of an actual participant, the poet does for this embedded narrator the same as he does for the teller of the frame-narrative. The strategies employed in both cases—appeal to (oneself as) an eyewitness, appeal to the Muses—are structurally identical. Both aim to overcome the risks of change and loss immanent in the course of oral transmission over time by invoking a fixed and incontestable presence to the events themselves.[83]

NOTES

1. Lord 1960, Detienne 1967, Zumthor 1990:196-209, Foley 1991, and references.

2. Along with the works cited in the preceding note, see also Goody & Watt 1968, Goody 1977, Ong 1982, Thomas 1989 (on forgetfulness); Svenbro 1976, Gentili 1988 (on "social control"); Austin 1966, Braswell 1971, Bourdieu 1972, Ingalls 1982, Edwards 1987b (on authorial innovation).

3. Pucci 1980:174-75, Segal 1983, Edwards 1985:71-93, Goldhill 1991:69-108.

4. Gouldner 1965, Svenbro 1976:78-80, Humphries 1978:209-41, Nagy 1979:213-52, Edwards 1985:11-13.

5. Goldhill 1991, with extensive references to other scholarship; and Ford 1992:90-125.

6. See Bal 1985:119 on the distinction between *narrator* and *author*: "When . . . I discuss the narrative agent, or *narrator*, I mean the linguistic subject, a function and not a person, which expresses itself in the language that constitutes the text. It hardly needs to be said that this agent is not the (biographical) author of the narrative. The narrator of *Emma* is not Jane Austen. The historical person Jane Austen is, of course, not without importance for literary history, but the circumstances of her life are of no consequence to the specific discipline of narratology."

7. Wilamowitz 1916:250-51, Sheppard 1922:27, Post 1939:174, Owen 1946:15, Segal 1971: 90-91.

8. Segal 1971:91. If Pucci (1977:40, note 34) is correct in characterizing the description of Nestor in *Il.* 1.247-49 as an instance of mild parody, the association between Nestor and Hephaistos might even suggest that the old man shares some of the god's buffoonery.

9. The unusual length of their descriptions is noted by Vester 1956:2-7, Lang 1983:140-41; cf. Kirk 1985:79.

10. Arend 1933:116-21, Lohmann 1970 and Hansen 1972.

11. In Nestor's case (*Il.* 1.245-48) the elements of this formula are distributed over several lines, in order to accommodate the description (cf. *Od.* 2.80-81) of the dashing of the scepter by Akhilleus, although the basic pattern of

Alternation—{X spoke}—{X sat down}—{Y stood up among them}—is preserved.

12. Other instances of introductory characterizations of a speaker—what de Jong (1987:199) calls "speaker-recommendations"—occur in the *Iliad* at 2.212-23 (Thersites), 13.216-18 and 15.281-84 (Thoas) and 18.249-52 (Poulydamas); shorter forms can be found at 6.76 (Helenos), 7.278 (Idaios), 7.325 = 9.94 (Nestor) and 7.366 (Priam). De Jong remarks (1987:198) that such instances "turn out, almost without exception, to have a function: they stress the quality in which a speaker is speaking."

13. See Bal 1985:100-13 for an extended discussion with examples, along with an attempted justification for the term "focalization" instead of the more familiar "point of view" or "narrative perspective"; also Genette 1980:189-94 and (in response to Bal) 1988:72-78. De Jong's succinct definition (1985:7) is also worth quoting here: "The text . . . is the result of the narrative activity of a *narrator*. The content of this text is the story . . . and the agent on this second level of the *focalizer*: it is with his/her/its eyes and in general through his/her/its perception that we . . . perceive the fabula. . . . This fabula consists of the chronological sequence of events, and the agents on this level are the *actors*." Rimmon-Kenan 1983 provides a useful synopsis of narratological theory. For its application to the text of the *Iliad*, see de Jong 1985 and 1987, especially 29-36.

14. Freidenberg 1930, Whitman 1958:161, Nagy 1979:263, Kirk 1985:138-42, Thalmann 1988, Martin 1989:109-10.

15. De Jong (1987:118-19) classifies the aside in *Il*. 2.220-21, along with such briefer remarks as that Zeus was "hateful" (στυγερός) to Hera (*Il*. 14.158), as instances of "implicit embedded focalization," and notes: "It is important to pay attention to the narrative situation in these cases, because it makes one aware that the qualification of an event or person is not necessarily universal (not all characters consider Zeus hateful. . .) or true, but may represent the opinion (focalization) of one character." Freidenberg 1930:243-44 notes the degree to which Thersites' argument repeats many of the points raised by Akhilleus in Book 1.

16. Martin 1989:110-13. On the ideology of appearance implicit in the notion of *kalokagathia*, see Junther 1930:113-14, Dover 1975:41-45;69-73, Donlan 1973 and 1980:106-07.

17. Compare *Il*. 12.233-37;241, *Od*. 2.178-82; and see below, Chapter 3.4, on the narrative pattern that the structures the rejection of a seer's advice.

18. The exact line describing the scope of Kalkhas' vision is unique in Homer, though the essential core of the formula (after the A2 caesura) recurs in Hesiod (*Thg*. 38; cf. *Thg*. 32), with reference to poetic vision. On its significance in both poets, see Pucci 1977 and 1980.

19. Kalkhas' speech therefore represents an instance of one type of *mise en abyme* or "embedded text," in the sense defined by Bal 1985:146: "When the primary fabula and the embedded fabula can be paraphrased in such a manner that both paraphrases have one or more elements in common, the subtext is a *sign* of the primary text." See also Bal 1981 and de Jong 1985, who refers to this trope as a "mirror story."

20. Genette 1968.

21. This is of course not to suggest that the invocation of the Muse is any less a narrative strategy than the Apollonian pedigree of Kalkhas' seercraft. See Svenbro 1976:16-35, Detienne 1967:9-27, Pucci 1990.

22. This is not to overlook or discount the scepticism about the honesty of individual prophets that is tolerated in the text of the poems. Despite the attitude evinced by a number of characters within the *Iliad* and *Odyssey*, however, it should be noted that nowhere in Homer are prophecies ever discarded without peril. On the narrative function of prophecy in the poems, see Peradotto 1974 and 1990:59-93.

23. See also de Jong 1987:29-31 and Prince 1987:65-66 (s.v. "Narrator").

24. Note that the pattern schematized above in §12, however rigorous its syntagmatic order, does not require that an expanded, "particularizing" description be given in every case. Compare, for example, *Il*. 7.365-67, where the introduction of Priam's speech during the Trojan Assembly omits the description altogether and thus instead exhibits the pattern §12(a)-(b)-(d). The prophet Helenos at *Il*. 6.76 is characterized simply by his epithet, as οἰωνοπόλων ὄχ' ἄριστος#.

25. Thalmann 1984:225, note 53.

26. I use these terms in the sense given to them by Genette 1980:40, who defines *analepsis* as "any evocation after the fact of an event that took place earlier than the point in the story

where we are at any given moment," and *prolepsis* as "any narrative maneuver that consists of narrating or evoking in advance an event that will take place." See Genette 1980:33-85; Bal 1985:49-68 (who prefers "flashback" and "flash-forward"), de Jong 1987:81-90 and Prince 1987:68 (s.v. "Order").

27. See de Jong 1987:68-81. I adopt the term "contrafactual" for the sake of convenience, despite her accurate distinction (68-69) between "normal counterfactuals," in which both clauses run counter to reality, and what she calls "*if-not* situations," where only one clause is contrary to fact. The example cited above in §18 is an instance of the second type.

28. Bassett 1938:100-02, Kullmann 1956:42-48, Reinhardt 1961:107-10, de Jong 1987:78-81.

29. De Jong concludes her account of contrafactuals with the claim (1987:80-81) that, far from serving as an index of what has been called (Genette 1969:92-93) "l'arbitraire du récit," namely the limitless number of avenues open to the narrator to continue his tale—thus confirming the events in his tale as purely *fictitious*—contrafactual tropes in Homer instead serve as indices of the alleged *reality* of the events he narrates, thus strengthening its versimilitude.

30. The following discussion of Tiresias' prophecy clearly owes much to Peradotto 1990:59-93.

31. Peradotto 1974.

32. This is even true in cases in which both the seer's age and his mastery of seercraft might be thought to earn for him a measure or respect from his audience. Compare the rough treatment received by both Halitherses and Mentor at the hands of the suitors in *Odyssey* 2.

33. See Genette 1969 on the distinction between *motivation* and *function* in narratives.

34. On the analogy between poetry and prophecy as kinds of "navigation," see Ford 1992:48, with note 92.

35. Or three? See *Od.* 3.245 and Kirk 1985:79.

36. Aristotle's subordination of both *diegesis* and *mimesis* to the category of the mimetic lies outside the scope of this study; see Genette 1980:163 and 172-73, Rimmon-Kenan 1983:106-07, de Jong 1987:5-8 and Kirby 1990.

37. Plato's full term for the narration of events or the reporting of speech through indirect discourse is διήγησις ἀπλῆ, "simple" or "pure" *diegesis*, namely *diegesis* that is

"unmixed" (397b: ἄκρατον) with representational elements. The sense of ἁπλῆ is a matter of some dispute; see Genette 1980:162, note 2, with the response of de Jong (1987:3-5), who prefers "single" or "single-layered" as a translation. Since this issue is of no special relevance here, I have chosen simply to contrast *mimesis* with *diegesis* in terms (cf. Genette 1980:163-64 and 1988:42-43) of an opposition between a "narrative of words" and a "narrative of events."

38. This qualification reflects the obvious fact, already acknowledged by Plato himself—who refers to the *appearance* of direct speech (393b: δοκεῖν . . . λέγοντα)—that the *mimesis* employed in nondramatic texts is in fact thoroughly diegetic. Although a character is made to speak "in his own person," as it were, namely by means of direct discourse, the (diegetic) narrative frame in which this speech occurs is not thereby suspended. Genette (1980:163-64) notes that "the very idea of *showing*, like that of imitation or narrative representation . . . is completely illusory; in contrast to dramatic representation, no narrative can 'show' or 'imitate' the story it tells. All it can do is tell it in a manner which is detailed, precise, 'alive,' and in that way give more or less the *illusion of mimesis*—which is the only narrative mimesis, for this single and sufficient reason: that narration, oral or written, is a fact of language, and language signifies without imitating." Compare de Jong (1985:8): "The narrating activity of the narrator is permanent throughout the whole text: it is his voice which is responsible for the diegesis as well as the mimesis." For a summary of the problem, see Rimmon-Kenan 1983:106-16.

39. For a complete list of embedded speeches, see de Jong 1987:160-79. Kelly 1990 examines the distinction between *diegesis* and *mimesis* in Homer from the standpoint of epic correption.

40. In this respect, they amount to a coalescence of the three narrative functions—"N[arrator]", "F[ocalizer]" and "A[gent]"—discussed by de Jong (1985:7), who remarks that such a "combination of three functions in one person (N=F=A) belongs to autobiography and therefore cannot be illustrated from an epic text."

41. Minton 1960, Block 1982, de Jong 1987:18-20, Richardson 1990:170-82, Ford 1992:72-82.

42. On focalization and distance as aspects of narrative "mood," see Genette 1980:162-73.

43. See Auerbach 1953:3-23, Conte 1986 on the omniscience of the epic narrator, and Ford 1992:6-7 on the "transparency" of traditional epic; and in particular, Richardson 1990:123-39.

44. De Jong 1987:x. She cites (171, with note 45) some twenty instances of embedded direct speech in the *Iliad*, excluding roughly the same number of cases of *oratio recta* embedded in messenger-speeches, then proceeds to examine representative examples (179-85).

45. Richardson (1990:165-66) remarks that while "Homer's objectivity is falsely stressed, . . . his personal feelings are only rarely expressed in overt commentary and even then the judgmental or the emotional element is not salient." His discussion—drawn from Booth 1961—of three senses of "objectivity" that fail to apply to the Homeric narrator work only at the diegetic level of the text, and ignore embedded focalizations.

46. In §22, it is an instance of "tertiary focalization"; see de Jong 1987:169-71.

47. De Jong 1987:174 contrasts the *oratio obliqua* at *Il.* 11.784 with 9.254-58—where Odysseus, speaking to Akhilleus, presumably gives a *direct* quote of Peleus' advice to the hero— and concludes: "Although it appears from L 767-8 that *both* Odysseus and Nestor were present in Phthia at the moment Peleus and Menoetius adhorted their sons and, therefore, must have heard the *same* speeches, they each pick out those elements which are best suited to context and addressee. . . . Due to the fact that [the principal narrator] does not provide us with the words of Peleus and Menoetius themselves, it is difficult to assess to what extent Nestor and Odysseus are faithfully quoting them." Her point is well taken, even if her suspicion may be somewhat overstated.

48. The Homeric paradigm is of course the "winnowing-fan" central to Teiresias' prophecy in *Odyssey* 11.See Peradotto 1974:823 and 1980:438, with note 12.

49. Svenbro 1976:21-25, Finkelberg 1987, Falkner 1989.

50. Collins 1988:13-26.

51. Notopolous 1938, Vernant 1965:51-94, Detienne 1967:9-28, Moran 1975.

52. Pucci 1980:178-81.

53.   Cp. also *Il.* 4.370-75, 20.200-17; and see de Jong 1987:160-62, Ford 1992:61-67.

54.   See Genette 1980:228-31. Though with slightly different terminology, Bal 1985:59 offers the following distinction: "Whenever a retroversion [or "flashback"] takes place completely outside the time span of the primary fabula, we refer to an *external analepsis,* an external retroversion. . . . If the retroversion occurs within the time span of the primary fabula, then we refer to an *internal analepsis,* an internal retroversion." The *oral* context of the *Iliad,* however, demands that a finer distinction be made here. For the fact is that these events all belong to "the absent narrative whole" on which the performance of the *Iliad* implicitly relies, and from which it gets its orientation for both singer and audience. In this respect, they fall well *within* the range of that broader story.

55.   Kirk 1985:167-68, Ford 1992:68-79.

56.   Van Groningen 1946, Rüter 1969, Redfield 1979, Lenz 1980, Heubeck-West-Hainsworth 1988:67-69, Ford 1992:18-23.

57.   Moran 1975.

58.   See Ford 1992:67-82 for full discussion and references.

59.   Minton 1960, Block 1982, de Jong 1987:18-20, Richardson 1990:170-82, Ford 1992:72-82.

60.   Ford 1990:20: "The mention of the divine will (especially Zeus's plan) is a signal that the invocation is beginning to conclude, and at this point the poet specifies where the tale is to begin."

61.   Clay 1983.

62.   See below, Chapter 3.3.

63.   Similar bifurcation characterizes the splitting of the ships back into local contingents after Geraistos (175-83), with Diomedes landing at Argos while Nestor himself continues on to Pylos; the parting between Nestor and Menelaos after Sunion (278-85); and the division of Menelaos' ships at Cape Malea (286ff.).

64.   On "paths of song," see *Od.* 8.72-75;479-81, 22.347-48, along with Becker 1937:36-37, Durante 1976:123-34 and Ford 1992:41-42.

65.   Ford 1992:44-48, with reference to Ong 1977. Reece (1993:190-92) considers the hospitality scenes in the *Odyssey* as a series of "signposts" in whose terms the poet shapes and recalls his narrative; cf. Yates 1966.

66. For further discussion and examples of external analepsis, see Genette 1980:49-50 and 61, Bal 1985:59; on its function in Homer, see Austin 1966, Gaisser 1969, Lang 1983 and especially de Jong 1985 and 1987:160-68.

67. On the paradigmatic function of tales in the *Iliad*, and of Nestor's in particular, see especially Andersen 1975, along with Sachs 1933, Willcock 1964, Austin 1966, Davies 1969, Gaisser 1969, Braswell 1971 and Pedrick 1983. See Segal 1971 for an analysis of Nestor's speech to Agamemnon and Akhilleus in Book 1; and also Whitman 1958:183-84, Atchity 1978:260-64.

68. Svenbro 1974, Gentili 1985.

69. Sachs 1933, Cantieni 1942, Vester 1956, Willcock 1964, Braswell 1971, Segal 1971, Andersen 1975, Atchity 1978:260-63, Pedrick 1983, Davies 1986.

70. See Pedrick 1983 on the problem of to whom Nestor's paradigmatic speech in Book 11 is actually addressed.

71. Coldstream 1976, Nagy 1979:114-17, 206-09.

72. See especially Willcock 1964, Braswell 1971, Segal 1971, Atchity 1978:260-63, Pedrick 1983, Davies 1986. Segal's account of the rhetorical dynamics of *Iliad* 1.247-84 is the most detailed on the issue of how narrative *exempla* are adapted to the needs of their immediate context and audience. "Innovation" may not be the best term, of course, especially since it implies our access to an "original" version upon which "variations" are then subsequently performed. See Svenbro 1974:11-15 and Nagler 1974:1-26 on the status of oral texts as "multiforms" or "allomorphs" of an inherently fluid narrative.

73. On the dialectical relation between tradition or *habitus*—defined (76) as a "socially constituted system of cognitive and motivating structures"—and personal interests, see Bourdieu 1977:72-95.

74. Richardson 1990:167-96.

75. Segal 1971:93.

76. De Jong 1987:41-53.

77. Krischer 1965, Barmeyer 1968, Lesher 1981, Murray 1981, Walsh 1984:3-21, de Jong 1987:51-53.

78. Pucci's understanding of this passage, inspired by a Derridean framework, of course raises doubts about the ultimate success of this strategy; see especially 1980:175-77, 180-83.

79.   As de Jong (1987:51) correctly notes (*contra* Murray 1981:91): "The contrast described in 485-6 . . . is not that between 'knowledge and ignorance' . . . but between two different degrees or kinds of knowledge of the past: *human* . . . based on hearing (oral reports), and *divine*, based on seeing (autopsy)."

80.   Murray 1981:92-94, Walsh 1984:8-19.

81.   Svenbro 1976:16-35.

82.   Atchity 1978:260.

83.   These essentially identical strategies of appeal to the Muses and recourse to autobiographical narration are responses to a markedly critical attitude within the poet's own audience towards its traditions, a self-consciousness about what constitutes narrative authority. It is in certain respects a unique one, inasmuch as the oral literature of other cultures only rarely exhibits as pronounced a concern with this issue; see e.g. Bowra 1952:40-41, Ford 1992:31-32. Despite the different and indeed more complex issues involved, it is tempting to compare the veridical function of the Muses in the Greek tradition with the *Gilgamesh* narrator's repeated reference to a fixed, inscriptional source for his tale of the hero; see Tigay 1982:143-46.

3

Nestor as Intercessor: Figures of Mediation

1. INTRODUCTION

Both Nestor and Thamyris *move* through much the same "epistemic" terrain. That is to say, the space they share is best thought of not as a fixed grid of intersecting attributes and lines of authority. This is far too static a picture, and the analysis in the preceding chapters has perhaps contributed to what is in fact a flawed view of Nestor's place in the poems. He instead fills a *dynamic* space. The formulas that shape his character encode specific narrative potential; they are *indices of action*, even if such action is never fully realized in any given performance, and remains instead merely virtual, the memory and promise latent in the terms in which characterization takes place. For a character to be described as such-and-such essentially amounts to an implicit claim that she or he can be expected to behave in such-and-such a way. And if characters in traditional narratives essentially *are* what they *do*, we might expect to find this identification even more prominently engaged at levels other than that of simple description.

This requires a shift in perspective from isolated words, cola and lines—by which the first two chapters were guided— to the higher level of narrative structures, type-scenes and functions. This shift is an important one methodologically, for a number of reasons. First, the sweetness, the fluidity and the allure of honey, wine, sleep, desire, music, mourning, voice, Nestor, Muse, *aoidos* and Siren in themselves do little more than isolate a paradigmatic set of attributes frequently predicated of these nouns in Homer. Their full significance can be shown only in terms of how they actually operate in the course of the poems, namely in terms of the actions they promote and the common effects these actions have. That is to say, and to select just one instance from many, if wine is not only "fluid" and "sweet" like sleep but also *works* like sleep to induce (say) forgetfulness or a relaxing of vigilance, then the features they both share are not simply metaphorical, but instead have the status of functional elements—one might even say, of agents—that can retard, advance or deflect the story along one path or another. This clearly occurs (again, to pick from among several examples) in the cases of Polyphemos drunk and vulnerable in his cave in *Odyssey* 9 and Zeus lulled by sleep on the hill above the plain in the course of the *Dios apatê* in *Iliad* 14. Here wine and sleep are functional analogues. In this sense, even simple adjectival modifiers (λιγύς, γλυκύς, ἡδυεπής) could enjoy the same functional status in the text as do characters and actual events, namely as *loci* of narrative potential. The present chapter will begin to address this issue.

The tale of Book 1 of the *Iliad* proceeds along a linear course punctuated by crises at which alternative paths successively come into sight; choices are made, as if at crossroads, and then the narrative continues along the path ostensibly determined by those choices. What more specifically structures its progress is a steady rhythm of Crisis, Mediation and Response, in which the latter event rarely marks a true narrative closure, but instead only opens out on further crises, paths that fork and fork again. A Priest's Appeal for restitution of his Daughter is rejected by a King, and Plague ensues. The Mediation of a Prophet leads on the one hand to Approval and the Propitiation of offended Deity, but on the other to Strife between Warrior and King. An Elder's attempt to mediate their conflict—in which the successful Intercession of a Goddess is itself embedded—fails to win acceptance, and the Warrior withdraws from society. This Crisis triggers a second divine Intervention in the form of an Appeal to the highest God, whose Acquiescence on the one hand subordinates all the subsequent narrative to the guidance of a Plan, at the same time as it generates Conflict with yet another Deity. The book closes with successful Mediation of their strife, with everything ostensibly right in heaven, though impending Disaster among mortal women and men.

This chapter will attempt to disengage the event of Mediation from its central place in this course of narrative in order to map its contours better. My point of departure—no more or less arbitrary than any beginning—is a formulaic line; we have already encountered it in Chapter 1, in passing reference to the trait of Goodwill that often characterizes elderly figures. The address-formula ὅ σφιν ἐϋφρονέων ἀγορήσατο καὶ μετέειπεν [With kind intention he spoke and addressed them], which appears on a total of fifteen occasions (9X, 6X) in both poems, introduces the intercessory speeches of Kalkhas (73) and Nestor (253) in *Iliad* 1; despite (and because of) their failure to mediate crisis, their influence on the progress and direction of the ensuing narrative is an important one. The formula not only implicitly adverts to functional parallels between them, but also situates both within a well-defined group of figures in Homer. A clear typology of the Mediator emerges from examination of the characters whose words are introduced by this line and the contexts in which it is used.

It will facilitate analysis to consider this formula in terms of three distinct but interrelated narrative categories. On the one hand, its reference to the psychological quality of Goodwill (ἐϋφρονέων) functions as an intentional marker that signals the presence of a certain *type* of character. Much like the noun-epithet formula in general, it identifies a specific *ethos* that in its turn promotes expectations of specific kinds of action. What does a character described as ἐϋφρονέων generally do? Next, and as one instance of the larger set of formulas in Homer that introduce speeches,[1] the line also designates a well-defined narrative *situation* (σφιν . . . ἀγορήσατο καὶ μετέειπεν) in which this *ethos* customarily arises. The nature of this situation in fact helps motivate Goodwill as a predicate; that is, it makes the attribution of this trait to such characters a significant rather than a merely arbitrary or "ornamental" one. When and where are "well-intentioned" characters generally found? Lastly, the full import of both *ethos* and *situation* can only be assessed in terms of the *response* they receive from other characters, thus by reference to their affect on the ensuing course of the tale. This is because, as I will argue, both of these categories are themselves subordinate to the *function* they serve in the unfolding of the narrative in one direction or another. How are such characters generally received, and what is the nature of their influence on others? I hope to show that the type-scene of Mediation in which these three elements of *ethos*, *situation* and *response* are involved is not only central to narrative emplotment, but also marks the point at which the activity of the narrator himself is most in evidence.

It should be noted, finally, that what follows does not intend to be either an exhaustive or even the definitive study of Mediation in the poems. The specific markers of *ethos*, *situation* and *response* that will orient this analysis are not the only ones in whose terms Mediation scenes are constructed. Characters can and indeed do act in intercessory roles without necessarily first being introduced, for instance, by an address-formula that adverts to their Goodwill. For that matter, the situation in which Mediators come to the fore—most notably, that of a formal Assembly convened to debate some critical issue—need not always be present to signal their arrival on the scene. Here, as always, and even in the absence of distinct formulaic cues, broad narrative *function* is the determining factor. What recommends our concentration on the address-formula ὅ σφιν ἐϋφρονέων ἀγορήσατο καὶ μετέειπεν is the fact that it forms the nexus of a complex of narrative stances and gestures that together offer privileged access to Mediation as a significant scenic pattern in the poems.

2. *ETHOS*

While the formula ὅ σφιν ἐϋφρονέων ἀγορήσατο καὶ μετέειπεν occurs nine times without variation in the *Iliad* (1.73, 2.78;283, 7.326;367, 9.95, 15.285, 18.253) and six in the *Odyssey* (2.160;228, 7.158, 16.399, 24.53;453),[2] in the latter poem it also accommodates a small number of allomorphs. The shape most frequently taken follows the "he addressed him with qualification" pattern studied by Edwards (1970:10-12), and in place of the opening hemistich #ὅ σφιν ἐϋφρονέων [with kind intention, he . . .] admits two instances (*Od.* 2.24, 24.425) of #τοῦ ὅ γε δάκρυ χέων [shedding a tear for his sake, he . . .], in lines widely separated in the text but thematically quite close. In each case, the qualifying phrase describes a father's grief in remembrance of his absent and deceased son—old Aigyptios for Antiphos in the first Ithakan Assembly in *Odyssey* 2, aged Eupeithes for Antinoos at the beginning of the informal gathering of islanders in Book 24—

and in the second of these two passages the opening phrase is repeated at the close of the speech that it was used to introduce (*Od.* 24.438). This apparent restriction of the formula {Qualification + ἀγορήσατο καὶ μετέειπεν} to instances of either Goodwill or Sorrow displayed by elderly figures is highly suggestive; its significance will be explored shortly. The other cases of ἀγορήσατο καὶ μετέειπεν# filling the last half of the line exhibit no prior qualification at all, and instead take the form of #τοῖσιν δ' — u u —, with the name of the speaker in the Nominative case—Alkinoos (3X), Amphinomos (3X), Antinoos (1X)—substituting for the descriptive {#Participle} or {#Noun + Participle} in the space between the A1 and B1 caesuras.

The characters whose speeches are introduced by ὅ σφιν ἐϋφρονέων ἀγορήσατο καὶ μετέειπεν all fit a consistent ethical pattern. The line in each case serves to mark the following speaker as one whose *ethos* is trustworthy and authoritative, and whose advice therefore implicitly deserves the attention and approval of his audience.[3] Moreover, it is important to note that respect accrues to the speaker in most instances because of his great age; fully two-thirds (10 of 15X) of all uses of the formula predicate it of old men. This is obviously the case with Nestor himself (*Il.* 1.253, 2.78, 7.326, 9.95, *Od.* 24.53), whose longevity forms the core of his ethical type, and with whom the whole-line formula is indeed most often used. But it applies equally to other elders as well: to Priam in the *Iliad* (*Il.* 7.367), and in the *Odyssey* to Halitherses (*Od.* 2.160, 24.453), Mentor (*Od.* 2.228) and the Phaiakian Ekheneos (*Od.* 7.153). I have argued (Chapter 1.2) that the type of the Elder comes to expression in Homer through recourse to a small and readily identifiable complex of formulaic semes, which in addition to the intentional markers of Goodwill (or Sorrow) also make reference to the command of persuasive speech, unusual powers of memory, circumspection and privileged knowledge of the past. The general range of these terms has already been discussed; here we need only briefly mention such "speaker-recommendations" (de Jong 1987:199) as appear in conjunction with the address-formula.

Note first the description of Priam as θεόφιν μήστωρ ἀτάλαντος# [equal of the gods in counsel] (*Il.* 7.365) at the opening of his speech in the Trojan Assembly; the phrase appears elsewhere only with reference to Patroklos (Il. 17.477, Od. 3.110) and Nestor's father Neleus (Od. 3.409). The expanded description preceding the two occasions on which the address-formula is used with Halitherses identifies him as a figure whose credentials are impeccable. In the first (Od. 2.158-59), as he rises to interpret the omen of the eagles sent by Zeus, his preeminence in reading birdflight is matched by his ability to put signs into words. The second passage (Od. 24.452) points to his prudence or circumspection by recourse to a formula—ὁ γὰρ οἶος ὅρα πρόσσω καὶ ὀπίσσω# [for he alone looked both before and behind]—that we have already (Chapter 1.2) had occasion to consider.[4] Although the figure of Mentor is not characterized by formulas shared by other elders, his association with persuasion (πειθώ) is an abiding one; this trait will occupy our attention when we come to examine the typical nature of responses to the advice of intercessors. Athene's frequent impersonation of Mentor at critical moments in the Odyssey (Books 2, 3, 22, 24) also emphasizes his prominence as a counselor. The aged Ekheneos (Od. 7.155-58), finally, "oldest of the Phaiakians," is likewise marked by his "possession" of speech (#καὶ μύθοισι κέκαστο).

The remaining five instances, though predicated of young or middle-aged men—Kalkhas (Il. 1.73), Odysseus (Il. 2.283), Thoas (Il. 15.285), Poulydamas (Il. 18.253), Amphinomos (Od. 16.399)—only serve all the more to confirm the priority of the Elder in the role of intercessor, since the traits by which they are characterized more properly belong to the formulation of aged figures. The cases of Thoas—equally skilled in both warfare and debate (Il. 15.281-85)—and Amphinomos—whose words most pleased Penelope (Od.16.394-99)—have already (Chapter 1.2) been examined; the others deserve only brief mention here. Of these, the Trojan Poulydamas calls for special comment because the terms of his characterization expressly match those of the elderly. To begin with, we saw that the formula designating circumspection—{Patronymic + ὁ γὰρ οἶος ὅρα πρόσσω καὶ ὀπίσσω} [. . .for he alone looked both before and behind]—is found only twice in the poems, with reference to Poulydamas (Il. 18.250) and also to the aged seer Halitherses in the Odyssey (Od. 24.452). Although much younger—he is in fact the same age as Hektor himself—

Poulydamas nonetheless enjoys precisely those traits commonly predicated of aged men (*Il.* 18.249-53):

§29

τοῖσι δὲ Πουλυδάμας πεπνυμένος ἦρχ' ἀγορεύειν
Πανθοΐδης· ὁ γὰρ οἶος ὅρα πρόσσω καὶ ὀπίσσω·
'Έκτορι δ' ἦεν ἑταῖρος, ἰῇ δ' ἐν νυκτὶ γένοντο,
ἀλλ' ὁ μὲν ἂρ μύθοισιν, ὁ δ' ἔγχεϊ πολλὸν ἐνίκα·
ὅ σφιν ἐϋφρονέων ἀγορήσατο καὶ μετέειπεν

The *prudent* Poulydamas spoke first among them,
Panthoös' son, *for he alone looked before and behind.*
He was Hektor's companion, both born on the same night,
but he was better with words, the other far better with the spear.
With kind intention he spoke and addressed them.

By evoking the traditional contrast between *mythos* and *ergon*, speech and action, line 452 identifies the framework on which his character is constructed as the same as what structures the *ethos* of elderly figures. Its terms thus assimilate Poulydamas to their ethical paradigm. The *mythos/ergon* contrast in fact underlies the stark opposition between his *ethos* and that of the impetuous Hektor, his *alter ego* throughout the *Iliad* (cf. *Il.* 12.210-50).[5] His advice to retreat into Troy at a critical juncture in the tale, despite the fact that it is rejected by Hektor, nonetheless wins the narrator's editorial comment ὃς ἐσθλὴν ἐφράζετο βουλήν# [who had devised sensible counsel] (*Il.* 18.313); and a similar expression consistently describes Nestor's own counsel as ἀρίστη, "the best" (*Il.* 7.325, 10.302; and cf. 2.55). A later section of this chapter will examine Poulydamas' role in greater detail. For the present, we need only recall the extent to which the formula for circumspection in its various forms (*Il.* 3.108-10, *Od.* 2.158-59) is emblematic of the Elder—played off against the frivolous minds (φρένες ἠερέθονται) of younger men (cf. §3)—to appreciate the type of figure Poulydamas represents here. In this respect, moreover, it may be no accident that his father Panthoös is himself numbered among the aged advisers to Priam (*Il.* 3.146) who, "no longer engaging in battle, but excellent speakers still," talk sweetly, "like cicadas," in the shade of the Skaian Gate (3.150-52).

The characterization of the prophet Kalkhas was a major focus of the preceding chapter, and his speech to the Assembly at the opening of the *Iliad* is prefaced by the first instance in the poem of the formulaic statement of Goodwill (*Il.* 1.73). Although Mediation most often occurs between human antagonists, the seer's position at the boundary between the mortal world and that of divinity marks him especially for an intercessory role. As we saw, the difference between the kinds of focalization that Prophet and Elder respectively embody turns on the issue of the temporality of the vision each enjoys. Whereas the elderly enjoy authority thanks to their diachronic link with the traditions that shape their communities, a vertical link with deity authorizes prophetic insight.

It is in fact tempting to locate the point of intersection between Prophet and Elder—with the exception of Theoklymenos in the *Odyssey* and (presumably) Kalkhas here, all Homeric prophets are older men—in the trait of "circumspection" signalled by the ὅρα πρόσσω καὶ ὀπίσσω# [looks before and behind] formula. The precise sense of the phrase is not so easy to determine. Whereas all nine of the occurrences of πρόσσω alone have a clearly spatial meaning, the instances of ὀπίσσω (49X) unevenly skew it between spatial (17X = 35%) and temporal (32X = 65%) reference. These numbers of course have no necessary bearing on the sense of the conjunction of the two in πρόσσω καὶ ὀπίσσω#, and the best that can be said is that the phrase simultaneously intends a "look" in both spatial and temporal directions. The ability "to see both before and behind" in the mortal world finds its counterpart in the far broader (and explicitly) temporal sweep of prophetic vision. Kalkhas alone in Homer is given the descriptive verse ὃς ᾔδη τά τ' ἐόντα τά τ' ἐσσόμενα πρό τ' ἐόντα [who knew the things that were, the things to come and the things past] (*Il.* 1.70), though the essential core of the formula recurs in Hesiod (*Th.* 38; cf. *Th.* 32).[6] The prophet's claim to immediate access to events that both precede and postdate his own temporal horizon—an access that thanks to the Muses (*Il.* 2.485) the poet himself can enjoy—represents "circumspective" vision at its fullest extent.

A synopsis is in order here. It will perforce be provisional and tentative. One insight that emerges clearly from the study of clustered formulas at all levels of their manifestation (colon, line, generic scene) is the interdependence of these elements. The traits associated with Mediation seem to cross and overlap with a variety of figures: Old Man, Young Man, Nurse, Double, Prophet and Herald. What must be especially resisted at this point is the temptation to grant priority to the *ethos* of a fictional character or character-type (and so to what may prove to be the fiction of autonomous agency itself) over the *context* in which that agency comes to expression—a temptation only strengthened by habits of reading and interpretation, to say nothing for the moment of deeper presuppositions these habits imply. This is in keeping with the claim made earlier (Chapter 1.3), with reference to a quotation from Barthes, that what we habitually read as character in narratives may well be merely the "nesting of adjectives" around an otherwise empty core. This is a core, moreover, that is chiefly defined by its potential for action: character *is* as character *does*. For reasons that only the conclusion of this study can hope to justify, the decision to present a typology of Mediation in Homer by first splitting up the unity of its object into an *ethos* and its contextual parameters—themselves in turn split further into parameters of *situation* and *response*—risks misrepresenting the true nature of the issue. Granted this proviso, undoubtedly still a little cryptic at this point, we can proceed with a summary account of traits that constitute the *ethos* of the Mediator.

Several have been isolated. The most prominent, given my choice of the formula ὅ σφιν ἐϋφρονέων ἀγορήσατο καὶ μετέειπεν as a starting point, bears on the quality of his intentions. Here many of the terms examined in Chapter 1.2 with reference to the generic type of the Elder come into full play. The Mediator is a kindly figure, fair-minded, and thus better capable of grasping a given situation without personal bias. Advanced age is privileged, but by reason of features that can also appear (precociously) in the young. Such features include first and foremost the quality that I have rendered as "circumspection"—a trait defined at least in major part in terms of the temporal range of a character's vision. Thanks to the experiential breadth that age has won for him, to prophetic

gifts or to "soundness of mind," the Mediator enjoys the ability
to "see both before and after" the present (and always critical)
situation. An analysis of the actual content of intercessory
speeches will show that this "sight" generally comprehends
either (1) the generic status of the present situation, thus
issuing in speeches whose rhetorical mode is that of the
parable or paradigm; (2) its specific aetiology, especially
when the Mediator is also a Prophet, and so too the proper
response it enjoins along with the consequences of failure to
respond properly; or else (3) a firm sense of ethical horizons,
namely of what the Mediator's community deems "right and
fitting" (κατὰ μοῖραν // κατ' αἶσαν).

At this point, it may also be fitting to speak to the
variation #του ὅ γε δάκρυ χέων [shedding a tear for his
sake] in two instances of the overall address-formula. In
addition to kindly intentions, we saw that a specific kind of
grief also marks the speech of many elderly figures. The
responsion between Aigyptios and Eupeithes, respectively at
the beginning and the end of the *Odyssey*, is a rich one indeed.
That the formula in each case thematizes memory is itself
important, not only in view of the temporal breadth enjoyed by
intercessory figures, but also in terms of the objectivity this
breadth suggests. What in fact relates Aigyptios and Eupeithes
along the axis of this formula is their antithetical reactions to
the same deep personal sorrow. Both have lost sons, and in both
cases Odysseus himself is to some degree (more or less directly)
to blame. Their responses could not differ more, however.
Aigyptios subordinates his grief to the welfare of the
community at large, which hinges on the return of its absent
King. No assembly has met on Ithaka since Odysseus left for
Troy, he says; may Zeus prosper the fortunes of whoever has
called them together now (*Od*. 2.25-34). This is a marked
expression of community, of piety, of resignation to the will of
Zeus despite intimate loss, in a tale in which the issues of
reverence and justice are paramount themes. Eupeithes' appeal
in Book 24 exhibits precisely the opposite attitude. For him the
(justified) revenge wrought on the suitors only demands another
round in a socially destructive cycle of vendetta. Personal
motives of grief and shame override his concerns for justice and
communal integrity (*Od*. 24.425-38). Absorbed by sorrow that
touches him no less deeply than does the sorrow of Aigyptios—

and despite even the index of divine sanction for Odysseus' revenge, to which Medon's speech (439-49) adverts—Eupeithes is incapable of the kind of acquiescence that Aigyptios shows. Precisely because of this he suffers the last death in the *Odyssey*—significantly, at the hands of a father who has also tasted the grief of an absent son.

There remains the association with persuasive rhetoric, by which all intercessory figures are without exception characterized. The absence of explicit reference to command of speech in the single case of Kalkhas (*Il.* 1.68-73) is not a true counterexample. Prophets have little need of eloquence, since—for cultural reasons that the narrative always endorses—their mantic status alone suffices to affirm the authority of what they have to say, to lend them sight "both before and after," and so to command obedience. Persuasion (πειθώ) in particular is a concept that exposes the distortion caused by my choice to examine Mediation under three separate headings, since it points up the interrelatedness of *ethos* and *response*. This is because the initial characterization of Mediators as persuasive is in some sense nothing more than a narrative prolepsis of the approval their advice later wins—and this approval in turn is already predisposed by just that characterization. Persuasiveness is essentially a perlocutionary attribute: the Active πείθειν [to persuade] necessarily implies the verb in its Middle Voice: πείθεσθαι [to obey]. We will see that this much is clear and perhaps even clearest in cases in which the Mediator's advice is in fact rejected.

3. SITUATION

If we turn now from the type of *ethos* signalled by the address-formula to the broader context in which it is used, we again find fundamental similarities among these fifteen passages. In by far the majority of cases, the situation in which ὅ σφιν ἐϋφρονέων ἀγορήσατο καὶ μετέειπεν appears is that of Debate, whether during an official Assembly (*Il.* 1.73;253, 2.78;283, 7.367, 9.95, *Od.* 2.160;228) or else on any occasion in which a problem or dispute arises without the formal trappings of a council (*Il.* 7.326, 18.253, *Od.* 16.399,

24.453). In the remaining three instances (*Il.* 15.285, *Od.* 7.158, *Od.* 24.53), something has occurred to contradict normal expectations or surpass the bounds of propriety, thereby causing anxiety, hesitation or even outright panic. What these fifteen passages all share in common is the fact that each marks a point in the narrative at which events have for one reason or another reached a critical impasse; this in turn cues the emergence of a Mediator whose advice is offered as a means of negotiating the crisis. Since frequent reference will be made to these scenes in the discussion that follows, it will be convenient to list them here in the form of the chart (§30) on the facing page.

Before examining these passages in greater detail, a brief synopsis of their content will be useful. The situation in which **SS1-2** occur is of course too familiar to need much comment. The Plague sent by Apollo in response to Agamemnon's refusal to return Khryseis threatens to destroy the Akhaian troops (*Il.* 1.11-52). Convening an Assembly, Akhilleus makes an explicit appeal to Kalkhas (**S1**), whose interpretation of the Plague's aetiology precipitates the quarrel between Agamemnon and Akhilleus that Nestor then (245-84) attempts to mediate (**S2**).

In Book 2, Agamemnon reports his "false dream" to a gathering of the Akhaian chiefs, and suggests convening a second Assembly to test the morale of the troops (*Il.* 2.41-75). Nestor's response (**S3**), though it hints at reservations as to its advisability, nonetheless confirms the plan. The effect of the *Peira* is of course both disastrous and comic: the Akhaians rush to man their ships for the journey home, and must be cajoled and compelled back into the Assembly by Odysseus (*Il.* 2.142-277). After dealing harshly with Thersites, Odysseus averts a mutiny by reminding them (**S4**) of Kalkhas' earlier prophecy at Aulis, which had forecasted the victory of the expedition.

The pair of scenes from Book 7 signal crisis in the Akhaian and Trojan camps, respectively. The stalemate reached in the single combat between Hektor and Aias leads to a victory celebration on both sides (*Il.* 7.54-322). Nestor advises (**S5**) that a truce be sought, given the great number of Akhaian dead on the battlefield, to arrange for their burial; and further suggests that a wall be built upon their single pyre in order to protect the Greek ships against eventual assault. This is followed

§30

S1	Plague sent by Apollo Mediator: **Kalkhas**	(*Il.* 1.68-73)
S2	Akhilleus vs. Agamemnon Mediator: **Nestor**	(*Il.* 1.245-53)
S3	Agamemnon's dream Mediator: **Nestor**	(*Il.* 2.76-78)
S4	Assembly to debate retreat Mediator: **Odysseus**	(*Il.* 2.278-83)
S5	Threat of Trojan assault Mediator: **Nestor**	(*Il.* 7.323-26)
S6	Trojan Assembly Mediator: **Priam**	(*Il.* 7.365-67)
S7	Embassy to Akhilleus Mediator: **Nestor**	(*Il.* 9.92-95)
S8	"Dead" Hektor returns Mediator: **Thoas**	(*Il.* 15.281-85)
S9	Trojans vulnerable on plain Mediator: **Poulydamas**	(*Il.* 18.249-53)
S10	First Ithakan Assembly Mediator: **Halitherses**	(*Od.* 2.157-60)
S11	First Ithakan Assembly Mediator: **Mentor**	(*Od.* 2.224-28)
S12	Odysseus sits in hearth Mediator: **Ekheneos**	(*Od.* 7.155-58)
S13	Plot to kill Telemakhos Mediator: **Amphinomos**	(*Od.* 16.394-99)
S14	Nereids at Akhilleus' pyre Mediator: **Nestor**	(*Od.* 24.50-53)
S15	Plot to kill Odysseus Mediator: **Halitherses**	(*Od.* 24.450-53)

immediately (345-78) by the tumultuous Assembly in Troy (**S6**), in which Priam mediates the conflict between Antenor and Paris over the restitution of Helen and her property.

By Book 9, Akhilleus' absence from the fighting has begun to take its toll on the Akhaians (*Il*. 9.1-91), and it is during an Assembly of chiefs that Nestor proposes (**S7**) sending the Embassy to persuade the hero to return to battle.

Some five books later (*Il*. 14.402-32), Hektor collapses when struck with a boulder by Aias. He is saved from death by Apollo, who infuses him with strength and leads his way back into combat. His unexpected reappearance throws the Danaans into panic, and the Greek line breaks before his advance (*Il*. 15.236-80). The Aitolian Thoas prevents a complete rout by encouraging the minor chiefs to close ranks and ward him off (**S8**).

In Book 18, the Trojans are encamped on the plain, their spirits raised by the death of Patroklos and the success of their advance against the ships, when the sound of Akhilleus' warcry throws them into confusion (*Il*. 18.196-248). During a hurriedly convened Assembly, Poulydamas advises them to leave the battlefield and take up defensive positions in Troy for the night (**S9**). Hektor opposes him, and the Trojans foolishly agree to remain in the field.

The next two scenes, virtually doublets, occur in the *Odyssey* during the Assembly on Ithaka, the first to be convened since Odysseus' departure for Troy. The first to speak is old Aigyptios, whose introductory speech-formula employs the allomorphic hemistich #του ὅ γε δάκρυ χέων, discussed in the previous section of this chapter. As tempers flare between Antinoos and Telemakhos, their argument is interrupted by the omen of two eagles that attack the crowd (*Od*. 2.15-156). Aged Halitherses, "keenest among them at reading birdflight," rises to interpret the sign (**S10**); his words are scornfully rejected by the suitor Eurymakhos (177-207). Another round of argument ensues until Mentor, whom Odysseus had left in charge of his household, reminds them of how gentle and fatherly Odysseus' kingship had always been (**S11**). This too falls on deaf ears, and the Assembly breaks up soon afterwards (242-59).

In Book 7, the unnamed Beggar in the palace of Alkinoos sues for passage home. In the presence of king and queen and assembled nobility, he sits down among the ashes of the central hearth (*Od.* 7.133-54). A shocked silence holds them all until Ekheneos, eldest of the Phaiakians, encourages them to give him a seat of honor and a share of the feast (**S12**).

Back on Ithaka, in Odysseus' courtyard, the suitors openly plot to murder Telemakhos (*Od.* 16.342-408). Amphinomos, conspicuous among them for the kindness of his intentions, dissuades them from acting on their plan until they have first consulted the gods (**S13**).

The last pair of scenes comes from the final book. Agamemnon in Hades recounts the funeral rites performed for Akhilleus. As the hero is laid on his pyre, Thetis and the Nereids keen in so unearthly a manner that the Greeks in terror turn to flee (*Od.* 24.35-50); Nestor alone restrains them (**S14**). Some four hundred lines later, the parents of the slain suitors convene an Assembly in which Eupeithes, the father of Antinoos—#του ὅ γε δάκρυ χέων—calls for vengeance against Odysseus and his house (421-38). The herald Medon reminds them that Odysseus had divine assistance for his actions, and aged Halitherses urges them to abandon their plan (**S15**).

Crisis thus distinctly marks each of these fifteen passages. This is not only apparent from the nature of the context in which each occurs, but in a significant number of instances it is also explicitly indicated as such in the text. The Trojan Assembly in Book 7 (**S6**) is convened in an atmosphere of grave anxiety; it is an ἀγορὴ . . . | δεινὴ τετρηχυῖα [greatly disturbed assembly] (*Il.* 7.345-46).[7] When the Akhaians see Hektor, presumed dead, back in the ranks of battle (**S8**), they are terrified, and their bravery collapses at their feet: τάρβησαν, πᾶσιν δὲ παραὶ ποσὶ κάππεσε θυμός (*Il.* 15.279-80). An even greater panic strikes the Trojans when they hear Akhilleus' shout in Book 18 (**S9**), and none dares sit down for fear of his immanent onslaught (*Il.* 18.246-48). The omen of the eagles in the Ithakan Assembly (**S10**) leaves everyone astounded and profoundly troubled with foreboding— θάμβησαν δ' ὄρνιθας . . . | ὅρμηναν δ' ἀνὰ θυμὸν ἅ περ τελέεσθαι ἔμελλον (*Od.* 2.155-56). Uneasy silence grips the Phaiakian nobility at the sight of the Beggar humbled in the ashes of the hearth (**S12**); and the identical formula—οἱ δ' ἄρα πάντες ἀκὴν ἐγένοντο σιωπῇ# (*Od.*

7.154 = 16.393)—describes the response of the suitors to Antinoos' proposal to murder Telemakhos *en route* back to Ithaka (**S13**).[8] The Akhaians are seized with trembling at the sound of the Nereids keening for Akhilleus (**S14**)—ὑπὸ δὲ τρόμος ἔλλαβε πάντας Ἀχαιούς# (*Od*. 24.49); had it not been for Nestor's intervention, they would all have raced back to their hollow ships (50-52). Finally, Medon's claim to have seen a divinity at Odysseus' side during his slaughter of the suitors brings "pale fear" (*Od*. 24.450: χλωρὸν δέος) down on the Ithakans as they plot their vengeance against the hero (**S15**).

These fifteen contexts also admit a variety of scenic structures. When it occurs within the framework of a formal Assembly, the Mediator's speech is prompted by the turn of events themselves, in which case it is most often the first speech in the series (**S5, S9, S10**) or else is preceded by a formal request for advice (**S1, S3**). Alternately, it may come as the third element in the pattern of Statement-Counterstatement-Reconciliation (A-B-C) proposed by Lohmann in his study of Homeric Assembly scenes (**S2, S4, S6, S7, S11, S13, S15**).[9] In five instances of the Goodwill formula in official Assemblies (**S1, S2, S3, S6, S11**), the Mediator is additionally marked by the presence of the formula introducing a change of speaker: Ἤτοι ὅ γ' ὣς εἰπὼν κατ' ἄρ' ἕζετο· τοῖσι δ' ἀνέστη [He spoke thus and sat down again, and among them stood up . . .] (*Il*. 1.68;245-48, 2.77, 7.365, *Od*. 2.224). We have already (Chapter 2.1) noted one case (**S2**) in which a variation on this pattern allows for expanded description of the actions of the previous speaker, but nonetheless preserves the essential elements {X spoke} — {X sat} — {Y stood up among them} (*Il*. 1.245-48;53):

§31

> Ὣς φάτο Πηλείδης, ποτὶ δὲ σκῆπτρον βάλε γαίῃ
> χρυσείοις ἥλοισι πεπαρμένον, ἕζετο δ' αὐτός·
> Ἀτρείδης δ' ἑτέρωθεν ἐμήνιε· τοῖσι δὲ Νέστωρ
> ἡδυεπὴς ἀνόρουσε . . .
> ὅ σφιν ἐϋφρονέων ἀγορήσατο καὶ μετέειπεν

> *Thus spoke* Peleus' son, and dashed to the ground the scepter
> studded with golden nails, *and sat down again*. But Atreides

> raged still on the other side, *and between them Nestor*
> the sweet-speaking *rose up . . .*
> With kind intention he spoke and addressed them.

Also noteworthy is the fact that instances **S1** (Kalkhas) and **S2** (Nestor) in *Iliad* 1 and **S11** (Mentor) in *Odyssey* 2 share the same overall pattern of expanded description of the speaker filling three or four lines between the alternation-formula {#῾῾Ὣς φάτο / #῎Ητοι + Name + κατ᾽ ἄρ᾽ ἕζετο· τοῖσι δ᾽ ἀνέστη} and the address-formula ὅ σφιν ἐϋφρο-νέων ἀγορήσατο καὶ μετέειπεν. The descriptions of Kalkhas and Nestor were examined in detail in the previous chapter. In Mentor's case, the expansion adverts to both his age and his long-standing association with Odysseus, in which his present authority is grounded (*Od.* 2.224-28):[10]

§32

> ῎Ητοι ὅ γ᾽ ὣς εἰπὼν κατ᾽ ἄρ᾽ ἕζετο· τοῖσι δ᾽ ἀνέστη
> Μέντωρ, ὅς ῥ᾽ Ὀδυσῆος ἀμύμονος ἦεν ἑταῖρος,
> καί οἱ ἰὼν ἐν νηυσὶν ἐπέτρεπεν οἶκον ἅπαντα,
> πείθεσθαί τε γέροντι καὶ ἔμπεδα πάντα φυλάσσειν·
> ὅ σφιν ἐϋφρονέων ἀγορήσατο καὶ μετέειπεν

> So he spoke and sat down, and among them rose up
> *Mentor, who was Odysseus' blameless comrade,*
> *to whom he entrusted the whole household when he left in the*
> *ships,*
> *for them to obey the old man and for him to guard them all well.*
> With kind intention he spoke and addressed them.

The pattern employed in all three cases ‛has already been charted above (§12); I repeat it here, with additional citation of passages from the *Odyssey*, for easier reference:

§33

(a) X finishes and sits; (Y) stands	*Il.* 1.68 / 1.245-48
(b) Naming of Y	*Il.* 1.69 / 1.248
(c) Expanded description of Y	*Il.* 1.70-72 / 1.249-52
(d) Address-formula (Goodwill)	*Il.* 1.73 = 1.253

It has been suggested (Lang 1980) that the expansion at §33(c) accommodates the description of a character who has not previously been mentioned in the story, and so provides a means for his introduction. The fact is that the three passages cited in

§33 do indeed coincide with the first appearance of Kalkhas, Nestor and Mentor, respectively, in the text of the poems. In the case of Priam (**S6**), already met long before the Trojan Assembly in *Iliad* 7, the §33(c) element is missing—though he is characterized as θεόφιν μήστωρ ἀτάλαντος [equal of the gods in counsel] (366)—and the scene instead follows the pattern §33(a)-(b)-(d) (=*Il.* 7.365-366-367). It thus seems plausible enough that the §33(c) slot could well be used to supply the audience of the tale with further information about a "new" character. Lang takes an extreme position on this issue, however, in her conclusion that Nestor does not belong originally to "the Trojan War story, or even . . . the *Iliad* itself," but is instead an "importation," and for this reason is given an "unprecedented and elaborate introduction" in *Iliad* 1 (1980:140-41).

Such an understanding of the expansion-element is flawed in at least two respects. To begin with, the assumption—a highly *textual* one—implicit in the notion of the "first appearance" of a character may well be inappropriate to oral literature. That we, as readers of this fixed, written version of the *Iliad* initially encounter Kalkhas or Nestor here in Book 1, for instance, is no guarantee that they had no place in the prior, oral versions of the tale that our text has now permanently supplanted. This much is obvious in the case of Kalkhas. Despite the chance, already noted, that his allegedly fictitious patrimony may well imply that the seer too is an "untraditional" figure, Kalkhas' involvement in events connected with though external to our *Iliad* narrative— namely, the prophecy delivered at Aulis, to which Odysseus refers analeptically (*Il.* 2.299-330)—makes this assumption unlikely. The same may be said on Nestor's behalf, unless we prefer to dismiss his account of his visit (along with Odysseus) to Peleus' house in order to recruit Akhilleus for the war (*Il.* 7.124-28, 11.765-90) as either an outright lie on the old man's part or else an attempt by the poet to engraft Nestor into a narrative tradition in which he had no authentic part. "Importation" thus seems no more legitimate an inference here that in the case, say, of the lengthy description of Poulydamas before his crucial speech in Book 18 (*Il.* 18.249-53). This latter instance, moreover—given the fact that it occurs as many as seven books after Poulydamas has "first" been "introduced" in the story (cf. *Il.* 11.57, 12.60)—should also suffice to discredit the idea that there is anything "unprecedented" about the "introduction" of Nestor in the first book of the poem.

It may risk less distortion to concentrate instead on the *function* that an expanded description serves both within its own narrative context and also in its relation to other passages that can be identified as multiforms. For a second and even more fundamental flaw in the suggestion that the expansion at §33(c) signals an "importation" is the privileged status it implicitly assigns to the *ethos* of a character in isolation from the part that character plays in the unfolding of the tale. These two elements cannot be separated from each other without damage to the narrative's tightly woven fabric. The fact is that the description in each case, far from being "introductory" and so perhaps merely "ornamental," instead anticipates a specific role for the character within a well-defined situation. That is to say, its function is that of a narrative cue. What it marks is not so much the arrival of some discrete and untraditional figure previously unknown to the audience—a stranger in need of a formal introduction, and for whom the expansion at §33(c) is a kind of calling-card—but instead the emergence of a whole narrative complex of descriptions and events. *Ethos* and *situation* together form a bundle of gestures and traits that embody specific possibilities for how the tale can proceed from this point onward. Their combination works both *anaphorically*—namely, to identify a familiar type of figure (Mediator) in a narrative context defined by familiar parameters (Crisis)—and at the same time, as the following section will show, as a *prolepsis* of the ensuing course of the tale. The terms of characterization deployed at §33(c) are determined by the *function* that the character exercises in the scene in which he appears.

Significantly, the remaining two instances of the alternation-formula {X spoke} — {X sat} — {Y stood up among them} also occur within the rhythm of Lohmann's Statement-Counterstatement-Reconciliation (A-B-C) pattern for Assembly scenes. They precede the speeches of Agamemnon (*Il.* 1.101) and Alexandros (*Il.* 7.354) respectively, each of whom rejects the advice of the previous speaker (Kalkhas-Akhilleus/Antenor) and thus implicitly signals the need for an intercessor (Nestor/Priam). Alexandros' case is the simpler of the two. While it lacks any explicit expansion corresponding to the element at §33(c), his response to Antenor's suggestion (*Il.* 7.347-53) to give Helen back to the Greeks is prefaced by the formula ὅς μιν ἀμειβόμενος ἔπεα πτερόεντα προσηύδα [In reply to him he spoke winged words] (356), which may be reserved for speeches of marked dramatic import.[11] Be that as it may, his rejection of the advice is answered by Priam's conciliatory speech (**S6**), structured by the §33(a)-(b)-(d) pattern.

Agamemnon's response to Kalkhas (*Il.* 1.101-105) is the more interesting, on the other hand, given the presence of the §33(c) element, but with a crucial difference at the level of its content:

§34
  (a) Ἤτοι ὅ γ' ὣς εἰπὼν κατ' ἄρ' ἕζετο· τοῖσι δ' ἀνέστη
  (b) ἥρως 'Ατρεΐδης εὐρὺ κρείων 'Αγαμέμνων
  (c) ἀχνύμενος. μένεος δὲ μέγα φρένες ἀμφὶ μέλαιναι πίμπλαντ', ὄσσε δέ οἱ πυρὶ λαμπετόωντι ἐΐκτην·
  (d) Κάλχαντα πρώτιστα κάκ' ὀσσόμενος προσέειπε

> He spoke thus and sat down again, and among them rose up
> Atreus' son the hero wide-ruling Agamemnon
> *raging, the heart within filled black to the brim with anger*
> *from beneath, but his two eyes showed like fire in their*
> *blazing.*
> *First of all he eyed Kalkhas bitterly* and spoke to him.

The variation at §34(c)-(d) demonstrates first how the alternation-formula in the abstract sequence §33(a)-(b) marks a point at which distinct choices are offered for the ensuing course of the narrative. One speaker finishes and sits (a), another rises and is identified, generally by way of a patronymic and/or a name + epithet formula (b). What he says may either affirm or reject the previous statement, and the sequence §33(c)-(d) encodes a prolepsis of the nature of his response by making reference to the basis for his authority—Kalkhas (**S1**): seercraft from Apollo; Nestor (**S2**): command of rhetoric, unusual longevity; Mentor (**S10**): responsibility delegated by Odysseus—and the quality of his intention (Goodwill) in speaking. The case of Agamemnon in §34 is conspicuous in the degree to which the imputation of malicious intent fills the entire §33(c) = §34(c) section. More than simply assigning a certain quality to his character, the description instead sets the stage for his dismissal of Kalkhas as a trustworthy authority, engaging a narrative subpattern— Rejection of Prophecy—that the following section of this chapter will examine in greater detail (§42). In terms of narrative logic, the colon κακ' ὀσσόμενος προσέειπε# [he eyed bitterly and spoke to him] in the address-formula at §34(d) follows "naturally" from the two lines that precede it, and *a fortiori* the same can be said of each instance of the formula ὅ σφιν ἐϋφρομέων ἀγορήσατο καὶ μετέειπεν in the passages charted above in §33.

Nestor's advice on the construction of a defensive wall out of the pyre of the cremated dead in *Iliad* 7 (**S5**)—a σῆμα [sign] whose monumentality threatens to eclipse the fame of the Trojan wall built by Poseidon and Apollo (*Il.* 7.443-63; 12.13-33)—can also be adduced here. His speech (*Il.* 7.327-43) is enframed by the formulas already identified as indices of Mediation: Crisis (the impending Trojan threat to the ships)— Assembly (informal, and for this reason lacking the formula for alternation of speakers)—Statement of Goodwill (325). Here #ὅ σφιν ἐϋφρονέων... is preceded by a set of lines (324-25) that advert to Nestor's role as a Counselor:

§35

τοῖς ὁ γέρων πάμπρωτος ὑφαίνειν ἤρχετο μῆτιν
Νέστωρ, οὗ καὶ πρόσθεν ἀρίστη φαίνετο βουλή.
ὅ σφιν ἐϋφρονέων ἀγορήσατο καὶ μετέειπεν

The old man began to weave his counsel before them first,
Nestor, whose advice had shown best before this.
With kind intention he spoke and addressed them.

These lines reappear a few books later (*Il.* 9.93-94) in the scene in which Nestor proposes the Embassy to Akhilleus (**S7**); and the second line is repeated, again with reference to Nestor, at *Odyssey* 24.52 (**S14**). Moreover, their match with the expansion-element at §33(c) is obvious. The function of this element as a marker not merely of the *ethos* of the speaker— and so as a way of "introducing" him—but also as a proleptic *situational* marker is equally clear from other instances of its use. The description preceding Poulydamas' advice in Book 18 (**S9**) has already been noted (§29). As well as serving to enhance the contrast between him and Hektor, his characterization at the same time represents an advance endorsement of the soundness of his counsel, thus marking Hektor's subsequent rejection as foolhardy and disastrous (cf. 18.310-13). In turn, Thoas' speech some three books earlier (S8) is preceded by the description of his balanced prowess in debate and warfare (*Il.* 15.282-84)—an explicit example of the heroic ideal to be "both a speaker of words and a doer of deeds" (cf. *Il.* 9.443). In neither of these two cases, moreover, is the character in question introduced "for the first time" in the narrative; the expanded description instead calls attention to his function as an Intercessor in a moment of Crisis.

Although falling outside the framework of Assembly scenes, the remaining instances of ὅ σφιν ἐϋφρονέων ἀγορήσατο καὶ μετέειπεν (*Il.* 15,285, *Od.* 7.158, 24.53) occur when the issue is no less critical, for they arise in situations that follow conspicuous violations of the natural or ethical order of things. The speech (S8) of Thoas in *Iliad* 15 is prompted by Apollo's sudden infusion of strength into the moribund Hektor, and succeeds in rousing the Greeks to defend themselves against the Trojan assault on their ships (285-99). Insofar as the intercession of Kalkhas in the first book (S1) is sought to account for the unexpected plague that strikes the Akhaians, it should also be grouped in this category; and the same can be said of the seer Halitherses' interpretation (S10) of the omen of the eagles that interrupt the Assembly on Ithaka (*Od.* 2.146-56). In *Odyssey* 24 (S14), the shade of Agamemnon recounts (35-59) how the unnatural keening of Thetis and the Nereids almost drove the Greeks to abandon Akhilleus' funeral rites until Nestor, παλαιά τε πολλά τε εἰδώς# [knowing many ancient things] (51), restrained them from taking flight in their ships. Finally (S12), when Odysseus concludes his initial appeal to the Phaiakians by withdrawing from their midst and sitting in the ashes of the hearth (*Od.* 7.153-54), the aged Ekheneos breaks the ensuing silence to draw attention to this breech of hospitality and demand a favorable response from Alkinoös. His advice expressly adverts to the unseemliness of allowing the Beggar to remain apart from them in disgrace—

Ἀλκίνο᾽, οὐ μέν τοι τόδε κάλλιον οὐδὲ ἔοικε, | ξεῖνον μὲν χαμαὶ ἧσθαι ἐπ᾽ ἐσχάρῃ ἐν κονίῃσιν [Alkinoös, this is not very seemly, nor is it proper for the stranger to sit on the ground by the hearth, in the ashes] (159-

60)—and reminds them of the sacred rights of suppliants, guaranteed by Zeus (165).

The homogeneity of the situations that mark the appearance of an intercessory figure makes their narrative contours fairly easy to map. In every case, the prior course of events in the story has reached a Crisis, a significant juncture at which possibilities for how the tale can continue fork in different directions. The alternative vectors are as distinct as they are antithetical: death by plague vs. remedy (**S1**), withdrawal vs. participation of Akhilleus (**S2, S7**), retreat vs. perseverance of the Greeks (**S3, S4**), neglect vs. performance of burial rites (**S5, S14**), defeat vs. defense (**S5, S8**), retention vs. restitution of Helen (**S6**), attack vs. defense (**S9**), disruption through anarchy (**S10, S11**) or vendetta (**S13, S15**) vs. social integration, death vs. survival of Telemakhos (**S13**), neglect vs. performance of the rites of hospitality (**S12**). A cursory glance at these alternatives (and a busier mind) could easily group them under fewer and more generic kinds of opposition. More important than their reduction to a single polarity, however— at the risk of overlooking the richness of innovation even within formal, formulaic constraints—is to notice once again the degree to which the *ethos* of a character is tightly bound up with the *situation* in which he appears.

Despite the prominent role played by ὅ σφιν ἐϋφρονέων ἀγορήσατο καὶ μετέειπεν (along with its reflexes) as the mark of an intercessory figure, that mark is itself conditioned by situational factors. This is clearest when—in nearly two-thirds of the cases in which it appears in formal Assembly scenes—the line is preceded by the formulaic alternation of speakers, expressed four times by the line Ἤτοι ὅ γ' ὣς εἰπὼν κατ' ἄρ' ἕζετο· τοῖσι δ' ἀνέστη and once (*Il.* 1.245-48 = §31) by a version of that formula stretched to accommodate additional description. Here the presence of a Mediator represents just one among several divergent possibilities opened up by the simple fact of Alternation. While it is true that there can be no intercession without the figure of the Mediator—which would seem to privilege *ethos* as the central element in the group—the latter's appearance is itself dependent on the specific situational parameters that call for intercession "in the first place." *Situation* and *ethos* are thus best understood not in isolation but rather as interlocking elements or, better, as the warp and woof of a single narrative fabric. Further, intercessors do not even arise necessarily from their context, but are instead included in a whole range of possibilities admitted by the situation thus far reached in the tale. The Other who gets up to speak next could indeed be an Antagonist instead, like Agamemnon in his reply to Kalkhas (*Il.* 1.101-02), or like Paris (*Il.* 7.354-55), who rises to challenge Antenor's advice in the Trojan Assembly (**S6**). In terms of the course of events in the narrative and the situations that crystallize in that course, Mediator and Antagonist in fact occupy alternative nodes through which the narrative can pass, and which in their turn (as we will see in the following section) offer further narrative options:

§36

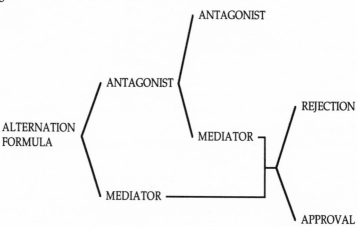

The possibility that the Antagonist's speech may be answered by yet another antagonistic figure instead of a Mediator is realized in the complex exchange between Agamemnon and Akhilleus in *Iliad* 1, comprising a total of six separate speeches in whose course the intercession of Athene (with an additional three speeches) is embedded. Moreover, it is important to recognize that Alternation in the above schema is itself just one of several possibilities engaged along the forking path of a far more extensive concatenation of events in Book 1, stretching back at least as far as Khryses' (rejected)

Appeal to Agamemnon—if not beyond it, into the unrecorded narratives that make up the vaster tradition of which our *Iliad* is a single fragment. Among other things, this tends to confirm the view of character proposed by Barthes, as discussed and modified earlier (Chapter 1.3). For viewed in terms of the interdependent relation it has with its context, *ethos* indeed seems less a privileged essence qualitatively distinct from the events in which it is embedded, and more like a simple event itself: a verbal construct, a node, a point of juncture in the overall narrative design of the story. An examination of the *response* to Mediation will carry these reflections farther.

4. RESPONSE

In the course of a critical situation that strains social harmony, custom or verisimilitude, an Elder—or one like him, precociously endowed with prudence and command of persuasive rhetoric—rises to speak. Narrative logic dictates that the response to his speech take one of three forms: (a) outright approval, (b) outright rejection or (c) some partial acceptance (along with partial rejection) of (all or part of) his advice by (all or some of) his addressees. Outright approval accounts for nine of the fifteen situations now under review (S3, S4, S5, S6, S7, S8, S12, S13, S14), with partial acceptance— taking the form of either acknowledgment of the soundness of the advice but failure to implement it (S2), or else approval under protest (S1)—comprising an additional two cases. The fact that nearly three-quarters of the speeches introduced by an address-formula that explicitly adverts to the speaker's Goodwill in Crisis earn a positive response marks that outcome with a high degree of probability in the narrative and thus, from the viewpoint of the audience, a high degree of expectation. As a narrative cue, then, the presence of a Mediator more often than not anticipates the likelihood that the tale will proceed along the lines projected by his counsel. In this respect, and just as in the case of the narrative function of prophecy in the poems, the advice proposed by a Mediator represents another instance of "the storyteller tipping his hand, showing us where the story can or will go, because he has already determined the end" (Peradotto 1990:67). In turn, the outright rejection of well-intentioned advice that occurs in the remaining four cases (S9, S10, S11, S15), given its lesser frequency, identifies them as unusual and "marked" situations, thus lending them a higher degree of dramatic intensity.

On the other hand, it should be noted that mere approval in itself of course says nothing about the ultimate soundness of the advice thus given and accepted. Good counsel may fall on deaf ears, but it is equally possible that advice that in the long run precipitates distress for those who follow it may initially win resounding approbation. "Unmarked" cases of Mediation are therefore not necessarily free from their own kind of narrative tension. They may in fact serve to open a potentially ironic rift between the (abstract) level of the story and that of the (concrete) narrative itself, since characters within the tale can be represented as unwittingly choosing a course that leads to their own demise. Thus Priam's compromised counsel (S6) to offer restitution of everything but Helen herself—yet another token of impaired judgement in his administration—only helps to confirm Troy's doom, despite the fact that the Trojans approve of it heartily (*Il.* 7.379). Nestor's advice to construct a defensive wall around the ships (S5) is hailed by the Akhaians (*Il.* 7.344), and in fact proves to be of no small tactical value, yet also draws down Poseidon's wrath when they fail to make proper sacrifice before building it—a procedural detail Nestor apparently overlooks mentioning. The most conspicuous example, however, is Patroklos' approval of Nestor's suggestion in *Iliad* 11 to borrow Akhilleus' armor and impersonate the hero in battle, which brings about his own death at the same time as it is essential in advancing the story of Akhilleus' return. "Ironic Mediation"—for lack of a better term, and with the understanding that the irony qualifies the narrator's discourse rather than the Mediator's intention—seems in fact to characterize much of Nestor's advice in the *Iliad*. I will return to this issue in the final section of this chapter, as well as throughout the next one.

Approbation can take a variety of forms—or better, comes to expression at a number of levels. Whether the Mediator's speech is followed by another speech expressing approval, or else by the description of actions that implement his advice, with or without some reference to the attitude of his audience, does not seem to matter greatly in the long run; the story advances through speech and action almost indifferently. In either case, acceptance is always marked by verbal echoes of the spoken advice. Thus Nestor's injunction (**S14**) to the terrified Akhaians at the funeral of Akhilleus (*Od.* 24.54: #ἔσχεσθ᾽, Ἀργεῖοι . . . [*Hold*, Argives . . .]) is answered by the description of their action following his speech (57: ῝Ως ἔφαθ᾽, οἱ ἔσχοντο φόβου μεγάθυμοι Ἀχαιοί [So he spoke, and the great-hearted Akhaians *held themselves* from flight]). The account of Alkinoos' response to the advice of Ekheneos in *Odyssey* 7 (**S12**)—ὦρσεν ἐπ᾽ ἐσχαρόφιν καὶ ἐπὶ θρόνου εἷσε φαεινοῦ | υἱὸν ἀναστήσας . . . [and raised him up from the fireside, and *set him in a* shining *chair*, making his son stand up . . .] (*Od.* 7.169-70)—is cast in language that echoes the old man's words (162-63: ἀλλ᾽ ἄγε δὴ ξεῖνον μὲν ἐπὶ θρόνου ἀργυροήλου | εἷσον ἀναστήσας [But come, raise the stranger up and *seat him on a* silver-studded *chair*]). A similar response follows the tempered advice (**S13**) that Amphinomos gives the suitors in *Odyssey* 16. The narrator's comment that Amphinomos *pleased* Penelope most *because of his words* (*Od.* 16.398: #ἥνδανε μύθοισι) is answered by the description of how the suitors receive what he says (406: ῝Ως ἔφατ᾽ Ἀμφίνομος· τοῖσιν δ᾽ ἐπιήνδανε μῦθος [So Amphinomos spoke, and *his word was pleasing* to them]). Although the line is exactly repeated at *Odyssey* 20.247, and is used (with substitution of names) once (*Od.* 13.16) of Alkinoos and four times (*Od.* 18.50;290, 21.143;269) of Antinoos, the responsion between *Odyssey* 16.398 and 406 is unique.

Most often, and at either level of the narrative, the vocabulary of approval centers formulaically on the activities of praise (ἐπαίνειν), harkening (κλύειν) and obedience (πείθεσθαι). There is of course nothing unusual in this; the expression of assent to speeches of any kind, with or without qualification of the intent of the speaker, in most cases has recourse to these verbs. Nearly half of the occasions of outright approval when that intention is marked as kindly (ἐϋφρονέων) are shaped according to the extensive pattern introduced by #῝Ως ἔφατ᾽ [thus he spoke] followed by a description of audience response. Two from this group (*Il.* 7.379

= 15.300) are noteworthy in that they belong to a set of speeches that win approval expressed by the formula ῾Ὣς ἔφαθ᾽, οἱ δ᾽ ἄρα τοῦ μάλα μὲν κλύον ἠδ᾽ ἐπίθοντο [So he spoke, and they listened well to him and obeyed him] (7X, 6X). As Muellner points out (1976:18-19), the line "is always used . . . after an order or exhortation by a man [or woman! (cf. *Od.* 6.247, 20.157)] in authority (master of slaves, leader of warriors) to a group of men [or women] (servants, warriors, etc.)." Priam's is the first instance (**S6**); the second is that of Thoas (**S8**), whose preeminence in debate among the Greek youth marks him with qualities conventionally reserved for older men. The same line is also used twice of the response to statements made by Nestor. One occasion (*Od.* 3.477), following his order for Telemakhos' chariot to be hitched, is not especially significant. No intercession properly so-called is involved—the formula #ὅ σφιν ἐϋφρονέων . . . is not used—and the passage serves mainly to identify the old man as someone whose commands should be obeyed. The other instance (*Il.* 9.79) bears more weight, however, since it describes the response of the Akhaian leaders to (rather mundane) advice from Nestor that directly precedes his raising of the far more delicate issue—in a speech (**S7**) introduced by #ὅ σφιν ἐϋφρονέων . . . —of reconciliation between Agamemnon and Akhilleus (92-113). It wins from Agamemnon the reply ὦ γέρον, οὔ τι ψεῦδος ἐμὰς ἄτας κατέλεξας [Old man, this was no lie when you spoke of my madness] (115), which is unique in the poems.

In one of the fifteen cases (**S2**), and in a few other passages directly associated with intercessory figures (Nestor, Priam) but lacking the formal markers of Alternation and/or Goodwill, a positive response is expressed by the formulaic ναὶ δὴ ταῦτά γε πάντα, γέρον, κατὰ μοῖραν ἔειπες [Yes, old man, all this you have said is right and fitting] (*Il.* 1.286, 8.146, 24.379; cf. *Od.* 3.331). The line as a whole—with substitution of different Vocative forms—accounts for well over a quarter (10 of 35X) of all instances of κατὰ μοῖραν [right and fitting] in the poems, and more than half of the cases (19X) in which κατὰ μοῖραν ἔειπ-# [spoke fittingly] completes the line. Four of the remaining occurrences show variations on a line concluding τοῦτο ἔπος κατὰ μοῖραν ἔειπ-# [spoke this word fittingly]; on five occasions the final colon is preceded by a conjunction (ἐπεί) or short adverbial modifier (e.g. οὐ). An allomorph of κατὰ μοῖραν ἔειπε-# appears four times in the phrase κατὰ μοῖραν κατέλεξ-# [recounted fittingly].

This is not the place to study the full range of this formula, for which an examination of κατὰ κόσμον [in right order] (13X) and κατ' αἶσαν [properly] (4X) would also be needed.[12] For our purposes, a few general observations will suffice. To make the data even more manageable, we can begin by excluding from consideration the four instances of κατὰ μοῖραν κατέλεξ-# [recounted fittingly] (*Od*. 3.331, 8.496, 10.16, 12.35), on the ground that the sense of the verb here refers more to the completeness or formal arrangement of a speech than to its actual content. Statements of approval incorporating the colon κατὰ μοῖραν κατέλεξ-# in this respect bear a closer resemblance to the use of κατὰ μοῖραν in the description of activities done in an orderly fashion, such as sitting in neat rows (*Il*. 19.256, *Od*. 4.783 = 8.54), tending flocks (*Od*. 9.309;342;352) or cutting meat (*Od*. 3.457). Five of thirteen instances of κατὰ κόσμον (*Il*. 10.472, 11.48, 12.85, 17.205, 24.622) also bear this sense. These occasions all imply a quasi-objective standard to which the activity in question is said to conform; and much the same notion is implicit in the use of κατὰ μοῖραν κατέλεξ-# as well, where the issue is that of the point-by-point completeness of a narrative account. It is accuracy and proper narrative order that Odysseus expects from Demodokos' tale of the Trojan Horse (*Od*. 8.496); and that characterize Odysseus' own recounting of the war to Aiolos (*Od*. 10.16), as well as of his experience in Hades, once he has returned to Kirke's island (*Od*. 12.35).

This does not seem to be the case with κατὰ μοῖραν ἔειπε-# [spoke fittingly], however. Its sense instead usually intends the far subtler standard of what should or ought to be done or said in a given situation, and so registers assent by reference to generally tacit assumptions about appropriateness and what is "fitting" in terms of custom or conventional morality. Thus Nestor's intercession (**S2**) in *Iliad* 1.275-84 amounts to a lecture on the rights pertaining to the man (Akhilleus) who is κάρτερος [stronger] (280) and the one (Agamemnon) who is φέρτερος [more authoritative] (281), respectively. It is a lesson in status, social hierarchy and privilege that elicits from Agamemnon the admission ναὶ δὴ ταῦτά γε πάντα, γέρον, κατὰ μοῖραν ἔειπες [Yes, old man, all this you have said is right and fitting] (286). The phrase is thus a highly abbreviated gesture that simultaneously evokes and endorses a whole system of mores and the social institutions that are built upon them.

Essentially the same lesson, though more succinctly expressed, informs Iris' advice to Poseidon to withdraw from battle rather than risk the anger of Zeus (*Il.* 15.201-04). Her suggestion that he back down from a confrontation takes the gnomic form of a statement that "even the minds of the great can be changed" (203; cf. *Il.* 13.115), followed by a somewhat darker reminder that the Furies always side with the elder brother. This wins a similar formulaic response: Ἶρι θεά, μάλα τοῦτο ἔπος κατὰ μοῖραν ἔειπες [Divine Iris, you spoke this word quite fittingly] (206). In turn, Diomedes acknowledges as much (*Il.* 8.146 = 1.286) in reply to Nestor's advice to retreat from battle. This is prompted by a bolt from Zeus thrown in front of their chariot, and couched in a homily on the disproportionate powers of gods and men: "No mortal can defend himself against the purpose of Zeus" (*Il.* 8.144; cf. 211). The compliment is returned twice: first, in the shortened form ἐπεὶ κατὰ μοῖραν ἔειπες [since you spoke fittingly], when Nestor approves (*Il.* 9.59) of Diomedes' commitment to fight in the belief that Greek victory at Troy is divinely sanctioned; and later in answer to the warrior's observation that younger men than Nestor should have the job of waking sleeping chieftains (*Il.* 10.169). Related to the first of these two instances is the disguised Hermes' use of ναὶ δὴ ταῦτά γε πάντα, γέρον . . . (*Il.* 24.379) to acknowledge the appropriateness of Priam's inference, based on the appearance of Hermes, that the gods approve his mission to Akhilleus.

Equally significant is the fact that over 60% of the time, κατὰ μοῖραν ἔειπε-# is used in situations in which there is a generational gap between the interlocutors. Here, as in the three passages from *Iliad* 1, 8 and 15 just mentioned, the term μοῖρα seems to preserve its original sense of "portion" or "allotment," since the issue is one of rights and privileges that accrue by virtue of one's age. Young or at least explicitly younger people (Agamemnon, Diomedes, Hermes in disguise, Leokritos, Athene as Mentor) use it of old ones (Nestor 3X, Priam, Mentor) five times (*Il.* 1.286, 8.146, 24.379, *Od.* 2.251, 3.331); on seven occasions (*Il.* 9.59, 10.109, 23.626, *Od.* 17.580, 18.170, 21.278, 22.486) it marks the approval (once ironic) given by an elderly figure (Nestor 3X, Eumaios, Eurynome, the Beggar, Eurykleia) to the proposal of a younger one (Diomedes 2X, Akhilleus, Telemakhos, Antinoos, Penelope, Odysseus). In the remaining instances (*Od.* 4.266; 9.351, 13.385, 20.37; 8.397), the formula appears where generational difference is not expressly at issue, but in contexts that nonetheless advert to a distinction in social status—husband/wife, mortal/god (3X), king/subject—which in turn implies different privileges and entitlements. Only once is it used between social and generational equals—the Phaiakians Euryalos and Laodamas (*Od.* 8.141)—though here too in response to a proverbial saying ("Nothing breaks down a man like the sea"). Twice it is reserved for expressions of approval which, although cast in the form of the narrator's own editorial voice—ἐπεὶ κατὰ μοῖραν ἔειπεν# [since he had spoken fittingly] (*Od.* 7.227 = 13.48)—are meant to reflect the opinions of characters (the Phaiakian nobles) within the narrative.

Two conclusions can be drawn from these statistics. The first obviously returns us to comments made earlier about traits that formulate the *ethos* of intercessory figures. Each is represented as trustworthy and authoritative, generally by reason of age and experience—compare καὶ ὃς προγενέστερος εἴη# [(X spoke sensibly,) like one who was older] (*Od.* 4.205; cf. *Il.* 2.555, 9.161, *Od.* 7.156, [11.342])—which is in turn reflected in the superior social position he occupies. What the phrase thus conveys is tacit acknowledgment of a hierarchical system of values and roles established through some procedure of apportionment (μοῖρα), and thanks to which the speaker's words enjoy authority. Moreover, advanced age not only gives the speaker purchase on the kind of moral (and circumspective) knowledge to which the phrase κατὰ μοῖραν ἔειπε-# refers, but also empowers him to recognize when others far younger also offer "fitting" counsel.

More important, however, is the fact that such approval always qualifies something said in harmony with the voice of tradition. Advice endorsed as κατὰ μοῖραν generally embodies an explicit evocation of conventional folk-wisdom, which lends itself easily to summary in gnomic form: *Respect authority. Don't abuse privilege. Yield to necessity. Old men do one thing, young men another. Even the mighty are flexible. Give honor to elders. Trust in the gods. Honor guests. Avoid bad company* . . . What is spoken κατὰ μοῖραν therefore appeals to and confirms the ethical values to which the speaker's addressees subscribe. Further, this community of fictional listeners within the narrative is implicitly always represented as entertaining the same moral expectations as the community in which their narrative itself is performed. They share essentially the same sense of scandal and approbation over essentially the same things. Their ethical horizons are thus roughly isomorphic, granted even qualitative differences (heroic/mundane) between them that in their turn make for experiential differences —the opportunity for direct intercourse with gods, for example—that maintain what has been called "epic distance."[13] By appealing to this common horizon of values, the formulaic colon κατὰ μοῖραν ἔειπε-# simultaneously contributes to the moral sense made by what transpires in the narrative—to what might be called its *ethical closure.*

The approval won nearly three-quarters of the time by the Mediator's speech is therefore assured both by the proleptic encoding of the grounds for that response—namely, through formulaic reference to Goodwill and, more generally, to the narrative possibilities inherent in patterns of Crisis and Alternation—and also by the degree to which that encoding assumes the same approval in the audience that receives the narrative. This tacit fusion of ethical horizons is in fact even clearer in those cases (**S9, S10, S11, S15**) in which the Mediator's advice is rejected.

Here more than in contexts in which expectations are fulfilled by a positive response to advice, the number and range of divergent narrative possibilities inherent in any given situation becomes especially apparent. This is of course not to suggest that the denial of expectations is any less traditional a feature of oral narratives, that denial is any less formulaic than fulfillment of expectation, or that it is not a possibility subject to formulaic encoding and thus an expectation capable of being prefigured and fulfilled. The fact is that the outright rejection of well-intentioned counsel occurs in roughly one-quarter of the scenes now under consideration, and twice (*Il.* 1.101-20; 18.284-313) is anticipated in the lines that precede the actual spoken denial. Although Agamemnon in *Iliad* 1 (**S1**) does in fact yield to Kalkhas' advice, his initial response is to reject it. This is foreshadowed, as we saw (§34), by the extended characterization of his ill-will towards the seer, extending from the #ἀχνύμενος with which it opens (*Il.* 1.103) to the address-formula (105) that closes with κακ' ὀσσόμενος προσέειπε# [he eyed bitterly and spoke to him].[14] In **S9**, Hektor's reply to Poulydamas' advice in *Iliad* 18 is introduced by the shorter but highly pregnant #τὸν δ' ἄρ' ὑπόδρα ἰδὼν προσέφη {name + epithet} [Then looking darkly at him, X spoke . . .] (*Il.* 18.284). Its resonance has been explored by Holoka, who concludes (1983:16) that the formula amounts to "a nonverbal cue fraught with judgmental significance," indicating that the speaker of whom it is used "deplores the willful traducing of rules of conduct governing relations between superordinates and inferiors." In this sense, it might be added, #τὸν δ' ἄρ' ὑπόδρα ἰδὼν προσέφη . . . represents a strong formulaic alternative to the approval expressed by the reply κατὰ μοῖραν ἔειπε-#. The same phrase characterizes Hektor's response to Poulydamas in an earlier scene (*Il.* 12.230), where the latter prudently counsels withdrawal at the very moment when the Trojans are about to break through the Akhaian defensive wall.[15] The fact that on both of these occasions the rejected advice subsequently proves to have been sound represents an ironic use of the formula that Holoka does not seem to appreciate fully.[16]

Hektor's confrontations with his Double throughout the *Iliad* indeed offer a prime example of a widespread pattern for Rejection of Advice; even at the expense of a slight digression, they will reward closer examination here. This is especially the case because the narrative relation between these two figures is entirely structured in terms of approved and rejected Mediation. The four scenes in which they appear together in fact exhibit a fine rhythmic alternation of Approval (**A**) and Rejection (**B**) that traverses the last half of the *Iliad* and reaches its climax in Book 18:

§37
A1	12.60-81
B1	12.210-50
A2	13.722-53
B2	18.249-313

The dictional and structural affinities among these four scenes are numerous, as the chart (§38) on the facing page attempts to show; the comments that follow will summarize the passages and underscore their parallels.

In all four passages, events in the narrative have reached a critical impasse, a dangerous threshold that inspires a temporary paralysis of will. In each case, moreover, this paralysis is graphically reflected in the Trojans' inability either to advance or retreat from their position. In the opening scene of *Iliad* 12 (**A1a**), their horses balk at crossing the ditch (*Il.* 12.50: τάφρον ἐποτρύνων διαβαινέμεν), broad and lined with sharp palisades, that the Greeks have dug at the foot of their wall. Some one hundred and fifty lines later (**B1a**), it is the Trojans themselves at the ditch who shrink back from their attempt to storm the ramparts (200=218: περησέμεναι μεμαῶσιν#), terrified by the portent of the eagle and the snake that Zeus has sent them (208-09). In Book 13 (**A2a**), they are caught in a crossfire, pinned down by the two Aiantes in front and a contingent of Lokrian bowmen who attack them from the rear (*Il.* 13.709-19). The arrows throw them into confusion, and none "remembers the joy of battle" (719-20). Finally, the war cry of Akhilleus so terrifies the Trojans encamped on the plain in *Iliad* 18 (**B2a**) that they violate the rules of Assembly by all standing *en masse* instead of sitting down and taking turns to rise and speak (*Il.* 18.246-47). This fact incidentally precludes use of the regular formula for Alternation—Ἤτοι ὅ γ' ὣς εἰπὼν κατ' ἄρ' ἕζετο· τοῖσι δ' ἀνέστη [So he spoke and sat down, and among them rose up . . .]—in the deliberation that follows; its presence here would otherwise assimilate this scene even more closely to the Assemblies in **S1**, **S3**, **S6** and **S10**.[17]

The address-formulas that in each case introduce the speech of Poulydamas are also closely interrelated. In the first two scenes (**A1b**, **B1b**) they are identical (*Il.* 12.60 = 210); while the third (**A2b**) differs only in the substitution of #εἰ μὴ for

	A1	B1	A2	B2
(a)IMPASSE	Horses balk at crossing Greek ditch (12.49-59)	Omen stalls Trojan advance at ditch (12.200-09)	Trojans pinned down by Aiantes and bowmen (13.701-22)	Akhilleus' cry terrifies Trojans (18. 243-48)
(b)ADDRESS	Πουλυδάμας θρασὺν ῞Εκτορα εἶπε παραστάς# [Poulydamas stood by bold Hektor and addressed him] (12.60) = (12.210) = (13.725)			Goodwill formula (18.253)
(c)APPEAL	ἀλλ' ἄγεθ', ὡς ἂν ἐγὼ εἴπω, πειθώ—μεθα πάντες [Come now, do as I say, let us all be persuaded.] (12.75)	ἐρέω ὥς μοι δοκεῖ εἶναι ἄρισ—τα# [I will say what seems best to me.] (12.215) = (13.735)		πίθεσθέ μοι· ὧδε γὰρ ἔσ—ται* [Believe me, for thus it will happen.] (18.266)
(d)RESPONSE	ἄδε δ' ῞Εκ—τορι μῦθος ἀπήμων# [and his counsel of safety pleased Hektor] (12.80)	#τὸν δ' ἄρ' ὑπόδρα ἰδὼν προσέφη [Then looking at him darkly he said...] (12.230)	= A1d (13.748)	= B1d (18.284)
(e)EDITORIAL	ø	ø	ø	#νήπιοι . . . [fools . . .] (18.311-13)

#δὴ πότε at the opening of the line. Here (*Il.* 13.723-25) the intercession of Poulydamas takes the form of the protasis of the contrafactual pattern "Then X would have happened if not Y" (28X)—ἔνθα κε λευγαλέως νηῶν ἄπο καὶ κλισιάων | Τρῶες ἐχώρησαν προτὶ Ἴλιον ἠνεμόεσσαν, | εἰ μὴ Πουλυδάμας θρασὺν Ἕκτορα εἶπε παραστὰς [Now pitifully the Trojans *would have* withdrawn from the shelters and the ships to windy Ilion, *had not* Poulydamas stood by bold Hektor and addressed him]—whose general function has been discussed earlier (Chapter 2.2). The pattern on the whole serves as an index of potential crisis, ostensibly marking the presence of alternate and antithetical paths along which the narrative could have proceeded. The fourth scene (**B2b = S9**) uses the formula adverting to the speaker's Goodwill: ὅ σφιν ἐϋφρονέων ἀγορήσατο καὶ μετέειπεν (*Il.* 18.253).

Similar echoes also characterize the opening lines of Poulydamas' speeches. In two scenes (**B1c, A2c**), his advice is prefaced by the hemistich ἐρέω ὥς μοι δοκεῖ εἶναι ἄριστα [I will say what seems best to me] (*Il*.12.215 = 13.735). The phrase appears twice elsewhere in the *Iliad* (3X in the *Odyssey*), once (*Il.* 9.103) during Nestor's speech proposing that a delegation be sent to Akhilleus (**S7**), in which the Goodwill formula also occurs; and in Akhilleus' reply to Odysseus during the Embassy itself (*Il.* 9.314). In turn, the line used in the first confrontation between Hektor and Poulydamas (**A1c**)—ἀλλ᾽ ἄγεθ᾽, ὡς ἂν ἐγὼ εἴπω, πειθώμεθα πάντες [Come now, do as I say, let us all be persuaded] (*Il.* 12.75)—appears often in the poems (8X, 2X); and its call for the approval and obedience of its audience is echoed in Poulydamas' appeal πίθεσθέ μοι· ὧδε γὰρ ἔσται# [believe me, for thus it will happen] (*Il.* 18.266) in the fourth scene (**B2c**).

The interlocking structure of these scenes is even clearer from the form taken by Hektor's reply in each instance. The two passages (**A1d, A2d**) in which his response to Poulydamas' advice is positive both employ the line Ὣς φάτο Πουλυδάμας, ἅδε δ᾽ Ἕκτορι μῦθος ἀπήμων [Thus spoke Poulydamas, and his counsel of safety pleased Hektor] (*Il.* 12.80 = 13.748). Here the adjective ἀπήμων [safe, secure] at one and the same time marks an editorial comment by the narrator and embeds an endorsement from Hektor's own point of view.[18] In the first of these scenes, further vindication of Poulydamas—specifically, of his suggestion to leave their chariots at the edge of the ditch and press their attack on foot (*Il.* 12.75-79)—appears in the subsequent account of the reckless and ultimately doomed attempt by Asios to lead a mounted assault against the wall (108-74). Alone among the Trojan leaders, he ignores the advice, and as a result meets with utter frustration.[19]

On the other hand, the formulaic τὸν δ' ἄρ' ὑπόδρα ἰδὼν προσέφη κορυθαίολος ῞Εκτωρ [Then looking darkly at him, Hektor of the shining helm spoke] (*Il.* 12.230 = 18.284) proleptically signals his rejection of advice in the other two scenes (**B1d, B2d**). The irony that characterizes both these instances of the "looking darkly" formula is an obvious one. In the climactic passage from Book 18 (**B2e**), the rashness of Hektor's reply, and no less that of the Trojans who cry out in their loud and misguided support of him, is the subject of a direct editorial remark (*Il.* 18.310-13):

§39

῍Ως ῞Εκτωρ ἀγόρευ', ἐπὶ δὲ Τρῶες κελάδησαν,
νήπιοι· ἐκ γάρ σφεων φρένας εἵλετο Παλλὰς ᾿Αθήνη.
῞Εκτορι μὲν γὰρ ἐπήνησαν κακὰ μητιόωντι,
Πουλυδάμαντι δ' ἄρ' οὔ τις, ὃς ἐσθλὴν φράζετο
βουλήν.

Thus spoke Hektor, and the Trojans shouted their approval;
the fools, since Pallas Athene had taken their wits away.
They gave praise to Hektor, whose counsel was bad,
but none to Poulydamas, who had spoken sound advice.

The precise range and force of the editorial comment #νήπιοι [fools] will concern us shortly. We have just noted its use in the Asios scene (*Il.* 12.113, 127) that follows on **A1**. Although it lacks any such explicit comment from the narrator, the other passage (**B1**) in which Poulydamas' counsel is dismissed nonetheless ultimately vindicates his cautionary advice, as the Greeks rally to the defense behind the two Aiantes, who finally succeed in pinning the Trojans down in a crossfire of arrows (*Il.* 13.701-22). This leads to Poulydamas' third intercession (**A2**), and Hektor's agreement that the bulk of the Trojan forces should indeed withdraw (748-53), a strategy that Poulydamas had in fact initially advised (**B1**).

A more detailed analysis of these passages reveals the degree to which the tension between Hektor and his Double turns out to be structured in terms of the contrast between the generic narrative types of Warrior and Counselor. Thus Poulydamas in **B1** (*Il.* 12.211-14) prefaces his interpretation of the omen with a reference to the fact that Hektor consistently opposes him despite the soundness of his advice—῞Εκτωρ, ἀεὶ μέν πώς μοι ἐπιπλήσσεις ἀγορῇσιν | ἐσθλὰ φραζομένῳ [Hektor, somehow you always rebuke me in assemblies, though I speak excellently]—and that it is improper for him to argue foolishly (οὐδὲ ἔοικε | . . . παρὲξ ἀγορευέμεν) in counsel and in matters of war. His speech in Book 13 (**A2**), following the vindication of his advice in that earlier passage, opens with a considerably more extensive lecture on the different gifts Zeus gives to different people (*Il.* 13.726-34):

§40

῞Εκτωρ, ἀμήχανός ἐσσι παραρρητοῖσι πίθεσθαι.
οὔνεκά τοι περὶ δῶκε θεὸς πολεμήϊα ἔργα,
τοὔνεκα καὶ βουλῇ ἐθέλεις περιίδμεναι ἄλλων·
ἀλλ' οὔ πως ἅμα πάντα δυνήσεαι αὐτὸς ἑλέσθαι.
ἄλλῳ μὲν γὰρ δῶκε θεὸς πολεμήϊα ἔργα,
ἄλλῳ δ' ὀρχηστύν, ἑτέρῳ κίθαριν καὶ ἀοιδήν,
ἄλλῳ δ' ἐν στήθεσσι τιθεῖ νόον εὐρύοπα Ζεὺς
ἐσθλόν, τοῦ δέ τε πολλοὶ ἐπαυρίσκοντ' ἄνθρωποι,
καί τε πολέας ἐσάωσε, μάλιστα δὲ καὐτὸς ἀνέγνω.

Hektor, you are incapable of being persuaded by arguments.
Because the god has given you prowess in warfare,
you also want to have wisdom surpassing others in counsel.
But you cannot choose to have all the gifts together;
for to one man god grants prowess in warfare,
to another dancing, to another the lyre and song,
and in another's breast Zeus of the wide brows puts excellent
wisdom, and many men take profit from him,
and he saves many, but he himself knows best of all.

The *topos* that Zeus generally grants an individual preeminence in only one sphere of life points out the difficulty in realizing the heroic paradigm of combining both martial and rhetorical prowess—thus of being "both a speaker of words and a doer of deeds" (*Il.* 9.443)—and confirms the fact that in this case, these two skills are indeed divided up between Hektor and Poulydamas (*Il.* 18.252): ἀλλ' ὁ μὲν ἄρ μύθοισιν, ὁ δ' ἔγχεϊ πολλὸν ἐνίκα [But the one far excelled in speeches, the other with the spear]. Born on a single night (251) each is the split image of that ideal.

Two additional aspects of this pattern call for further comment here. The first concerns the presence in §38 (**B1**) of an element that identifies an important subgroup of critical situations that include Mediation among their possibilities, and also serve to draw the figures of Counselor and Prophet even closer together. Though the majority of Mediators are not professional seers, the boundary between these two types always remains a flexible one, and is drawn as much by their *function* in context than by reference to some fixed set of credentials. Thus as the parameters of the situation require, the role elsewhere reserved for adepts like Khalkas (*Il.* 1.92-100), Halitherses (*Od.* 2.146-76) and Theoklymenos (*Od.* 20.345-57) can be shifted to figures such as Poulydamas (*Il.* 12.215-29) and Nestor (*Il.* 8.130-44)—and, for that matter, Amphinomos (*Od.* 20.240-46) as well. In the case of Poulydamas (**B1**), in fact, the identification is quite explicit, for the Trojan concludes his reading of the portent of the eagle and the snake with the claim ὧδέ χ' ὑποκρίναιτο θεοπρόπος, ὅς σάφα θυμῷ | εἰδείη τεράων καί οἱ πειθοίατο λαοί [So an interpreter of the gods would answer, one who knew in his mind the truth of portents, and whom the people believed in.] (*Il.* 12.228-29). Once again, *ethos* and *situation* are not entirely distinct, but instead seem to be made of interwoven strands.

A pair of instances (**S9, S10**) involving the dismissal of an intercessor's advice also match this pattern of Omen—Mediation—Approval/Rejection. Both occur during the Ithakan Assembly in *Odyssey* 2, and represent the abusive response of suitors to attempts at Mediation by Halitherses and Mentor, respectively, each of whose speeches is introduced by the formula ὅ σφιν ἐϋφρονέων ἀγορήσατο καὶ μετέειπεν (*Od.* 2.160 = 228). The close proximity of these two scenes—separated only by the speech of Telemakhos (208-23)—

along with their essential identity of content and structure, in fact suggest the doubling of a single pattern:

§41
(a)	Omen (eagles)	146-56
(b)	Mediator (Halitherses = Prophet) speaks	157-76
(c)	Antagonist (Eurymakhos) rejects (b)	177-207
(d)	Telemakhos speaks	208-23
(e)	Mediator (Mentor = Elder) speaks	224-41
(f)	Antagonist (Leokritos) rejects (e)	242-56
(g)	Assembly dissolved	257

The doubling of the elements §41(b)-(c) in (e)-(f) is obvious, and this is reinforced by the status of Leokritos in the second group. Unlike Eurymakhos (30X), who takes second place only to Antinoos (56X) for prominence among the suitors, this Leokritos (Euenorides) is a genuine nonentity, merely the shadow Eurymakhos casts in this type-scene. Apart from his speech here, his only other appearance in the poem comes twenty books later at the moment of his perfectly formulaic death (*Od.* 22.294-96): speared from behind by Telemakhos, kidney and diaphragm pierced, face flat in the dust.

Equally striking is the similarity between §41(a)-(f) in its full form and the overall (though far more complex) narrative pattern of Omen—Mediation—Rejection in the Akhaian Assembly in *Iliad* 1. This is especially true with regard to the sequence of types of intercessory figures (Prophet→Elder :: Kalkhas/Halitherses→Nestor/Mentor) that appear in both scenes. In each case, it is an elderly character who (unsuccessfully) attempts to mediate the conflict arising from a prophecy that is unfavorable to an individual (Agamemnon) or group (suitors) in power. A further parallel between the two Assemblies is perhaps worth noting at §40(f), where Agamemnon's approving response to Nestor (*Il.* 1.286: κατὰ μοῖραν ἔειπες#) is inverted in Leokritos' jibe at Mentor, σὺ δ' οὐ κατὰ μοῖραν ἔειπες# [You did not speak fittingly] (*Od.* 2.251).

Even more significant, however, are structural features that the abusive replies to prophetic Mediation share in these two passages, with which Hektor's speech to Poulydamas in **B1** should also be compared. Agamemnon's rejection in *Iliad* 1,

Hektor's in *Iliad* 12 and that of Eurymakhos in *Odyssey* 2 all take the fixed form of (a) an initial impugning of the wits and competence of the Prophet/Counselor, followed in the latter two scenes by (b) a dismissal of the mantic value of the omen in question, and (c) the antagonist's boastful claim to possess prophetic skills more acute and more accurate than those of the Mediator:

§42
(a)	*Ad hominem*	*Il.* 1.106-08 / 12.233-34 / *Od.* 2.178-79
(b)	Omen discounted	*Il.* 12.237-40 / *Od.* 2.181-82
(c)	Claim to mantic skill	*Il.* 12.235-36;241 / *Od.* 2.180

The effect of redundancies like the one embedded in the structure of the Assembly scenes in *Iliad* 1 and *Odyssey* 2—not to mention the A-B-A-B patterning of Hektor's relation to Poulydamas throughout the *Iliad* (§38)—is generally to emphasize its message. The repeated rejection of a Mediator's sound advice only draws attention to how great a violation of conventional narrative conduct has taken place, and so amounts to an implicit justification of the retribution that inevitably follows. This is why a kind of tautology governs all scenes of Mediation. Once it is formulaically established that the Other who rises to speak in Crisis is indeed a Mediator—and not, for instance, another Antagonist (cf. §36)—the outcome stemming from the rejection or approval of his advice takes a predetermined course. Acceptance always leads to Success, Dismissal always ultimately issues in Failure. The necessity of the outcome is clearer in the case of Rejection than Approval, if only because the former possibility is less usual and certainly more scandalous, a disruption of traditional values that demands that balance be restored by a reassertion of the proper order of things. Clearest of all in Homer is the ineluctability of disaster that follows the rejection of a Mediator who is also a Prophet, since nowhere in either poem are prophecies ever disregarded with impunity.[20] The response-pattern (§42) that links dismissal of the Prophet/Mediator with dismissal of prophecy itself or with the unjustified arrogation of the vision of prophets by the characters (Hektor, Eurymakhos) who reject their advice only emphasizes this point.

A second and final observation to be made with reference to the table of passages at §38 concerns the editorial comment on the Trojan rejection of Poulydamas' advice in **B2e** (= §39). Its phrasing—νήπιοι· ἐκ γάρ σφεων φρένας εἵλετο Παλλὰς 'Αθήνη [the fools, since Pallas Athene had taken their wits away] (*Il.* 18.311; cf. 9.377)—ironically recalls Hektor's own earlier reproach of Poulydamas six books earlier in **B1**—εἰ δ' ἐτέον δὴ τοῦτον ἀπὸ σπουδῆς ἀγορεύεις, | ἐξ ἄρα δή τοι ἔπειτα θεοὶ φρένας ὤλεσαν αὐτοί [If in all seriousness this is your true argument, then the gods themselves have ruined the brain within you] (*Il.* 12.233-34). Uttered then from the limited perspective of a man who is "intractable to reasoned persuasion" (*Il.* 13.726), the taunt later turns back on him from the narrator's omniscient and thus more authoritative viewpoint. Moreover, this couplet of lines in fact appears once earlier (*Il.* 7.359-60), significantly enough in Alexandros' rebuke of Antenor in the Trojan Assembly scene (**S6**). The ethical contrast that structures the relationship between Hektor and Paris throughout the poem collapses here into a telling identity.

These ironies within the narrative open on a larger sort of irony, however. The editorial #νήπιοι in *Iliad* 18 belongs to a large group (31%) of the total number of the occurrences of this noun (15 of 48X) in the poems, which in turn amounts to an even larger percentage (62%) of all instances of the noun in initial position (24X). In all of these cases, as in Hektor's rejection of Poulydamas in *Iliad* 18, the editorial #νήπι- marks a point in the text at which the narrative is interrupted by the storyteller's judgement of a character's misunderstanding of the situation in which he finds himself, generally as the result of bad counsel or false optimism; this misreading in turn issues in his decision to pursue a specific course of action. The editorial judgement amounts to an imbedded prolepsis, a foreshadowing of the disastrous outcome to which that decision leads.[21] As with all dramatic irony, it indicates a clash between different focalizations, and turns on an issue of knowledge, contrasting an ignorant with an informed perspective. This contrast generally occurs along the seam dividing different narrative levels, namely between events within the narrative on the one hand, and its overarching frame on the other. Put more succinctly, the editorial #νήπι- exposes a rift in the text between the concrete tale and the unfolding of the abstract story. In this respect it serves the same function (though with opposite sense) as the contrafactual pattern "Then X would have happened if not Y" alluded to above with reference to the third scene (**A2**) charted in §38. Both mark a textual irony, an opening in which competing narrative paths are disclosed.

More on this shortly. Let me return to my appraisal of scenes in which the Mediator's advice is rejected, which was suspended by my digression on Hektor and Poulydamas. The final instance (**S15**) occurs in *Odyssey* 24, at the gathering of aggrieved Ithakans who meet after burying their sons to plot vengeance against Odysseus. Repeating Aigyptios' anguish at the opening of the first Assembly, Eupeithes addresses them in sorrow over his loss (*Od.* 2.24 = 24.425; cf. 438) and demands retribution. The pity (438: οἶκτος) that seizes his audience quickly modulates into astonishment (441: τάφος) and then dread (450: δέος) as first Medon and then Halitherses intervenes to address the crowd. While Medon prudently (442) draws attention to the fact that Odysseus' slaughter of the suitors was divinely sanctioned (443-49), Halitherses, "speaking with kind intention" (452), rebukes them for their failure to restrain their sons. His exclamation οἳ μέγα ἔργον ἔρεξαν ἀτασθαλίῃσι κακῇσι [(sons) who performed outrageous acts in their wicked folly] (458) tellingly echoes what Eupeithes has just said of Odysseus—ὦ φίλοι, ἦ μέγα ἔργον ἀνὴρ ὅδε μήσατ' Ἀχαιούς [Friends, what an outrageous act this man has devised against the Akhaians] (426)—in a formula elsewhere reserved for the expression of astonished disapproval (*Od.* 4.663 = 16.346, 11.272, 12.373).

The response to his advice to abandon all thought of vendetta is a mixed one. Although the majority shouts its approval, a great many are displeased (465: #οὐ γάρ σφιν ἅδε μῦθος ἐνὶ φρεσίν) and opt instead to side with Eupeithes; their decision ironically plays on his name: ἀλλ' Εὐπείθει | πείθοντ' [but they were persuaded by Persuader]. Once again, as the Ithakans rush to arms and muster at the gates of the town, an editorial comment confirms that Eupeithes' rejection of the Mediator will bring about his own demise (470-71):[22]

§43

φῆ δ' ὅ γε τίσεσθαι παιδὸς φόνον, οὐδ' ἄρ' ἔμελλεν
ἂψ ἀπονοστήσειν, ἀλλ' αὐτοῦ πότμον ἐφέψειν.

He claimed he would avenge his son's murder, but he was not
going
to return home again, for doom would overtake him.

In a narrative concerned with the return of fathers and sons
and with the consequent reunification of the family, it is
striking that Eupeithes' death in an attempt to avenge his
errant child should be represented as a loss of *homecoming*
(ἀπονοστήσειν). He is joined with Antinoos in death at the
very moment that Laertes and Odysseus, Odysseus and
Telemakhos are brought together again.

5. IRONIC MEDIATION

The preceding analysis has shown that the nature of the
specific *response* (Approval/Rejection) to Mediation is
sufficient in and of itself to determine and thus also to
foreshadow the nature of the ultimate *outcome* (Success/
Failure) of the action. A stable (if limited) narrative pattern
with strong predictive value thereby emerges. Rejection of a
Mediator's advice always precipitates disaster for those who
spurn it: Agamemnon (**S1**), whose mistake is admitted (*Il.*
19.76-144) only after the slaughter of countless Akhaians;
Hektor (**S9**), who acknowledges only too late (*Il.* 22.99-103) the
soundness of Poulydamas' prudent counsel; Eupeithes (**S15**),
aggrieved father bent on revenge and last casualty in the
Odyssey. The case of the suitors in Book 2 of that poem (**S10,
S11**) in fact suggests something of the range of this pattern, and
also the ways in which narratives can be motivated by
interlocking combinations of formally different patterns that
nonetheless point towards the same end. There is a sense, after
all, in which the suitors' fate is implicitly already sealed by
their dismissal of Mediation in the Ithakan Assembly scene,
despite the fact that it does not finally overtake them until
some twenty books later. Yet that conclusion is also determined
and justified by any number of other patterns that all spell

disaster for an agent who also, for instance, violates the ties of hospitality by overstaying his welcome, devouring his host's livelihood, suborning his servants, plotting against him, and the like. Nor is it only failure and death that bear this kind of overdetermination, since Approval leads just as inevitably to the success of an endeavor in the cases in which it occurs. The following simple schema results:

§44

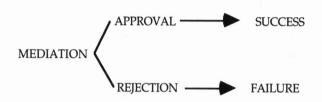

I have suggested that a number of ironic possibilities can complicate this schema, however. For in the event that the advice proposed by a Mediator itself proves to be in some sense unsound—either flawed or perhaps even possibly deceptive—its acceptance by others can ultimately have the same result as unimpeachably good advice that is rejected or bad advice that wins approval. Accommodating this possibility, the full range of options would map out as follows:

§45

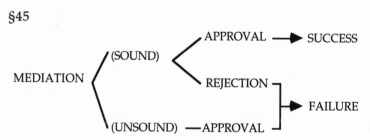

A relatively simple example has already been noted. Priam's intercession in the tumultuous (*Il.* 7.346) dispute between Paris and Antenor in Book 7 (**S6**) "bears a functional resemblance" (Kirk 1990:280) to Nestor's address to Agamemnon and Akhilleus in the Assembly at the opening of the poem (*Il.* 1.247-84). The similarities go not much farther than echoes at the level of the formulas—namely those of Alternation and Goodwill—used to introduce their speeches, in keeping with the pattern charted above (§35). In terms of their content and general tenor, however, the two speeches differ markedly. While Nestor aims at a genuine compromise between the antagonists, by spelling out the different privileges to which each can legitimately lay claim in terms of the status they each enjoy, Priam simply acquiesces to Alexandros' insistence that he will not return Helen. He chooses to ignore the validity of the argument advanced by Antenor (*Il.* 7.350-52), that the Trojans now stand in violation of the oaths they swore prior to the duel in Book 3, and instead uncritically supports his son's proposal (374) to offer restitution only of the goods stolen from Sparta. This wins the assent of the Trojans—ὣς ἔφαθ', οἱ δ' ἄρα τοῦ μάλα μὲν κλύον ἠδ' ἐπίθοντο [So he spoke, and they carefully listened and obeyed him] (379)—and the herald Idaios is sent to deliver the decision to the Greeks. The offer of course meets with the rejection it deserves (398-404), and Idaios' own personal asides during the course of his message indirectly condemn it by *ad hominem* references to its author. Paris, "for whose sake this strife has arisen" (388 = 374), should have perished long before, he remarks (ὡς πρὶν ὤφελλ' ἀπολέσθαι [390]); and he even represents the refusal to give Helen back as a course of action opposed by the majority of Trojans—οὔ φησιν δώσειν· ἦ μὴν Τρῶές γε κέλονται [He says he won't return her, though the Trojans urge it] (393). His interjections thus serve essentially the same function as explicit editorial comments by the narrator (e.g. #νήπι-) on other occasions on which unsound advice is approved and implemented.

The support Nestor gives to Agamemnon's plan to test the morale of the troops in *Iliad* 2—the famous *Peira*, simultaneously comic and disastrous—is another case in point, and a somewhat more complex one. This scene (**S3**) raises a number of textual problems that are not especially germane here.[23] Even before the Council of Chiefs at which the old man rises to speak "with kind intention" (*Il.* 2.78), the figure of Nestor insinuates itself into the narrative in the form taken by Agamemnon's "false" dream, which stands over his head Νηληΐῳ υἷι ἐοικώς, | Νέστορι, τόν ῥα μάλιστα γερόντων τῖ' 'Αγαμέμνων [in the likeness of Neleus' son Nestor, whom Agamemnon honored above all elders] (20-21). The editorial comment in the closing hemistich clearly intends to motivate this particular guise.[24] Kirk remarks that the dream "assumes Nestor's likeness in order, presumably, to give itself credibility" (1985:116); and the high opinion of Nestor that Agamemnon elsewhere expresses (cf. *Il.* 3.371-74) would tend to corroborate this. At the same time, as has been suggested,[25] the dream's guise—μάλιστα δὲ Νέστορι δίῳ | εἶδός τε μέγεθός τε φυήν τ' ἄγιστα ἐῴκει [in appearance and stature and shape it most closely resembled splendid Nestor] (*Il.* 2.57-58)—may also have the proleptic function of preparing for Nestor's prominent role in Book 2 as a whole. It is equally possible that this prolepsis more specifically foreshadows the irony of the ensuing scene, as the Greek leaders meet beside Nestor's own ship. There (55-71) Agamemnon repeats what Nestor/Dream has told him, and appends to his account the unexpected proposal of staging an Assembly in which he himself will disingenuously argue in favor of retreat and the other chiefs will play their part by dissuading the troops from this course of action (73-75).

Nestor's response—athetized by Aristarkhos on various grounds,[26] none especially substantial—is essential for the degree to which it amplifies the irony of the entire Dream episode (79-83):[27]

§46

ὦ φίλοι, 'Αργείων ἡγήτορες ἠδὲ μέδοντες,
εἰ μέν τις τὸν ὄνειρον 'Αχαιῶν ἄλλος ἔνισπε,
ψεῦδός κεν φαῖμεν καὶ νοσφιζοίμεθα μᾶλλον·
νῦν δ' ἴδεν ὃς μέγ' ἄριστος 'Αχαιῶν εὔχεται εἶναι·
ἀλλ' ἄγετ', αἴ κέν πως θωρήξομεν υἷας 'Αχαιῶν.

Friends, leaders and counselors of the Akhaians,
if any other of the Akhaians had told of this dream
we would have called it false and would rather reject it;
but now he who claims to be best of the Akhaians has seen it.
So come then, let us see if we can arm the sons of the Akhaians.

The irony of course resides in the fact that the dream was indeed false and deceptive to begin with; and this in turn ironizes Agamemnon's characterization as "best of the

Akhaians," here offered as grounds on which the dream should be accepted as true vision. This is clearly an instance of *dramatic* irony, moreover, embodying a contradiction between what the audience already knows from the opening scene of the book—reinforced by the narrator's editorial statements (35-40), which incorporate the formulaic judgement #νήπιος [fool] (38)—and what the characters themselves believe to be the case. It is presumably unintended by Nestor himself, who is here made the unwitting mouthpiece of an irony that only narrator and audience are properly positioned to appreciate. At the same time, the dream represents a falsity compounded by the farce that Agamemnon, on his own initiative, suggests they perpetrate on the troops. The backfire of this plan, as the Akhaians joyfully accept the feigned counsel and rush to their ships (142-54), mirrors the greater failure they will suffer in attempting to implement what Nestor/Dream had actually proposed to "the best of the Akhaians."

Nestor is the pivot on which this deception turns. Just as his authority as a respected counselor (21) motivates the guise assumed by Dream in order to manipulate Agamemnon, the same authority is presumably also what convinces the assembled leaders to approve the latter's foolish plan when Nestor himself supports it. His argument that Agamemnon's status guarantees the truth of his vision in fact embodies the same general principle adduced in Nestor's attempt to mediate the conflict between Atreides and Akhilleus in the preceding book (*Il.* 1.277-81), namely that obedience is due to Agamemnon thanks to his privileged (φέρτερος) position as a sceptered king. Nestor's implication in this double round of irony—deliberate in the case of Nestor/Dream, unintentional when he speaks *in propria persona*, and in both cases leading to disaster for those who are persuaded by him—makes him a potentially ambiguous Mediator in the narrative. Moreover, as later considerations will suggest, this ambiguity may well itself be deliberate on the narrator's part.[28]

Nestor's advice in *Iliad* 7 (S5) to build a defensive wall upon the burial mound of the slain Akhaians may represent yet another instance of Ironic Mediation. The difficulties surrounding this passage too are familiar ones, and the general consensus seems to be that it is an interpolation.[29] Its situation and opening lines have been discussed earlier (§35); what is important to note here is that despite the approval the old man's suggestion wins from the Greek leaders (*Il.* 7.344 = 9.710), the advice again proves to be flawed and futile in the long run. To begin with, the wall provokes the anger of Poseidon, who complains that its construction was completed without the required sacrifices—οὐδὲ θεοῖσι δόσαν κλειτὰς ἑκατόμβας# (450)—and that its fame will eclipse that of the wall he himself and Apollo had built for Troy (451-53). The first charge is repeated with expansion at the opening of Book 12, this time in the form of an external prolepsis in the voice of the narrator (*Il.* 12.3-9):

§47

οὐδ' ἄρ' ἔμελλε
τάφρος ἔτι σχήσειν Δαναῶν καὶ τεῖχος ὕπερθεν
εὐρύ, τὸ ποιήσαντο νεῶν ὕπερ, ἀμφὶ δὲ τάφρον
ἤλασαν, οὐδὲ θεοῖσι δόσαν κλειτὰς ἑκατόμβας,
ὄφρα σφιν νῆάς τε θοὰς καὶ ληΐδα πολλὴν
ἐντὸς ἔχον ῥύοιτο· θεῶν δ' ἀέκητι τέτυκτο
ἀθανάτων· τὸ καὶ οὔ τι πολὺν χρόνον ἔμπεδον ἦεν.

> nor would the Danaans'
> ditch hold them back nor the wide wall above it
> they had built for the sake of their ships, driving a deep ditch
> around it, *and they had not given the gods splendid hekatombs*
> so that it might protect their swift ships and the great spoils
> within it. It was built despite the will of the immortal
> gods, and so was not going to remain secure for a long time.

The scene concludes with the famous account of the gods' destruction of the wall after the fall of Troy and departure of the Akhaians (10-35), just as Zeus had initially suggested (*Il.* 7.459-63). In her survey of the various theories proposed to make sense of this "farthest reaching of all analepses" in the *Iliad,* de Jong offers the following "intra-textual interpretation" of the passage (1987:88):

> [T]he Greek wall is going to be the centre of the events in book M (which was called τειχομαχία in antiquity). Normally, the [principal narrator] underlines the importance of an object by telling its *history*, i.e. through an external analepsis, e.g. concerning Agamemnon's scepter in B 101-8. Since the Greek wall had only recently been built the [principal narrator] here turns to another device, telling the *future* of the object involved.

> The effect is to illustrate to the [audience] the fragility of human
> existence, the tininess . . . of human enterprises, even those of
> semi-divine men, when set against the eternity of nature and the
> immortal gods.

This is certainly correct, especially given the extended
description of the forces of river, ocean and rain later brought to
bear on the wall by Apollo, Poseidon and Zeus (*Il.* 12.19-33),
completely erasing its presence, making the beach smooth
again (30) and hiding all trace of human workmanship beneath
mounds of sand (31). The effect is foreshadowed even before the
wall's final obliteration, in the ease with which Apollo
tramples part of it down some three books later, like a child
who wrecks his own sand-castle (*Il.* 15.355-66).[30]

What this interpretation tends to scant, however, is the
reason initially given for the gods' displeasure. The wall has
been built without the proper offerings to consecrate it;
Poseidon's complaint to this effect, as we saw, is echoed by the
narrator himself (*Il.* 7.450 = 12.6). To be sure, it is absurd to
speculate whether the wall *would have* remained standing *if
only* the Greeks had performed hekatombs upon it. This would
be to confuse *motivation* with *function*, for whatever the stated
reason for the wall's inability to hold—including Poseidon's
concern that it will outlast the work of his own divine hands—
the fortifications *must* fall in order to initiate the narrative
sequence of events that run from Hektor's firing of the ships
through Patroklos' death and the return of Akhilleus to battle.
Despite this function in the story, however, the reason stated
within the narrative draws explicit attention to the flaw
inherent in Nestor's original advice to build the wall in Book 7,
and so once again seems to cast a shadow of doubt over the
nature of his role as a Mediator. After Hektor has broken
through the defenses, Nestor laments their failure to fulfill
the purpose he intended for them: τεῖχος μὲν γὰρ δὴ
κατερήριπεν, ᾧ ἐπέπιθμεν | ἄρρηκτον νηῶν τε καὶ
αὐτῶν εἶλαρ ἔσεσθαι [For the wall has fallen, which we
expected would be unbreakable and a protection for us and our
ships] (*Il.* 14.55-56; cf. *Il.* 7.338). However prudent it appears at
the time, then, and however much it wins the approval of its
audience as the "best counsel" (cf. *Il.* 7.325), his suggestion
embodies a sin of omission that is at least partly responsible for
the failure of the project.

Consideration of other and more crucial instances of the ambiguity surrounding Nestor as an intercessory figure will occupy the following chapter. Here a few conclusions can be ventured on what has been an admittedly incomplete study of the event of Mediation in Homer. Its very incompleteness is in fact itself a point worth dwelling briefly on.

Despite the emergence of a number of relatively stable formulaic contours for Mediation, its full extent remains largely uncharted. This is partly because the pattern of Mediation is by no means limited to those scenes in which the address-formula ὅ σφιν ἐϋφρονέων ἀγορήσατο καὶ μετέειπεν appears; this served at best as a convenient point of departure. Moreover, analysis is further complicated by the fact that each instance of specific responsion among cola, lines and generic scenes only seems to open on ever wider and more intricate and more interdependent patterns of responsion. These call for further study, but at the same time also implicitly challenge the approach taken in this chapter. Structurally, the different elements of the pattern of Mediation are governed by what can be called *coimplication*, namely by the fact that they stand in intimate relation to one another, as interwoven strands in a single narrative fabric. And it is thanks to this that an approach in terms of the categories of *ethos, situation* and *response* remains at best a very rough heuristic strategy.

To take only the most striking example, I have suggested that the category of *ethos* apparently enjoys no special privilege in these type-scenes. Its boundaries are so flexible— shifting among the figures of Youth and Elder, Prophet, Counselor, Nurse, Double, Father, Husband, Herald, King— that it is tempting to conclude, along with Barthes, that what passes for character in narratives is indeed merely a cluster of "semes"—goodwill, memory, sorrow, prudence, command of persuasive speech, circumspection, soundness of mind—to which a proper name is attached. The latter, in its turn (and far from signifying some unique essence), may well only mark as it were an empty *locus* of narrative potentials. What strengthens this impression is the degree to which *ethos* itself in all its flexibility seems to be a function of specific contextual constraints. Mediator no less than (say) Antagonist rises to speak or fails to rise only within and by reason of possibilities embedded in a certain *situation*. It is the fact of Crisis, after all, that makes the attribution of Goodwill to a certain character a significant rather than simply an ornamental predicate. *Situation* is in turn no independent variable either, but instead is plausibly determined by prior concatenations of events in the narrative, which stretch back towards some vanishing-point in the tradition of the story. This is why a great number of passages in the text of the poems are no less valid instances of Mediation despite their lack of many or even most of the explicit formulaic cues (Debate, Alternation, Ethical Expansion, Goodwill) that initially seemed so definitive. What chiefly counts is the *function* they serve in the narrative development.

NOTES

1. Edwards 1970.

2. Kirk (1985:78, 146) mistakenly claims that it appears only in the *Iliad*.

3. De Jong 1987:199 remarks that such introductory speech formulas all "serve to *recommend* the speaker" to his addressees.

4. The hemistich ὁ γὰρ οἶος ὅρα πρόσσω καὶ ὀπίσσω# at *Od.* 24.452 shows the variant reading ὁ γὰρ ὥρα πάντα πρόσω καὶ ὀπίσσω# [for he saw everything past and future] in one large family of codices in the manuscript tradition. This allomorph is understandable in terms of his role as a seer, and under the pressure exerted by the nearly identical lines that introduce him earlier in the *Odyssey*. Compare 24.451-53 and 2.157-60, where Μαστορίδης· ὁ γὰρ οἶος ὁμηλικίην ἐκέκαστο | ὄρνιθας γνῶναι καὶ ἐναίσιμα μυθήσασ-θαι [Mastor's son, for he alone of his generation knew how to understand bird flight and interpret signs] (2.158-59) "substitutes" for and "expands" on the line Μαστορίδης· ὁ γὰρ οἶος ὅρα πρόσσω καὶ ὀπίσσω (24.452).

5. Redfield 1975:143, Willcock 1976 (at 11.57-60).

6. Compare *Il.* 7.43-53, where Helenos is inspired with a (partial) vision of Hektor's destiny, or at least of the fact that the hero is not yet fated to die and so can risk an encounter in single combat with "the bravest of the Akhaians." The seer characterizes his knowledge as something heard from the gods (53: ὣς γὰρ ἐγὼν ὄπ' ἄκουσα θεῶν αἰειγενετάων).

7. The same term characterizes the earlier Assembly of Akhaians—#τετρήχει δ' ἀγορή (*Il.* 2.95) [the assembly was in tumult]; see Kirk 1990:280.

8. The formula is used extensively (10X, 6X) to describe astonishment and shock at a speaker's words.

9. Lohmann 1970:9-11. See also Arend 1933:116-21 and Edwards 1980.

10. Heubeck 1988:145.

11. For a survey of scholarship on "winged words," see Edwards 1988:32-34.

12. Diller 1956, Walsh 1984:8-9, de Jong 1987, Ford 1992:121-25. On κατὰ κόσμον, see, most recently, Pratt 1993:55-94.

13. For a representative view, see e.g. Bakhtin (1981:11), who claims that "an absolute epic distance separates the epic world from contemporary reality, that is, from the time in which the singer (the author and his audience) lives." The claim, like the terminology, is borrowed from the Neoclassicism of Schlegel, Goethe and Schiller; see Todorov 1984:85-91. How implicitly readerly and textual a perspective it embodies is clear from such statements as (Bakhtin 1981:17) "the epic past is locked into itself and walled off from all subsequent times by an impenetrable boundary, isolated . . . from the eternal present of children and descendants in which the epic singer and his listeners are located. . . . The epic world is constructed in the zone of an absolute distanced image, beyond the sphere of possible contact with developing, incomplete and therefore re-thinking and re-evaluating present." The "slippage" between Nestor's moral horizon an that of the narrator himself—and, by implication, the horizon of values still shared by the audience of the *Iliad*—does much to demolish this "impenetrable boundary." See also Goody and Watt 1968:31-34 and Ong 1982:46-49 on the homeostasis of traditional societies.

14. With this passage, Iris' denial of such an intent towards Priam in the line οὐ μὲν γάρ τοι ἐγὼ κακὸν ὀσσομένη τόδ᾽ ἱκάνω [I come *not eyeing you with evil intention*] (*Il.* 24.172) should be compared.

15. Holoka 1983:6-7.

16. Holoka (1983:16) acknowledges its use "to good ironic effect in scenes where an individual, erroneously thinking himself to be superior, looks darkly and thereby commits the very offense he intends to castigate—unseemly behavior vis-à-vis a superior (*Odyssey* 17.459; 18.388)." To limit the ground for irony to a character's mistaken claim to superior social status excludes those equally ironic occasions on which, *despite his recognized superiority*, a character dismisses legitimately good advice.

17. The pattern (§37B2) in *Iliad* 18 thus amounts to an allomorph of the scene outlined above in §33, with the expanded (three-line) description of Poulydamas' *ethos* (*Il.* 18.250-52) matching the §33(c) element and the line τοῖσι δὲ

Πουλύδαμας πεπνυμένος ἦρχ' ἀγορεύειν [First to speak among them was the prudent Poulydamas] (249) replacing the alternation- formula, to form the sequence §33(a₁)-(b)-(c)-(d).

18. De Jong 1987:204-06.

19. Note the high frequency of editorial commentary in his passage: Asios is a "fool" (*Il.* 12.113: νήπιος), as are the troops who follow him (127); in his pride he was not destined to evade death and return to Ilion safely (113-15); and his lament to Zeus falls on deaf ears (173-74). For more on Asios as a type of the frustrated (and doomed) hero, see Lohenstam 1981:38-43, 77-83.

20. Stockinger 1959, Peradotto 1974 and 1980.

21. De Jong (1987:86-87) remarks that #νήπι- "is mostly found wedged in between mention of a character's *optimistic* expectations and the [narrator's] description (often prediction) of the true (disastrous) course of events. Signaling the contrast between hope and delusion, it expresses and elicits pity, despite the fact that the delusion is often brought about by the character's own tragic error."

22. See de Jong 1987:66 (with note 55), 86-87 for discussion and a citation of other passages exhibiting internal prolepses in the negative form οὐδ' ἄρ' ἔμελλεν#.

23. Kirk 1985:116-24.

24. See de Jong 1987:211-12, who rightly takes issue (note 38) with Kirk's claim (1985:121) that the relative clause is intended "to introduce [Nestor] to the audience."

25. Shipp 1972:232; and cf. Kirk 1985:116, 121.

26. Kirk 1985:123.

27. Compare the similar passage later in the poem (*Il.* 24.220-22), where Priam argues for the credibility of the vision that advised him to visit Akhilleus, and in which 24.222 = 2.81.

28. Among the sounder reasons given for Aristarkhos' rejection of Nestor's entire speech before the Council of leaders (*Il.* 2.76-83) is the fact that its excision from the text would allow the epithet ποιμένι λαῶν in the lines οἱ δ' ἐπανέστησαν πείθοντό τε ποιμένι λαῶν | σκηπτοῦχοι βασιλῆες [and the sceptered kings rose, obeying the shepherd of the people] (85-86) to refer to Agamemnon, who is more usually characterized as such; the phrase is applied to Nestor only once elsewhere (*Il.* 23.411), in what Kirk (1985:124) styles "untypical circumstances." If so, its presence here might

represent the trace of an uneven splice of Nestor's speech into a scene in which Agamemnon's proposal was followed immediately by the description of its approval by the other kings. This would in turn raise the question of what function such a deliberate insertion is meant to serve.

29. Scodel 1982a, Davies 1986, de Jong 1987:88-89 and 153, Kirk 1990:276-80 and 288-92, Ford 1992:147-57.

30. Nor are the Trojans much impressed by the wall, it should be noted. Hektor dismisses it scornfully: νήπιοι, οἳ ἄρα δὴ τάδε τείχεα μηχανόωντο | ἀβλήχρ᾽ οὐδενόσωρα (*Il.* 8.177-78) [Fools, who devised these fortifications— flimsy things, not worth a thought].

4

Nestor as Host:
Nostos & Hospitable Death

χρὴ ξεῖνον παρεόντα φιλεῖν, ἐθέλοντα δὲ πέμπειν.
Entertain a guest at hand, but speed him when he wants to go.
(*Od.* 15.674)

1. INTRODUCTION

Examination of a single narrative pattern for the type-scene of Mediation in the previous chapter has not only confirmed Nestor's role as an intercessory figure, but has also noted that this role is sometimes an ambiguous or "ironic" one. On a number of occasions, the well-intentioned (ἐϋφρονέων) advice he offers subsequently proves to have been flawed, resulting in distress or sometimes even disaster for those who assent to it. This ambiguity is well worth more consideration. This is especially so in light of the fact, as earlier chapters have shown, that Nestor's characterization in the poems is in certain striking respects isomorphic with that of the Homeric *aoidos*—that Nestor himself is the type of a "self-singer." For our findings thus far have suggested that Mediation is a distinctly *authorial* strategy. Like prophecy, it represents a point in the narrative at which the narrator's controlling influence can be seen without suffering his direct intervention in the form of an aside or some other explicit commentary—". . . and then X *would have* happened if Y *had not* . . ."—on the unfolding of the action. It embeds that influence, on the one hand masking it in the form of choices exercised by characters *within* the tale, at the same time as it exposes its extranarrative source by projecting the ends those choices will realize even despite what the characters themselves intend in so choosing, and certainly despite the far more limited perspective from which their choices are made. This exposure, we have noted, is often an implicit one, a result of the anaphoric power of oral narratives. Like other formulaic narrative structures, the type-scene for Mediation deploys gestures and patterns heavily charged with traditional significance, proleptic of certain definite outcomes, and therefore geared to encourage very definite expectations from their audience; these have been charted above (§45). Mediation tacitly reveals divergent paths along which the tale can proceed, thus laying bare the causal framework on which the storyteller constructs his narrative.

This is particularly true where Mediation is ironized, since there the disparity between intention and outcome, motivation and function, concrete tale and abstract story is most in evidence. In Nestor's case, I have already suggested that this irony represents a deliberate manipulation of his character in the interest of furthering the story. As we saw, the clearest example occurs in the opening scene of *Iliad* 2, along with the Council that follows it, where Nestor's identification with the deceptive Dream sent by Zeus—in itself a problematic conflation[1]—allows for his use as a mouthpiece for the dramatic irony that marks his speech some fifty lines later, and that also characterizes the ultimate outcome of Agamemnon's farcical *Peira*. Here the old man is a tool employed in the service of the developing plot, a disguise used once—and so *a fortiori* also twice—by the narrator to motivate disaster for the Akhaians. Or rather, he is but one in a whole panoply of superimposed guises that the narrator himself assumes in this passage: first masked as Zeus who, while gods and mortals alike take their rest, broods sleeplessly over the best way to advance his overarching Plan (*Il.* 2.3-6)—

§48

ἀλλ' ὅ γε μερμήριζε κατὰ φρένα ὡς 'Αχιλῆα
τιμήσῃ, ὀλέσῃ δὲ πολέας ἐπὶ νηυσὶν 'Αχαιῶν.
ἥδε δέ οἱ κατὰ θυμὸν ἀρίστη φαίνετο βουλή,
πέμψαι ἐπ' 'Ατρείδῃ 'Αγαμέμνονι οὖλον "Ονειρον.

But he was pondering in his heart how he might bring honor
to Akhilleus, and destroy many beside the Akhaian ships.
Now to his mind this seemed to be the best plan,
to send evil Dream to Atreus' son Agamemnon.

—then as Dream itself, his avatar ἀμβροσίην διὰ νύκτα [through ambrosial night] (57), who in turn appropriates the shape and figure of Nestor (20, 57-58) to stand over Agamemnon's head, speak to him with the words of a trusted counselor (21), and thus encompass his folly.

It is of course true that in some sense *every* character in the tale, and certainly every one who speaks "in his own person"— namely, every character portrayed through "the *illusion of mimesis*" (Genette 1980:164)—ultimately represents a cipher of the narrator, who "assimilates his manner of speech as nearly as he can to that of the character concerned" (Plato, *Rep.* 393c). What distinguishes intercessory figures such as Nestor, however, is that in their case the disguise is much thinner, as it were, the impersonation more transparent. They tend to appear at critical moments, points at which the tale has reached a crossroads, to negotiate Crisis by influencing the progress and direction of the tale with their advice. In this respect, and whether or not their advice wins approval, they exert control over the narrative in ways that other characters do not. They shape and steer its course with an authorial hand. Moreover, as with Nestor's participation in the Council of leaders in *Iliad* 2, their hand sometimes moves in such a way as to reveal that of the narrator himself. The irony of his presence there stems from the fact, as we noted, that it echoes his presence to Agamemnon in the opening Dream sequence. This dramatic irony—accessible at the oral, performative level—is also underscored in our *written* text by traces indicating that his speech before the Council is in all likelihood an "insertion" into that scene, which mirrors in turn his odd conflation with evil Dream in the earlier episode. For us as *readers* of the *Iliad*, then, if not for its original audience, these traces come very close to exposing the old man as a deliberate tool of the storyteller.

Other instances of Ironic Mediation involving Nestor are the focus of the present chapter. At the same time as their analysis will contribute to a better appreciation of his often ambiguous role in the poems, it will also raise issues that touch the nature and function of Greek epic narrative.

2. PATROKLOS AT THE THRESHOLD

The type-scene for Visitation—describing the Arrival, Recognition, Greeting and Entertainment of a Guest—is among the most basic patterns in the formulaic inventory of the Homeric poems; and unsurprisingly so, since it encodes a *praxis* institutionalized (even ritualized) within Greek society itself.[2] As Edwards has shown, building on the work done by Arend in his early and influential *Die Typischen Scenen bei Homer*, the pattern of Visitation amounts to an elaboration of elements within a more generic type of scene, to which Arend gives the name Arrival (*Ankunft*).[3] It encompasses in turn a well-defined set of discrete narrative units that allow for a certain amount of variation within a fixed syntagmatic order. The complete pattern runs as follows:[4]

§49
   (a)   a Visitor stands at the entrance
   (b)   someone (generally the Host) sees him
   (c)   the Host gets up from his seat
   (d)   the Host takes his hand and greets him
   (e)   the Host conducts him inside
   (f)   the Host offers him a seat (usually in a place of honor)
   (g)   food and drink are served
   (h)   conversation ensues

Each of these elements, with the exception of §49(g)-(h), which can themselves be expanded into full-fledged Bath and/or Feast scenes,[5] generally fills no more than a single verse. The same is true of the entire sequence §49(d)-(f), which often appears as the formula ἐς δ' ἄγε χειρὸς ἑλών, κατὰ δ' ἑδριάασθαι ἄνωγε [and took him by the hand, led him in and told him to sit down] (*Il.* 11.646;778, *Od.* 3.35). The offer of food at §49(g) generally allows for the greatest expansion, and may range from an almost cursory mention—e.g. ξείνιά τ' εὖ παρέθηκεν, ἅ τε ξείνοις θέμις ἐστίν [and properly set out hospitality, as is the guest's right] (*Il.* 11.779), in which the final gnomic hemistich (6X, 4X) explicitly marks what precedes it as the "zero degree" of Hospitality, so to speak[6]— to elaborate descriptions of the utensils and their setting, the preparation and serving of the meal.

In his 1975 study, Edwards charts the wide range of variations—in the form of omission, juxtaposition, condensation and expansion—admissable in this specific pattern and in those of Arend's more comprehensive types, with a view towards resolving apparent "inconsistencies" in the text of Homer. Insufficient attention has been paid, however, to a less common but significant divergence from the pattern of Visitation. The arrival of a Visitor at another's home follows the fixed and predictable syntax outlined in §49 only when (as in most cases) the Host's offer of entertainment is indeed welcomed and accepted. When it is not—in a narrative pattern that I will call Hospitality Declined—the regular sequence of elements is interrupted and issues are raised that are represented as far more compelling than the social and religious obligations that bind Guest and Host together.

The simplest instance of Hospitality Declined in the poems, and the one that most closely conforms to the sequence charted above, occurs in Book 11 of the *Iliad*. Patroklos has been sent by Akhilleus to discover the identity of the wounded soldier whom Akhilleus saw rush by in a chairot (*Il.* 11.607-15). On his errand, he arrives at Nestor's tent (644-52):

§50

(a) Πάτροκλος δὲ θύρῃσιν ἐφίστατο, ἰσόθεος φώς.

(b-c) τὸν δὲ ἰδὼν ὁ γεραιὸς ἀπὸ θρόνου ὦρτο φαεινοῦ,

(d-f) ἐς δ' ἄγε χειρὸς ἑλών, κατὰ δ' ἑδριάασθαι ἄνωγε.

(*g) Πάτροκλος δ' ἑτέρωθεν ἀναίνετο εἶπέ τε μῦθον·

(*h) "οὐχ ἕδος ἐστί, γεραιὲ διοτρεφές, οὐδέ με
πείσεις.

(*i) αἰδοῖος νεμεσητὸς ὅ με προέηκε πύθεσθαι
ὅν τινα τοῦτον ἄγεις βεβλημένον· ἀλλὰ καὶ αὐτὸς
γιγνώσκω, ὁρόω δὲ Μαχάονα, ποιμένα λαῶν.
νῦν δὲ ἔπος ἐρέων πάλιν ἄγγελος εἶμ' Ἀχιλῆϊ."

And Patroklos stood, godlike man, in the doorway.
Seeing him, the old man rose from his shining chair,
took him by the hand, led him in and told him to sit down,
(*) but Patroklos from the other side declined, and said:
(*) "No chair, old man nurtured by Zeus; you won't persuade me.
(*) Honored and quick to find fault is he who sent me to learn
(*) who this wounded man was you were bringing. Now I myself
(*) know, and I see it is Makhaon, shepherd of the people.
(*) Now I go back as messenger to tell Akhilleus."

The sequence proceeds as far as Nestor's formulaic insistence that his guest take a seat (=§49[f]), at which point its normal course is interrupted when Patroklos turns the offer down. Asterisks mark the divergent elements in §50, resulting in the following schematic pattern for Hospitality Declined:

§51

(a)   a Visitor stands at the entrance
(b)   someone (generally the Host) sees him
(c)   the Host gets up from his seat
(d)   the Host takes his hand and greets him
(e)   the Host conducts him inside
(f)   the Host offers him a seat (usually in a place of honor)
(*g) address-formula indicating the Visitor's Refusal
(*h) the Visitor declines the offer of a seat (= Refusal to Sit)
(*i) the Visitor gives a reason for refusing (= Haste to Depart)

The Visitor's Refusal to Sit (§51[*h]) characterizes all other instances of this alternate type-scene in the poems, and in fact amounts to the formulaic "switch" or "pivot" on which Visitation turns into Hospitality Declined. Consider the scene (*Il.* 23.198-211) in which the messenger Iris rejects a similar invitation from Zephyros and Boreas at the House of the Winds. Although this passage lacks the complete set of elements listed above (§§49/51), its conformity to the basic pattern of {Arrival at the Threshold}—{Recognition}—{Rise of the Host}—{Request to Sit}—{Refusal} is clear (*Il.* 23.201-07):

§52

(a)   ...θέουσα δὲ Ἶρις ἐπέστη
(a-b) βηλῷ ἔπι λιθέῳ· τοὶ ὡς ἴδον ὀφθαλμοῖσι,
(c/f) πάντες ἀνήϊξαν, κάλεόν τέ μιν εἰς ἑ ἕκαστος·
(*g)   ἡ δ᾽ αὖθ᾽ ἕζεσθαι μὲν ἀνήνατο, εἶπε δὲ μῦθον·
(*h-i) "οὐχ ἕδος· εἶμι γὰρ αὖτις ἐπ᾽ Ὠκεανοῖο ῥέεθρα,
        Αἰθιόπων ἐς γαῖαν, ὅθι ῥέζουσ᾽ ἑκατόμβας
        ἀθανάτοις, ἵνα δὴ καὶ ἐγὼ μεταδαίσομαι ἱρῶν."

                    ...and Iris stopped running and stood
          on the stone sill; but when their eyes saw her,
          all sprang to their feet, and each asked her to sit beside him.
     (*) But she in turn refused to sit, and she said:
     (*) "No chair; for I'm going back to the streams of Ocean
     (*) and the Aithopians' land, where they perform hekatombs
     (*) to the immortals, so that I too can partake of the sacrifices."

Three other scenes also merit consideration here, no less for the issues they raise than the responsion they exhibit. On his way to visit Andromakhe in *Iliad* 6, Hektor turns aside to enter the house of Alexandros; he pauses at the door of their room (*Il.* 6.318-19) and rebukes the coward for hanging back from the fight, a charge his brother does not dispute. The latter urges him to wait until he has armed himself for battle—ἀλλ' ἄγε νῦν ἐπίμεινον, 'Αρήϊα τεύχεα δύω (340)—but Hektor does not reply.[7] Helen then contributes some famous words of her own by way of self-reproach, and concludes by offering Hektor the hospitality of a seat: ἀλλ' ἄγε νῦν εἴσελθε καὶ ἕζεο τῷδ' ἐπὶ δίφρῳ [But come now, enter and sit on this chair] (354 = §51[f]). His response is to decline (*Il.* 6.360-63):[8]

§53

(*h)   "μή με κάθιζ', 'Ελένη, φιλέουσά περ· οὐδέ με
        πείσεις·
(*i)   ἤδη γάρ μοι θυμὸς ἐπέσσυται ὄφρ' ἐπαμύνω
        Τρώεσσ', οἳ μέγ' ἐμεῖο ποθὴν ἀπέοντος
        ἔχουσιν."

(*)   "Don't make me sit, Helen, though you love me. You
        won't persuade me.
(*)   For already my heart is hastening to defend
(*)   the Trojans, who long for me greatly in my absence."

Hektor's refusal here is preceded some one hundred lines earlier by an essentially similar scene in his father's palace (*Il.* 6.242-68).[9] There he is met by his mother Hekabe, who in a formulaic line (6X, 5X) clings to his hand and addresses him: ἔν τ' ἄρα οἱ φῦ χειρὶ ἔπος τ' ἔφατ' ἔκ τ' ὀνόμαζε (253). Her subsequent offer is not of a seat but rather of wine— ἀλλὰ μέν', ὄφρα κέ τοι μελιηδέα οἶνον ἐνείκω [But stay while I bring you honey-sweet wine] (258)—which he declines on the ground that to drink it would make him "forgetful of strength and courage" (cf. *Il.* 22.282) and thus deflect him from his present aim (*Il.* 6.264-68):[10]

§54

(*h) "μή μοι οἶνον ἄειρε μελίφρονα, πότνια μῆτερ,
(*i) μή μ' ἀπογυιώσῃς μένεος ἀλκῆς τε λάθωμαι·
      χερσὶ δ' ἀνίπτοισιν Διὶ λείβειν αἴθοπα οἶνον
      ἄζομαι· οὐδέ πῃ ἔστι κελαινεφέϊ Κρονίωνι
      αἵματικαὶ λύθρῳ πεπαλαγμένον εὐχετάασθαι. "

(*) "Lift me no honeylike wine, honored mother,
(*) lest you unnerve me, and I forget strength and courage.
(*) To pour bright wine to Zeus with unwashed hands
(*) would shame me; a man cannot pray to the dark-misted
(*) son of Kronos if he is spattered with blood and mire."

Finally, the same overall pattern informs Priam's initial
refusal to sit and dine with Akhilleus in *Iliad* 24. Here
Akhilleus' offer echoes Helen's in Book 6—#ἀλλ' ἄγε δὴ
κατ' ἄρ' ἕζευ ἐπὶ θρόνου [But come, sit down upon this
chair] (*Il.* 24.522; cf. 6.354 = §51[f])—and the old man's response
is cast in much the same language used then by Hektor (*Il.*
24.553-56):

§55

(*h/i) "μή πώ μ' ἐς θρόνον ἵζε, διοτρεφές, ὄφρα κεν
             Ἕκτωρ
         κεῖται ἐνὶ κλισίῃσιν ἀκηδής, ἀλλὰ τάχιστα
         λῦσον, ἵν' ὀφθαλμοῖσιν ἴδω· σὺ δὲ δέξαι ἄποινα
         πολλά, τά τοι φέρομεν."

(*) "Don't make me sit on a chair, Zeus-nurtured one, while
          Hektor
(*) lies abandoned among the shelters, but quickly
(*) give him back, so my eyes may see him; and accept the
          ransom
(*) we bring you, which is great."

Various formulaic echoes interlace all these scenes. The
initial colon #οὐχ ἕδος ἐστί {εἰμι} is unique to the two
passages (*Il.* 11.648 = 23.205) quoted above, in the reply of
Patroklos (§50) and Hektor (§52), respectively. The cola #μή
με κάθιζε (*Il.* 6.360 = §52), #μή μοι οἶνον ἄειρε
μελίφρονα (*Il.* 6.264 = §54) and #μή πώ μ' εἰς θρόνον ἵζε
(*Il.* 24.553 = §55) each appear nowhere else in either poem. On
the other hand, the closing hemistich οὐδέ με πείσεις# (*Il.*

11.648 = 6.360 = §§50/53) is fairly common (6X, 1X), and—coupled with a verb of restraint—twice elsewhere marks a character's refusal to be turned aside from his purpose. Thus it occurs in Akhilleus' speech to Thetis in Book 19—μηδέ μ' ἔρυκε μάχης φιλέουσά περ· οὐδέ με πείσεις [Don't hold me back from battle, though you love me; you won't persuade me] (*Il.* 19.126; cf. 6.360)—as well in as Priam's response to his wife's opposition to his plan to visit Akhilleus in the final book of the poem: #μή μ' ἐθέλοντ' ἰέναι κατερύκανε... | ...οὐδέ με πείσεις# [Don't hold me back when I would be going... You won't persuade me] (*Il.* 24.218-19).

More important than responsion at the level of line or phrase, however, are the narrative features these passages share in common. To begin with, in two scenes (§§50/52) the Arrival of the Visitor comes during the course of a meal already in progress. This is a fairly common occurrence, of course; it is frequently the case that a newcomer's appearance on the scene coincides with the performance of some ritual—feast (*Od.* 1), sacrifice (*Od.* 3), wedding celebration (*Od.* 4), council meeting (*Od.* 7) or ordinary mealtime activities (*passim*)—and this coincidence is worth brief comment. Whatever its extranarrative history and function, it is likely that the ceremonial context serves on the one hand, and within the tale itself, to identify the Host by displaying the kinds of rituals that define him. It situates him within a certain cultural and moral horizon, which can range from the urbane civility of the Spartan court (*Od.* 4) to the inhospitable violence encountered in the Kyklops' cave (*Od.* 9). One indeed thinks here especially of how prominent an issue this identity is in the *Odyssey*, where the character of each new potential Host is of no small concern to the traveller—ἦ ῥ' οἵ γ' ὑβρισταί τε καὶ ἄγριοι οὐδὲ δίκαιοι, | ἦε φιλόξεινοι, καί σφιν νόος ἐστὶ θεουδής; [Are they outlaws, savages without justice? Or kind to strangers, with a godfearing disposition?] (*Od.* 13.201-02; cf. 6.119-26, 9.172-76). On the other hand, participation in ritual is also the primary means whereby the Vistor first becomes assimilated; it helps negotiate his transition from Alien to Guest. The formulaic gestures of Offering and Accepting Hospitality both symbolize and practically effect his inclusion into the host community.

The appearance of Patroklos at Nestor's tent is preceded by the lengthy description (*Il.* 11.618-43) of the return there of Nestor and Makhaon shortly beforehand, along with their ensuing entertainment and conversation. It could be argued that his Refusal of Hospitality is partly motivated here by narrative constraints, on the ground that the repetition of two meal scenes back to back within such a short space of verse would be tedious or awkward. This claim is not especially convincing, for reasons to be taken up presently. Iris likewise visits the house of Zephyros while the Winds are engaged in feasting, a fact indicated by a single line (*Il.* 23.200-01)—again, an instance of a type-scene in its "zero degree." This is not true of Hektor's brief visit with his brother (§53), since his arrival merely interrupts routine domestic chores: Helen supervising the weaving, Paris toying idly with his bow (*Il.* 6.321-24). The scene between Priam and Akhilleus in *Iliad* 24 is remarkable in a number of respects that have been studied closely elsewhere.[11] For our purposes here it is enough to note that his arrival coincides with the end of a meal (whose preparation has not been described) enjoyed by Automedon and Alkimos (*Il.* 24.471-76), but in which Akhilleus himself has not taken part.

Far more pertinent than any alleged desire on the storyteller's part to avoid repetition of meal scenes in too close proximity to each other—for after all, he was presumably under no constraint to serve dinner before the new Guest arrives—is the latter's function in each of these passages, along with the contrast of priorities revealed by his refusal to be entertained. The Visitor in all cases examined above in fact appears in the role of Messenger. With respect to Patroklos (§50), Iris (§52) and Priam (§55), each has been explicitly dispatched by someone else on an official mission (cf. *Il.* 11.608-15, 23.192-99, 24.143-59;173). Hektor himself is under no special injunction to visit Paris (§53)—he merely drops in on his way to see Andromakhe—though both his rebuke of Alexandros (*Il.* 6.324-31) and his response to Helen's Offer to Sit (360-62) make his own sense of mission quite clear. This suggests that the passages in question represent "mixed" types such as those studied by Edwards, namely the condensation of Arend's Arrival (*Ankunft*) + Visitation (*Besuch*) with Messenger (*Botschaft*) scenes. The initial sequence for "Simple Arrival" or *Einfache Ankunft* ({Setting Out—Arrival—Encounter}) + *Besuch* (§49[1-5]) proceeds as far as the Offer and Refusal of

Hospitality, at which point the scene coalesces with the standard pattern for *Botschaft*.[12] Here, in its purest form, the appearance of the Messenger is followed immediately by (1) his standing beside the addressee (*not* "at the threshold"), and (2) the delivery of the message, after which—with or (rarely) without the response of the addressee—(3) the Messenger departs.

This modulation—or better: this juxtaposition, given the abruptness of the shift between types—serves in each instance to focus attention on a conflict of priorities, thus highlighting the purpose by which the Visitor is motivated. For Hospitality Declined is in every case motivated by an equally formulaic expression of the Visitor's Haste to Depart (§51[*i]). The Offer to Sit is always refused in the interest of values deemed higher than the social obligation of allowing oneself to be entertained, and so *a fortiori* more urgent than the social and religious values that structure the relation between Host and Guest. Hektor's loyalty to the defense of Troy (§53), outlined more sharply by contrast with his brother's idleness, and no less explicit in his refusal of wine from Hekabe (§54); Patroklos' mission (§50) to report the identity of the wounded soldier to Akhilleus; the appeal of Iris to the Winds (§52) in response to Akhilleus' prayer, when the pyre of Patroklos will not burn and release him to death; the desperate dignity of Priam (§55), who will not sit with his son's killer while Hektor's corpse lies unattended and unburied, though he has only just (*Il.* 24.477-79) kissed those murderous hands—all these scenes throw critical values into high relief, revealing commitments and duties from whose fulfillment nothing can deter the Visitor.

In three of the five passages now under review, these prior obligations are immediately honored. Hektor turns from Alexandros and Helen with no less resolve than he left his mother moments earlier, and goes on his way, while Hekabe hastens to offer prayer to Athene (*Il.* 6.286-310) and Paris for once shakes off his erotic sloth and prepares to return to the battlefield (503-19). Iris speaks briefly and departs, and the Winds leap up from their seats to do her bidding (*Il.* 23.212-16). In Priam's case, the higher values of reconciliation and forgiveness—more urgent than hatred, much harder to learn—require that he finally yield to Akhilleus' offer, and sit to dine with him. Despite his initial Refusal, the demands of

Hospitality *must* prevail. Only through their participation in the ritual meal can any true healing come about.[13]

With Patroklos (§49), however, the situation is markedly different. On the one hand, his Refusal to accept Hospitality—specifically, his decline of the Offer to Sit—is ostensibly honored by Nestor. In the absence of contrary indications, we must imagine that he remains standing throughout the monologue that ensues. On the other hand, the alleged urgency of his need to be on his way (*Il.* 11.649-52) is ignored by his Host. Rather than being allowed to turn quickly and leave—as are Hektor (§§53-54) and Iris (§52)—Patroklos is detained an inordinate length of time from returning to Akhilleus by what amounts to Nestor's most extensive monologue (*Il.* 11.655-803) in the poems, namely his tale of the cattle-raid against the Eleians, and his visit (along with Odysseus) to the house of Peleus, followed by his famous advice to Patroklos concerning Akhileus' armor.

This scene is worth considering in detail,[14] especially as it represents a striking instance of what the previous chapter identified as Ironic Mediation. Its narrative background is familiar. Book 11 of the *Iliad* recounts the steady reversal of Greek fortunes in the war. Agamemnon's *aristeia* in the first two hundred and fifty lines, though initially successful, stalls when he is hit by a spear cast by Antenor's son Koön (*Il.* 11.248-54). Though the latter is killed in the exchange that follows, the wound soon compels Agamemnon to retire from the fighting (264-83); and his withdrawal marks the sign from Zeus—as conveyed to Hektor by Iris—that the Trojans will now enjoy power to prevail until they reach the Akhaian ships and the sun goes down (187-94 = 202-09). Their onslaught is temporarily checked when Diomedes and Odysseus both rally against them. Diomedes, however, is soon forced to retreat when struck by Alexandros' arrow (369-400); and Odysseus, sustaining a wound to the ribs, must be rescued by Menelaos and Aias (428-88). In the ensuing skirmish, the physician Makhaon is hit (502-20)—his conveyance off the field by Nestor forming a bridge to the scene in which Patroklos pays a visit to his tent—then Eurypylos (575-95), and Aias himself is beaten back into the ranks of his men. At this point, the narrative shifts to Akhilleus' perspective from high on the stern of his ship, as he watches Nestor rush by in a chariot, conveying someone off the battlefield. Patroklos answers his summons from inside the shelter—an action marked by the editorial prolepsis κακοῦ δ' ἄρα οἱ πέλεν ἀρχή# [and this was the beginning of evil for him] (604)—and is dispatched by Akhilleus to discover the wounded man's identity.

Arriving at Nestor's tent (§49), he finds him enframed in a tableau of domestic ritual: at table with Makhaon, served by his attendant Hekamede, engaged in the pleasure of talk over wine, pale honey, bread and onion (618-44). The curious fact that the physician, hurt seriously enough to require being taken out of battle (502-15), can nonetheless now enjoy a hearty meal without any apparent discomfort, has long been characterized as inconsistent;[15] and other elements in this and surrounding passages have likewise raised suspicions. The entire sequence of events—from the initial wounding of Makhaon (502) through Akhilleus' summons and Patroklos' visit (599-654), the old man's so-called *Nestoris* (655-803) and Patroklos' encounter with Eurypylos at the end of the book (806-48)—is indeed a troubled one in many respects, and has led some to brand the whole scene as a late interpolation.[16]

Here as elsewhere, however, and despite whatever problems of *motivation* may exist at the level of the narrative, a *functional* approach will yield the best results, taking its lead from Wilamowitz' observation (1920:200) that Machaon's sole purpose in the narrative is to occasion Patroklos' visit to Nestor.[17] From this perspective, two interrelated questions need to be addressed; the first relatively easy to answer, the other somewhat more complex. Precisely why—and why precisely now—must Patroklos be sent to Nestor's tent by Akhilleus? And why is it specifically to Nestor rather than to some other character that Patroklos is sent?

To begin with, he is sent by an Akhilleus whose curiosity about the name of a wounded man implies anxiety that undercuts the firmness of his resolve to stay out of battle (cf. *Il.* 16.17-19, 18.6-14).[18] This is in fact the first we have seen of the Hero since the close of Book 9, in which his final words to the embassy state his expectation to remain aloof until Hektor slaughters his way as far as the Myrmidonian encampment (*Il.* 9.650-55):

§56

οὐ γὰρ πρὶν πολέμοιο μεδήσομαι αἱματόεντος,
πρίν γ' υἱὸν Πριάμοιο δαίφρονος, Ἕκτορα δῖον,
Μυρμιδόνων ἐπί τε κλισίας καὶ νῆας ἱκέσθαι
κτείνοντ' Ἀργείους, κατά τε σμῦξαι πυρὶ νῆας.
ἀμφὶ δέ τοι τῇ, ἐμῇ κλισίῃ καὶ νηῒ μελαίνῃ
Ἕκτορα καὶ μεμαῶτα μάχης σχήσεσθαι ὀΐω.

For I will not think again of bloody fighting
until brilliant Hektor, son of wise Priam
reaches the Myrmidons' ships and shelters,
killing the Argives and burning the ships with fire.
But around my own shelter and black ship
I think Hektor will be held, though hot for battle.

The interpretation that Diomedes puts on this message
when it is delivered to the Council of leaders at the end of the
same book (697-703)—that the offer of gifts has only stiffened
Akhilleus' pride—concludes with the advice that the best
plan is simply to ignore him, "for he will fight again,
whenever his heart in his breast urges him and the god impels"
(702-03: τότε δ' αὖτε μαχήσεται, ὁππότε κέν μιν |
θυμὸς ἐνὶ στήθεσσιν ἀνώγῃ καὶ θέος ὄρσῃ). The scene
two books later, where Akhilleus eagerly watches the "steep
work and sorrowful tumult" (*Il.* 11.601) of war from the deck of
his ship, betrays the first signs of just such an urge; though the
compulsion here has its ultimate source in no god's hand, but
rather in that of the narrator himself. For the Hero's
understanding of what he has seen leads him to think that the
moment has arrived when the Greeks will supplicate him to
return (*Il.* 11.608-15):

§57

δῖε Μενοιτιάδη, τῷ ἐμῷ κεχαρισμένε θυμῷ,
νῦν ὀΐω περὶ γούνατ' ἐμὰ στήσεσθαι Ἀχαιοὺς
λισσομένους· χρειὼ γὰρ ἱκάνεται οὐκέτ' ἀνεκτός.
ἀλλ' ἴθι νῦν, Πάτροκλε Διὶ φίλε, Νέστορ' ἔρειο
ὅν τινα τοῦτον ἄγει βεβλημένον ἐκ πολέμοιο·
ἤτοι μὲν τά γ' ὄπισθε Μαχάονι πάντα ἔοικε
τῷ Ἀσκληπιάδῃ, ἀτὰρ οὐκ ἴδον ὄμματα θωτός·
ἵπποι γάρ με παρήϊξαν πρόσσω μεμαυῖαι.

Splendid son of Menoitios, delight to my heart,
now I think the Akhaians will stay at my knees
in supplication, for an unendurable need has come upon them.
But go now, Patroklos beloved of Zeus, ask Nestor
who is this wounded man he brings out of battle.
From behind, at least, he looked in every way like Makhaon,
son of Asklepios, but I did not see the man's face,
since the horses racing ahead passed on by me.

Akhilleus' anticipation in lines 608-10 has been condemned on the ground that it ignores the *Embassy* of Book 9; or conversely, and with wider consensus, taken as evidence that Book 9 was a later addition to the "original" poem; and the scholarly response from some quarters has been to point out that the ambassadors do not *actually* get down on their knees to beg the hero.[19] This is hardly convincing. What is worth attending to here is the apparent abruptness—even awkwardness—with which Akhilleus proposes that Patroklos visit Nestor. Despite the fact that the basis for his proposal has been laid some one hundred lines earlier (*Il.* 11.504-06) in the description of Makhaon's wounding, the transition between his reading of the situation (608-10) and his request to Patroklos (611-15) still seems sudden, almost a *non sequitur*. Can the fate of one doctor really be worth so much to the Greek war-effort that the injury to Makhaon can represent for Akhilleus an "unendurable need" that has smitten all the Akhaians?

As in other scenes already discussed, the logical gap between these two parts of his speech—symbolized by the inconsequential nature of this casualty[20]—in fact exposes a rift between narrative levels, namely between the concrete tale and the abstract story that guides its progress. Makhaon's wound is exaggerated, nothing a good breakfast of bread, honey, onion and wine won't cure. The relation between what Akhilleus sees and what he is made to conclude from it is disproportionate, and can only be explained in terms of a disjunction between narrative *motivation* and the *function* it is meant to serve in the advancement of the story.

So much for both why and why now Patroklos is sent on his innocent errand—that is, as far as it is possible to account for any poet's choice of means and moment; ultimately, one can only acknowledge it and assess its plausibility in terms dictated by shifting verisimilitude. Diomedes' confidence at the end of Book 9 (*Il.* 9.707-09) has proved groundless, thanks to the Plan of Zeus. The foremost warriors among the Akhaians have been wounded (Agamemnon, Diomedes, Odysseus)—and in this respect, the injury that Makhaon sustains may indeed legitimately symbolize the failure of their collective resistance. The others (Aias) are in dire straits; and Hektor ineluctably approaches the wall he will finally breach at the end of *Iliad* 12. It is time to prepare for Akhilleus' Return, now that the conditions of his claim in Book 9 (§56) seem on the verge of fulfillment; hence his inference—or wish?—at 607-09 in Book 11.[21] Precisely why that Return entails that *another* be led to *Nestor's* tent must now be asked.

Why *another* goes, and not Akhilleus himself, has been addressed convincingly by Pedrick (1983). Her analysis of Nestor's tale of his own heroism in the Pylian border war with the Epeians (*Il.* 11.670-761) focuses on the degree to which that account takes the traditional shape of an epic *aristeia*. With only slight variation, it exhibits most of the basic elements and formal conventions that characterize the narrated exploits of prominent fighters (Diomedes, Agamemnon, Patroklos, Hektor, Akhilleus) elsewhere in the *Iliad*, from his initial triumph over named opponents to his break of the enemy lines and wholesale rout of their troops.[22] Even more, his feats in fact eclipse those of his younger peers—or at least they do so in this telling.[23] The epic inflation that marks his account— specifically, his claim (746-48) to have killed fifty pairs of men in chariots, while the best anyone else can manage in the *Iliad* is to dispatch but three (*Il.* 11.93;102;127)—will concern us shortly. What is important to note here is Pedrick's assessment (1983:66) of the part played by Nestor's tale within the development of Book 11 as a whole:

> . . . just when the Greeks need a champion to step forth, when Aias and Eurypylos must retire, an aristeia occurs. A brilliant young warrior embraces his people's need and completely routs the enemy. It is a moment of grim irony, for we are not on the Trojan battlefield, but in the quiet of a tent, listening to an old man's voice. His aristeia is intoxicating, but it only underscores how desperate the Greeks' plight is. Their one victorious moment that day is there, their hope of relief as fleeting as the past. . . .

The ironic value of this movement from battlefield to shelter is especially significant because of the shift it represents from the sphere of action to that of speech, from direct experience to memory. *Diegesis* yields to *mimesis*—

albeit to the *mimesis* of yet another diegetic act—and *ergon* is displaced into *mythos*. For just when the need is greatest, the tale of Akhaian misfortunes in war turns back on itself, so to speak, to its narrative origins—namely back to the paradigmatic function that tales of the valorized past aim to fulfill on every occasion of performance in "traditional" communities. At a moment of Crisis, formulaic narrative negotiates this shift, taking form in the words of an old man endowed with lucid speech, poetlike, "from whose lips the voice ran sweeter than honey" (*Il.* 1.248-49). Immediacy recedes, and the narration of the past assumes again its undisputed value as the pattern in whose form the present should unfold. A welter of confusions relaxes its grip, giving way to an ancient tale told in the still space of a tent amid the simple objects and gestures of domestic ritual; what emerges thereafter is refigured and informed with new purpose. ῝Ως φάτο, τῷ δ' ἄρα θυμὸν ἐνὶ στήθεσσιν ὄρινε [So he spoke, and stirred the feeling in the other's breast] (*Il.* 11.804). What ultimately stirs Patroklos is the vision of a bygone *aristeia* wholly constructed by words; its events—along with the values they embody—give shape to his present situation and suggest a course for future action.

Moreover, this shift also highlights the enframing tale's own status *qua* narrative. The strategy here is one of doubling or surrogation, and operates at a number of closely interwoven levels. In lieu of an act of heroism to rescue the Greeks from the brink, we find instead the *mythos* of a similar act, in the form of the so-called *Nestoris*. The relation between the main storyteller and his audience is thus mirrored in the narrative itself, as an agent within the tale becomes the addressee of another tale that purports to show him how his own life's tale should unfold. The fact that scholarship has so often been tempted to treat the *Nestoris* as an "independent" or "interpolated" *epic* lay[24]—whatever the merits of that argument—at least implicitly acknowledges this mirroring of the frame-narrative in its embedded story. For in terms of performative situation, general content, horizon of values and even formulaic style,[25] Nestor's tale replicates that of the principal narrator. Moreover, it should be noted that Nestor's rhetorical credentials and authority as a narrator in his own right, especially as one whose advice deserves attention and approval, have already been obliquely established in the course of the biographical identification of the servant Hekamede, whom the Akhaians after sacking Tenedos gave Nestor οὕνεκα βουλῇ ἀριστεύεσκεν ἁπάντων [because he always surpassed all others in counsel] (*Il.* 11.627). It remains to be considered at the conclusion of this chapter whether this mirroring also extends to the effect each story has on its respective audience.

At the same time, of course, this surrogation is also thematic to the tale of the *Iliad* itself. For in place of Akhilleus, whom Pedrick has shown is the proper addressee of Nestor's paradigm, it is instead Patroklos who hears and responds to its message (1983:67-68):[26]

> Achilles senses that Nestor's emergence from battle signifies a grave crisis and, he imagines, another appeal for his help. . . . But the appeal was not to be as Achilles imagined it; the Greeks are not coming to him in supplication. Once they sent Phoinix with the gloomy lesson of Meleager, but now Nestor is waiting in his tent with an exhortation. . . . Achilles misses this truth, for he does not go to hear it himself but sends his best friend. Patroklos goes and learns the lesson meant for someone else. . . . When the appeal Achilles expected finally comes, it is simply a choice from Patroklos: relent and go yourself, or send me.

At this point begins the doubling that will finally result in Patroklos' impersonation of Akhilleus in *Iliad* 16; the significance of the moment is marked by the proleptic editorial comment κακοῦ δ' ἄρα οἱ πέλεν ἀρχή# [and this was the beginning of evil for him] (*Il.* 11.604). I have also suggested that this shift in agency appears to coincide with—or at least seems causally related to, perhaps metaphoric of—an equivalent detour made by the course of the narrative itself in Book 11 from battlefield to shelter, action to *mythos*. Before tracing out this path in any further detail, however, it will be best to retrace our steps a little and stand with Patroklos at the threshold of the old man's tent.

Here we rejoin our earlier discussion of the conventional patterns of Hospitality and its variant, Hospitality Declined. Though he initially turns down the Offer to Sit and be entertained (§50[*g]-[*h]), Patroklos is nonetheless detained by Nestor's longest reminiscence in the poem. The tale of his splendid *aristeia* at Pylos (*Il.* 11.670-762) eventually comes full circle to recall his arrival once at the house of Peleus while the latter was performing sacrifice to Zeus (765-79):[27]

§58

ὦ πέπον, ἦ μὲν σοί γε Μενοίτιος ὧδ' ἐπέτελλεν
ἤματι τῷ ὅτε σ' ἐκ Φθίης 'Αγαμέμνονι πέμπε.
νῶϊ δὲ ἔνδον ἐόντες, ἐγὼ καὶ δῖος 'Οδυσσεύς,
πάντα μάλ' ἐν μεγάροις ἠκούομεν ὡς ἐπέτελλε.
Πηλῆος δ' ἱκόμεσθα δόμους εὖ ναιετάοντας
λαὸν ἀγείροντες κατ' 'Αχαιΐδα πουλυβότειραν.
ἔνθα δ' ἔπειθ' ἥρωα Μενοίτιον εὕρομεν ἔνδον
ἠδὲ σέ, πὰρ δ' 'Αχιλῆα· γέρων δ' ἱππηλάτα Πηλεὺς
πίονα μηρία καῖε βοὸς Διὶ τερψικεραύνῳ
αὐλῆς ἐν χόρτῳ· ἔχε δὲ χρύσειον ἄλεισον,
σπένδων αἴθοπα οἶνον ἐπ' αἰθομένοις ἱεροῖσι.
σφῶϊ μὲν ἀμφὶ βοὸς ἕπετον κρέα, νῶϊ δ' ἔπειτα
στῆμεν ἐνὶ προθύροισι· ταφὼν δ' ἀνόρουσεν
Αχιλλεύς,
ἐς δ' ἄγε χειρὸς ἑλών, κατὰ δ' ἑδριάασθαι ἄνωγε,
ξείνιά τ' εὖ παρέθηκεν, ἅ τε ξείνοις θέμις ἐστίν.

My child, this is certainly what Menoitios told you
on the day he sent you from Phthia to Agamemnon.
The two of us, brilliant Odysseus and I, were there inside
and listened carefully to everything he said in the halls.
For we had come to the strongly built house of Peleus
mustering troops throughout fertile Akhaia.
There we then found Menoitios the hero inside,
and you, and Akhilleus beside you; and the aged horseman
Peleus
was burning fat thighs of an ox to Zeus who loves to thunder,
in the enclosure of the courtyard. He was holding a gold tankard
and tipping out bright wine over the burning sacrifice.
You two were attending to the ox's meat, and we two then
came and stood at the threshold. Akhilleus rose up in wonder,
took us by the hand and led us in, and told us to sit down,
and set hospitality properly before us, as is the guest's right.

This passage is worth quoting in full if only for the richness of its details. Somewhat like the Beggar in the *Odyssey*, whose speeches enumerate particulars that lend an aura of credibility to what he says, Nestor recalls with special vividness the circumstances of his visit once to Phthia. At the same time, and unlike the Beggar's words, the representation here is more generic than unique. Its particulars—the courtyard, burning fat, the gold vessel, poured wine, both the stance and activity of the various characters present—all coalesce into a ritual, stylized scene of Sacrifice and Hospitality.[28] Nestor's entire speech is structured by ring-composition, beginning (*Il.* 11.655-69) with reference to Akhilleus, and rounding off the *Nestoris* by returning to mention the Hero again (762-64). This has been noted before;[29] what has not been duly emphasized, however, is that the closing of this ring also intersects two different narrative levels—namely primary and secondary ("mimetic") *diegesis*—in the repetition of line 646 in line 778. The responsion here is exact, with Nestor's rising up to take Patroklos by the hand when he first appears (as related by the principal narrator) echoed in Akhilleus' reaction to Nestor in the old man's own (embedded) narrative: ἐς δ' ἄγε χειρὸς ἑλών, κατὰ δ' ἑδριάασθαι ἄνωγε [and took {him/us} by the hand, led {him/us} in and told {him/us} to sit down]. In this respect, the details and circumstances of Nestor's recollection of Phthia more immediately and more properly recall those of the scene that Patroklos himself interrupts when he arrives at the old man's tent (*Il.* 11.618-44) to find Nestor and Makhaon at table over sweet honey, wine, bread and onion. The bridge between heroic *mythos* and its performative situation is therefore literally built on the formulaic gesture with which a Visitor is received (§49[d]-[f]). Moreover, the *traditional* grip of that gesture is evident in the tag-line ξείνιά τ' εὖ παρέθηκεν, ἅ τε ξείνοις θέμις ἐστίν [and set hospitality properly before us, as is the guest's right] (779), which marks what was earlier described as the "zero degree" of Hospitality—the abbreviated reference to a panoply of familiar, ritual acts whose particulars the audience can easily supply for itself on the basis of its own direct experience, as well as its experience through narratives.

This formulaic bridge unfolds within the space of Hospitality (§49[h]). Across it, the tale of exemplary glory in the *Nestoris* moves next to recollection of Menoitios' charge to Patroklos to protect the young Akhilleus when they are at Troy (785-90):

§59

σοὶ δ' αὖθ' ὧδ' ἐπέτελλε Μενοίτιος, Ἄκτορος υἱός·
"τέκνον ἐμόν, γενεῇ μὲν ὑπέρτερός ἐστιν Ἀχιλλεύς,
πρεσβύτερος δὲ σύ ἐσσι· βίη δ' ὅ γε πολλὸν ἀμείνων.
ἀλλ' εὖ οἱ φάσθαι πυκινὸν ἔπος ἠδ' ὑποθέσθαι
καὶ οἱ σημαίνειν· ὁ δὲ πείσεται εἰς ἀγαθόν περ."
ὣς ἐπέτελλ' ὁ γέρων, σὺ δὲ λήθεαι.

But Menoitios, Aktor's son, spoke to you in turn as follows:
"My child, by right of blood Akhilleus is higher than you,
though you are elder; but he is greater by far in strength.
Speak sound words to him, and give him good counsel,
and show him the way. If he listens it will be for his good."
This is what the old man said, but you have forgotten.

These lines have already been cited above (§22) as an instance of "tertiary focalization," the embedding of *mimesis* within yet another *mimesis* of a character's speech. Their exhortatory function makes Nestor's direct quotation of Menoitios that much more effective a rhetorical device than would a paraphrase of what the son of Aktor said to his own son in Peleus' halls.[30] "As if he were someone else"—ὥς τις ἄλλος ὤν (Plato, *Rep.* 3, 393c)—Nestor assimilates himself to Menoitios, adopting a paternal voice to lecture the young hero, with a view toward convincing him to fulfill the obligation enjoined on him then by his father. It is geared precisely to remind him of his duty as the elder and more experienced of the pair; and quotation *verbis ipsis* quite literally strengthens the point. Nestor's famous concluding advice (now *in propria persona*) is that, if Akhilleus proves intractable to persuasion, Patroklos should borrow his armor, impersonate the Hero, and so win for the Greeks some "breathing-space" (ἀνάπνευσις) in the fight to defend their ships (*Il.* 11.794-803). The entire sequence of substitutions— Patroklos for Akhilleus as the addressee of the old man's tale, the *Nestoris* for the expected *aristeia*, Nestor himself for Menoitios, and Patroklos once more for Akhilleus—is thereby completed; and "this was the beginning of evil for him" (604: κακοῦ δ' ἄρα οἱ πέλεν ἀρχή#).

His response is given by the line Ὣς φάτο, τῷ δ' ἄρα θυμὸν ἐνὶ στήθεσσιν ὄρινε [So he spoke, and stirred the feelings in his breast] (804); the formula (5X, 1X) often serves to denote a tumultuous or even distressed reaction to a speaker's words.[31] As a result of his staying to hear Nestor's reminiscence and the advice that follows it—which at the level of type-scenes amounts to a breach of the pattern Hospitality Declined + Haste to Depart—Patroklos is deflected from his original aim and set on a narrative path that leads ineluctably to his demise. Four books then intervene, recounting the fated advance of the Trojans against the Akhaian ships, before this line of the narrative resumes in *Iliad* 16 with the implementation of Nestor's advice. When Patroklos finally returns to the Myrmidonian camp after this "hiatus,"[32] it is not to report the information he was initially sent out to discover—namely, the identity of the wounded fighter glimpsed by Akhilleus. Indeed, the fact that his original mission has apparently been forgotten is often cited as further evidence of the suspect authenticity of the entire Makhaon-Patroklos-Nestor episode in Book 11.[33] Instead, it is to entreat Akhilleus to lend him his armor and allow him to fight in his place.

This lacuna is bridged by the simple device of repetition; except for the change of pronouns and the variation of a single line (*Il.* 11.799/16.40), his appeal to Akhilleus precisely echoes the old man's earlier counsel (11.794-803 = 16.36-45). Repetition has the effect of collapsing the distance separating these two narrative moments, thus effecting a return to the initial situation in *Iliad* 11; at the same time, it also marks at least the formal coalescence of Nestor and Patroklos as speakers. It is in fact tempting to entertain the possibility that this merger of voice through one character's direct repetition of another's words when both speak in the narrative—itself the standard trope in messenger speeches[34]—works here as the figure for a kind of merger of agency as well. For we saw that Patroklos' innocent route from Akhilleus' ship to Nestor's encampment simultaneously crosses a border between *ergon* and *mythos*, leaving present action on the battlefield behind and passing over into a mediated world of narrative, whose contours are defined by the walls of a tent and the ritual gestures of Hospitality. He emerges from that world "als ein Verwandelter" (Reinhardt 1961:264), inspired by a paradigm of heroic accomplishments that was meant for *someone else* to hear and act upon. Specifically, what inspires him is the folktale of the youngest son—alone surviving the death of his brothers (*Il.* 11.690-93)—who, eluding his father's efforts to protect him from harm (717-19), rallies his people against their haughty and powerful enemy, kills their leader (737-46) and singlehandedly slays another fifty men or more (747-49), thereby winning an unparallelled victory and such honor as belongs to an immortal (761).[35] Less relevant than the details, of course, is the general pattern of the triumph of the untried warrior at a moment of communal crisis and in the face of overwhelming odds. This is precisely the pattern that the old man's tale, in all its epic inflation,[36] implicitly sets for the young one to emulate, despite the fact that Nestor himself may only "see him as providing a moment's respite (11.800)" (Pedrick 1983:68, note 53). When Patroklos leaves the world of narrative, it is to assume the paradigm that narrative holds out him, to clothe himself in *mythos* by donning Akhilleus' armor.[37]

Patroklos' request for that armor (*Il.* 16.35-45) elicits an editorial comment that recalls the narrator's earlier prolepsis of doom (46-47; cf. 11.604):

§60

῎Ως φάτο λισσόμενος μέγα νήπιος· ἦ γὰρ ἔμελλεν
οἱ αὐτῷ θάνατόν τε κακὸν καὶ κῆρα λιτέσθαι.

So he spoke, supplicating, *the great fool*; this was
his own death and evil destruction he was entreating.

The judgement μέγα νήπιος is a strong one.[38] It occurs in this precise form only here, though allomorphs of the phrase in the same position appear on four other occasions, with various particles filling out the space before the noun. In all but one case (*Od.* 19.530), which describes an infant child, the comment adverts to utter foolishness portending catastrophe: Odysseus' crew drunk on the beach while the Kikonians muster their troops (*Od.* 9.44); blind Polyphemos duped by the ruse of the sheep (*Od.* 9.442); the suitors, who take the death of Antinoos from the Beggar's arrow for an accident (*Od.* 22.32), and who stupidly devour Odysseus' stores, unmindful of the master's return (*Od.* 22.370). The closing hemistich ἦ γὰρ ἔμελλεν#— with variants οὐδ᾽ ἄρ᾽ (5X) or τῷ δ᾽ ἄρ᾽ and different inflections of the verb—is likewise reserved for proleptic reference to unseen disaster. Its sense is contrafactual, drawing attention to grief or else total demise that is chosen unwittingly, hence to the ironic distance between expectation and outcome. The defensive wall of the Greeks proposed by Nestor (S5) was not destined to stop the Trojan assault (*Il.* 12.3); Dolon's boast to return unscathed from his espionage behind enemy lines would prove a hollow one (*Il.* 10.336); on the verge of death, Hektor acknowledges that his hopes for mercy from Akhilleus had been empty (*Il.* 22.356); Odysseus' return from Troy was fated to be painful and prolonged (*Od.* 4.107); the fair west wind that blew from Aiolos' island to Ithaka was only to fail him just within sight of home (*Od.* 10.26); Eupeithes sought sweet vengeance but in so doing incurred his own death (*Od.* 24.470).

What links these passages together, and to Patroklos' attempt to impersonate Akhilleus, is the rift they all signal between narrative motivation and function. In the present case, it also returns us to the typology of Mediation outlined in the previous chapter and, specifically, to the issue of Ironic Mediation. I have already styled Nestor's intercessory role as a sometimes ambiguous one, and have further suggested that it seems plausible to see the figure of Nestor as a cloaked authorial presence in the narrative, exercising control over its course from within its narration. This is corroborated by the part the old man plays in *Iliad* 11. For what emerges from the preceding analysis is that Nestor here ultimately acts in the service of the abstract story, despite how his actions are motivated in the tale itself. However dire the significance of Makhaon's wound is initially represented as being—"for a physician is worth many men" (*Il.* 11.514-15)—and however credible Akhilleus' request for information about the injured soldier—for example, as a sign that he is not at all indifferent to the suffering of the Greeks—from the viewpoint of emplotment, Patroklos' mission is of course a bogus one.[39] Its actual function, as Wilamowitz (1920:200) saw, is to supply the pretext for his encounter with Nestor. In turn, Nestor's role at this critical juncture in the tale is to motivate the Sacrifice of Patroklos and the consequent Return of the Hero.

The intercession of Nestor in Book 11 thus emphasizes, even more strikingly than the other passages examined in Chapter 3, the function of the Mediator throughout the poems as a kind of "switch" located at a critical point in the narrative and— more than other character-types—in the direct employ of the story that guides the unfolding of the narrated events. Plague vs. remedy, social disruption vs. social harmony, defeat vs. victory, ritual propriety vs. neglect of obligations that bind mortals to the gods—the Mediator arises always and only whenever the course of events has reached a fork that leads the tale along divergent paths toward divergent ends: failure (often death) on the one hand, success—sometimes death too, but always measured by the specific closure toward which the story moves—on the other. The editorial comment μέγα νήπιος in *Iliad* 16 therefore only announces more explicitly a prolepsis of disaster already inherent in the Mediator's advice four books earlier, and inhering potentially in all advice given, whatever the authority of its source, whenever another rises to speak or else to take a Visitor's hand in Hospitality, to lead him in and ask him to sit down.

3. TELEMAKHOS AT PYLOS

Despite its far greater preoccupation with comings and goings, with hasty farewells or departures·forestalled and tardy or unexpected returns—comprising frequent Arrival, Messenger and Visitation scenes and also scenes structured by a character's eagerness to leave—the *Odyssey* exhibits no instances of the precise combination of the patterns Hospitality Declined + Haste to Depart that have been examined so far. Where Haste to Depart does occur, it is always after Hospitality has already been accepted and enjoyed, and the Visitor (sooner or sometimes very much later) expresses a desire to be on his way again. This is clearly often the case with Odysseus himself, in his dealings with Aiolos (*Od.* 10.17-18)— where his request for permission to depart represents the motif in the "zero degree"—Kirke (*Od.* 10.467-89), Kalypso (*Od.* 5.81-84;160-224) and the Phaiakians (*Od.* 7.146-52;331-33, 8.465-66, 13.28-35).[40] It is also featured prominently in the visits of Telemakhos to Sparta (*Od.* 4.594-99, 15.64-74) and Pylos (*Od.* 15.195-214), where the pattern raises issues that have direct bearing on the present argument.

Much of the *Telemakheia*, mirroring the larger and parallel tale of Odysseus, gets its narrative rhythm from the pattern of Arrival—Hospitality—Departure; formulaic rituals

of Greeting and Farewell enframe the various tales
Telemakhos hears of his father and others in both Pylos and
Lakedaimonia. Moreover, both men's journeys also coincide
thematically in that each encounters obstacles to his successful
return home.[41] The language of restraint vs. release, delay or
detention vs. easy departure, stasis vs. mobility, constraint vs.
volition is in fact prominent in the passages in which each
attempts to extricate himself from the bonds of one or another
form of Hospitality. In turn, these bonds themselves may be
cruel or gentle, violent or seductive, coercive or compelling—as
brutal and stark as the boulder that blocks all exit from the
Kyklops' cave on the one hand, as alluring as Kirke's company
on the other. And while Telemakhos' journey hardly takes him
as far into a world of the fabulous as his father's does, the
young man nonetheless encounters traps along his way that are
potentially no less problematic despite the ordinary, mundane
forms they assume.

After his arrival, entertainment and conversation with
Menelaos in the opulent Spartan court, Telemakhos responds to
his Host's insistence—ἀλλ' ἄγε νῦν ἐπίμεινον ἐνὶ
μεγάροισιν ἐμοῖσιν [But come now, stay in my house]—
that he remain there "eleven or twelve more days" (*Od.* 4.587-
92) by politely declining the offer (594-99):

§61

　　'Ατρείδη, μή δή με πολὺν χρόνον ἐνθάδ' ἔρυκε.
　　καὶ γὰρ κ' εἰς ἐνιαυτὸν ἐγὼ παρὰ σοί γ' ἀνεχοίμην
　　ἥμενος, οὐδέ με οἴκου ἕλοι πόθος οὐδὲ τοκήων·
　　αἰνῶς γὰρ μύθοισιν ἔπεσσί τε σοῖσιν ἀκούων
　　τέρπομαι. ἀλλ' ἤδη μοι ἀνιάζουσιν ἑταῖροι
　　ἐν Πύλῳ ἠγαθέῃ· σὺ δέ με χρόνον ἐνθάδ' ἐρύκεις.

　　Son of Atreus, don't keep me here any longer.
　　Indeed I'd stay sitting beside you all year,
　　nor would longing for home or parents ever seize me:
　　for listening to your tales and words remarkably
　　delights me. But my men already grow restless for me
　　in sacred Pylos, and you keep me here too long.

The explicit connection between fascination with speech
and deferral or forgetfulness of aim recalls issues raised much
earlier in this study; they will receive more attention in what

The extent to which the depiction of Nestor in the *Odyssey* links him with the performance of communal rites has often been noted. "Sacrifice is much emphasized in this book (cf. 338 ff., 390 ff., 418 ff.), and the detailed description of the ritual at 445 ff. is of outstanding importance for our knowledge of Greek sacrificial practice."[57] Less attention has been paid, however, to how this link affects (or, better: reflects) Nestor's overall characterization. In addition to establishing his piety—"an aspect of his character not particularly noticeable in the *Iliad*" (Heubeck-West-Hainsworth 1988:160), or at least not as explicit—the framing of the old man within the structure of such conventional *praxeis* as Sacrifice and Hospitality also and more generally confirms his allegiance to tradition. We recall that an essentially similar tableau—wine, onion, honey, bread and pleasing conversation—greeted Patroklos at the door of Nestor's tent in *Iliad* 11, and helped to symbolize a shift from the immediacy of battle to the quieter—but in some respects no less dangerous—world of *mythos*.

In one sense, of course, this allegiance is hardly surprising, and in fact owes much to the generic terms in which Elders are characterized in both poems. After all, they are privileged conduits of their community's ancestry, as much in the actions they perform as in their predilection for talk and in the content of their speeches. At the same time, as analysis of the scene in Book 11 of the *Iliad* suggested, there is also a sense in which traditional gestures can be endowed with an almost sinister quality. At the very least, they can be deployed in the tale in ways and circumstances that prompt one to ask what ulterior function they have been enlisted to serve. Though latent in the other poem, this becomes especially clear in the *Odyssey*, especially in light of the degree to which the unfolding of its tale is guided by the theme of Obstacles to Return; and, more generally, in terms of its implicit polemic against the far more traditional world of the *Iliad* narrative.[58]

In this context, and in view of the narrative motif of Hospitality Declined, the pattern of the scene that ensues between Telemakhos and Nestor in *Odyssey* 3—following hard on the lines just quoted above (§66)—is worth a closer look. After the wine has been drunk and the sacrificial fires are finally extinguished on the beach, the Visitors turn away to go back to their ship (*Od.* 3.342-44), but the old man restrains

(κατέρυκε) them—Νέστωρ δ' αὖ κατέρυκε καθαπτόμενος ἐπέεσσι [But Nestor in turn put his hand out and held
them back, with the words . . .] (345)—to insist most strenuously
on his duties and rights as a Host (346-55):

§67

Ζεὺς τό γ' ἀλεξήσειε καὶ ἀθάνατοι θεοὶ ἄλλοι,
ὡς ὑμεῖς παρ' ἐμεῖο θοὴν ἐπὶ νῆα κίοιτε
ὥς τέ τευ ἢ παρὰ πάμπαν ἀνείμονος ἠὲ πενιχροῦ,
ᾧ οὔ τι χλαῖναι καὶ ῥήγεα πόλλ' ἐνὶ οἴκῳ,
οὔτ' αὐτῷ μαλακῶς οὔτε ξείνοισιν ἐνεύδειν.
αὐτὰρ ἐμοὶ πάρα μὲν χλαῖναι καὶ ῥήγεα καλά.
οὔ θην δὴ τοῦδ' ἀνδρὸς 'Οδυσσῆος φίλος υἱὸς
νηὸς ἐπ' ἰκριόφιν καταλέξεται, ὄφρ' ἂν ἐγώ γε
ζώω, ἔπειτα δὲ παῖδες ἐνὶ μεγάροισι λίπωνται,
ξείνους ξεινίζειν, ὅς τίς κ' ἐμὰ δώμαθ' ἵκηται.

May Zeus forbid, and all the other deathless gods,
that you return to your swift ship while in my domain,
as if in that of a man entirely short of clothing and penniless,
who has no abundance of blankets and rugs in his house,
and where neither he nor his guests can sleep in luxury.
But I do have many good blankets and rugs.
Certainly not: the dear son of Odysseus, of all people,
will not sleep on the deck of a ship, at least as long as
I myself live, and there are sons in my palace after me
to entertain guests, whoever arrives at my house.

As West remarks (Heubeck-West-Harrington 1988:183),
Nestor "treats [Athene-] Mentor's move to depart as based on a
misconception of both his resources and his moral standards."
These standards seem in fact to be the more pressing motivation
here. Good blankets and rugs, entertainment and (doubtlessly)
the occasion for still more talk are matters of obligation and
honor in whose fulfillment old Nestor will brook no denial. If
only in terms of its proximity to that other passage, these lines
call for comparison with Menelaos' earlier homily on Guest-
Host relations (§63). The difference is striking. On the one
hand, an urbane and genteel (even "modern") recognition of the
priorities that can lead a Visitor to sue for quick farewell—
"Entertain a guest at hand but speed him when he wants to go"
(*Od.* 15.74)—priorities even more compelling than the
elaborate, time-honored, institutional choreography of *xenia*.

On the other, an imperious assertion that the ritual simply *must* be performed, with no consideration at all for whether the Guest might well have other liens on his time, because ultimately it redounds to the Host's social and ethical status and—what is perhaps more important—validates the institution itself. Here Nestor stands firmly on the side of the traditional, established (κατὰ μοῖραν) way of things; its rites entail demands that are autonomous and self-evident, at least to him, and that serve to orchestrate fixed social roles along with their corresponding social identities. That the Visitor has places to go, that he is moved by intimate desires whose urgency conflicts with the leisurely pace of convention, is simply irrelevant. The ritual seems to be all that counts.

In light of this difference, it is interesting to note a change of meaning or a kind of revaluation that implicitly modifies the physical gesture that accompanies Nestor's speech at §67. The Visitors turn away from Sacrifice, now that its predictable closure has been reached; but as they move toward the ship, where an untried crew waits on the challenge of some new destination across the wide sea (*Od.* 3.360-66), something reaches out to hold them back. The very same formulaic hand that on other occasions takes another's hand in Hospitality, to lead him in from the often lawless world outside and offer him a place to sit (§49[d]-[f])—ἐς δ' ἄγε χειρὸς ἑλών, κατὰ δ' ἑδριάασθαι ἄνωγε (*Il.* 11.646;778, *Od.* 3.35)—followed by a bath and meal and the obligatory talk of genealogies and precedents, is now a hand that touches to restrain (*Od.* 3.345: κατέρυκε καθαπτόμενος) the Visitor, even though the time has come for him to set his sights for home again (336: νέεσθαι). This is precisely the hand that Telemakhos later (§64) fears will hold him back against his will (ἀέκοντα) in sandy Pylos, ἱέμενος φιλέειν [desiring to entertain] (*Od.* 15.201; cf. 9.261, 15.69).[59] Its grasp—the grip of tradition, far-reaching and tenacious, oblivious of or else indifferent to the individual's most pressing "need" (*Od.* 15.201: χρέω)—is just what Telemakhos seeks to evade when he proposes to his age-mate that Peisistratos leave him at the ship instead of driving past it to the old man's palace. It is the hand that draws Patroklos into the space of a tent erected—and into a world constructed mythically—on the shifting line of battle in the

Iliad. And it is also the same hand that—in fact or
metaphorically, and smoothly or with naked force—keeps
Odysseus himself on so many occasions, in so many distant caves
or halls, from reaching Ithaka again. In all these cases, the
formulaic gesture of Hospitality modulates darkly into one
that threatens Detention.

Mentor-Athene acknowledges (*Od*. 3.356-58) the propriety
of Nestor's offer. It is "fitting" (ἔοικε) that the young man
yield to persuasion and stay the night in the comfortable
portico of the house instead of on the hard deck of a ship.
What the old man has said was "said well"—#εὖ δὴ ταῦτά
γ' ἔφησθα, γέρον φίλε (357)—namely in agreement with
how social convention prescribes how the Visitor should be
treated; and we recall that elsewhere Nestor's advice often
earns the judgement that it was spoken κατὰ μοῖραν [right
and fittingly] (cf. 331). On her own behalf, however, she
politely and firmly declines the offer on two grounds. Among
all the crew, she is the only one who can lay claim to the status
of an elder (362: γεραίτερος), and so must provide the others
with guidance; besides, she has important business to attend to
among the Kaukonians (356-70). She then departs in the famous
epiphany, leaving Telemakhos to enjoy (and endure) the old
man's hospitable care.

Let me now switch back—and also forward, as abruptly as
the narrative itself, perhaps—to Telemakhos' move to
forestall the anticipated offer of Hospitality in Book 15 (§64).
As in the case of Patroklos in *Iliad* 11, it can be argued with
some justification that his hasty departure from Pylos is
motivated by the narrator's desire to avoid what would be an
awkward and otiose repetition of a Hospitality scene. It is of
course true that Telemakhos has already been entertained
there—though some twelve books "earlier"—and has gleaned
from Nestor what precious little information the old man has
about Odysseus' whereabouts. By the same token, however, it
should be noted that the Guest-Host relation between them has
not yet not been cemented by the customary (almost obligatory)
presentation of a Gift.[60] This by itself could support a claim
that the storyteller "had every reason" to bring Telemakhos
and Nestor together one last time. Once again, though, the
narrative function of the pattern of Hospitality Declined or
Preempted carries far more weight than the kinds of arguments

by which the scholiasts seem absorbed. The convention of the *geras* (gift-exchange) is superseded, and the promise to Menelaos broken, by the far more urgent motif of Haste to Depart in the face of the risk of detention and loss of homecoming. More important than the fact that he leaves Pylos empty-handed is that Telemakhos escapes falling into Nestor's hands a second time and so manages to leave at all.

4. NESTOR AMONG THE SIRENS

Speech like song, like that of the Muse or Bard, but also like that of the Sirens; sweet interminable words born of memory but somehow causing forgetfulness; a lucid voice flowing smoothly like honey, wine, lamentation, sleep and the mists of death to draw and deflect its listener from his journey home—the traits discussed in Chapter 1.4 now intersect with issues raised by the preceding discussion of the pattern of Hospitality Denied + Haste to Depart. For in terms of that type-scene, Nestor's intercessory function clearly emerges as that of a Detainer. In *Iliad* 11, he holds Patroklos back from fulfilling his ostensible mission, and releases him only to follow a very different narrative path than the one that led him first to the Elder's tent. In that case, as I suggested, he plays an essentially *authorial* role in initiating a course of events that will bring the story—of the *Iliad* no less than of Patroklos himself—to its final destination.

His Mediation there is cloaked and ironic. This is true not simply in a *dramatic* sense, as a function of the audience's privileged knowledge that this errand to Nestor is "the beginning of evil for him" (*Il.* 11.604). It is also because the relation between Nestor and Patroklos ostensibly mirrors the one that traditionally obtains between the principal narrator himself and his audience. For Telemakhos in the *Odyssey*, Nestor's Hospitality in turn figures as a threat to both his successful Journey out and Return back again. The protraction of the Sacrifice in Book 3, relatively harmless in itself, nonetheless serves as a token of how long-winded the old man can be, and how tenacious in insisting on his traditional rights as a Host. Less harmless—even if couched in the language of implicit parody (§66)—is the obstacle he poses to Telemakhos on his way home. Earlier sections of this chapter have concentrated on the part played in both scenes by the formulaic pattern that governs the Arrival of a Visitor at another's house. In each, the familiar type-scene is enlisted in the service of ends—emplotment on the one hand, broader thematic concerns on the other—that belong to a level deeper than that of the surface tale in which they are deployed. What the present section must begin to address is the role of narrative in both cases of Detention.

Especially in the *Odyssey*, this role depends on the link so often expressed in that poem between storytelling and seduction. This issue is of course much larger than the figure of Nestor himself. Deeper than the level of events in the tale, it belongs to the dynamics of the story that controls the representation of Nestor's character; and deeper still, it ultimately derives from an implicit psychology of pleasure to which the narrator and his community subscribe.[61] In what follows, it will suffice to recall the extent to which narrative is depicted in the poems by recourse to language that often draws its terms from the spheres of erotic and magical influence,[62] as well as how frequently the main effect of the charm it works is to induce forgetfulness in its listener. Sweet is whatever allures and soothes, but what allures also poses the risk of loss of and deflection from one's aim; and chief among the sweet things that detain and defer—in fact, "sweeter even than honey" (*Il.* 1.249)—is the exquisite pleasure of narrative.[63]

In this respect, the temptation represented by Nestor's words embodies a danger that for Telemakhos in Book 15 is as great—always allowing for exaggeration through parody—as the threat posed to Odysseus by the Sirens. I have already noted the associations between Nestorian and poetic speech in general, in terms of such attributes as sweetness, clarity and allure. The Sirens too, of course, enjoy similar or identical traits. Kirke (*Od.* 12.38-54) warns Odysseus of the danger they represent to his homecoming in words that give special emphasis to the quality of the sound (φθογγή) of their voice—four of eleven instances of this noun in the poems refer to the Sirens (*Od.* 12.41;159;198, 23.326)—and their seductive song (ἀοιδή). The other term (ὄπα) frequently used for their voice shows a similar distribution, with over half of its occurrences reserved for the Sirens (4X) and divine voice in general (10X).[64] The remainder are given over to human voices in what seem to be marked and emotionally charged circumstances—in expressions of grief (*Il.* 22.451,*Od.* 11.421, 20.92) and pitiless rage (*Il.* 11.137, 18.222, 21.98)—and in situations that advert to its exceptional beauty. Such is the case of the Trojan Elders, who speak like cicadas drone (*Il.* 3.152); and of Odysseus himself (*Il.* 3.221), whose words falls like flurries of snow. In all these instances, the immediate effect of the voice is to command its listener's awe and full attention, to turn him aside from his prior course, to stun and absorb or even to render him immobile.[65]

Its quasi-magical nature is central to how it is characterized. It should be remembered in this context that Kalypso is said to hold Odysseus back (κατερύκει), always *bewitching* him with soft and flattering words—αἰεὶ δὲ μαλακοῖσι καὶ αἱμυλίοισι λόγοισι | θέλγει (*Od.* 1.56-57; cf. 3.264-65)—so that he will *forget* Ithaka (ὅπως Ἰθάκης ἐπιλήσεται); and that θελκτήρια [charms, bewitchments] is how Penelope styles the lays of Phemios (*Od.* 1.337). Eumaios (*Od.* 17.514-21), moreover, recommends the Beggar to Penelope for the degree to which his tales, like those of a skilled bard, have the power to *enchant* their audience—οἷ' ὅ γε μυθεῖται, θέλγοιτό κέ τοι φίλον ἦτορ. The Sirens clearly represent this influence in the highest and most lethal degree, which is indeed directly proportionate with the sheer pleasure (*Od.* 12.52;88) that listening to them brings to their audience. For whoever gives them ear will never come home to see wife and children again (41-43), since he will be *bewitched* by their "lucid song"—Σειρῆνες λιγυρῇ θέλγουσιν ἀοιδῇ [the Sirens charm with their clear singing] (44; cf. 40)—into remaining until the flesh rots from his bones (45-46). The paralysis induced by how and what these creatures sing is in fact prefigured by the sleeplike doldrum that falls on the ship when it passes their island—ἄνεμος μὲν ἐπαύσατο ἠδὲ γαλήνη | ἔπλετο νημενίη, κοίμησε δὲ κύματα δαίμων [the wind ceased, and a windless calm came on, and a divinity laid the waves to sleep] (168-69). This gentle sleep is of course both permanent and final—the end of all wandering, the loss of home, and a *nostos* unto death. Further, this specific effect differs only in degree, not in kind, from the immobility induced by the charm of Muse-inspired poetic song; as Eumaios remarks (*Od.* 17.518-20):[66]

§68

ὡς δ᾽ ὅτ᾽ ἀοιδὸν ἀνὴρ ποτιδέρκεται, ὅς τε θεῶν ἐξ
ἀείδη δεδαὼς ἔπε᾽ ἱμερόεντα βροτοῖσιν·
τοῦ δ᾽ *ἄμοτον* μεμάασιν ἀκουέμεν, ὁππότ᾽ ἀείδη

As when a man gazes at a singer, one who knows
from the gods and sings words that please men;
when he sings, his audience is *motionless*, eager to hear him.

I will return to this parallel. Others are worth considering more closely at present, however, in light of the type-scenes of Hospitality Accepted, Declined, and Forestalled. To be sure, the analogy here operates at a more abstract level than that of the ritualized formulaic gestures charted above (§§49/51). It is rather as a multiform of some far broader narrative pattern of Detention—albeit still cast in the language of Hospitality— that their role in *Odyssey* 12 must be understood. In a certain sense, for that matter, the brand of Hospitality they promise in fact amounts to an inversion of many of the features that normally characterize that motif. For the Sirens have no threshold at which the Visitor can stand while awaiting recognition (§49[a]), apart from the dangerously smooth surface of the stilled waves that surround them (169). Nor do they rise up from their seats (§49[c]) to take his hand (§49[d]), lead him inside (§49[e]) and offer him a chair (§49[f]); the Guest instead sits out of doors in open meadow ground (45: ἐν λειμῶνι). No food is served (§49[g]); or what nourishment they give is at the very least weird and paradoxical—uncanny fare that somehow feeds on life instead of bringing it true increase (45-46). The mesmerized Visitor listens as his own flesh wastes away. The image of course resembles nothing as much as an inverted image of the ancient, cicadalike speakers at the Skaian Gate in *Iliad* 3, whose body likewise slowly melts into a sweet liquid burble, "the seductive pleasure of language stipped down to a mantra's hum" (Ferrari 1987:28). Finally, it is with no formulaic hand that the Sirens reach out to welcome and also to detain their Visitor—with neither the hand at the tent on the Iliadic battlefield, nor even the hand that stays the travellers on

Pylos' sandy beach—but instead only with their honey-sweet voices; the strength of the grip is more than sufficient. As Odysseus' ship glides near their island home, the wind suddenly drops and they call to him (*Od.* 12.184-91):

§69

Δεῦρ' ἄγ' ἰών, πολύαιν' 'Οδυσεῦ, μέγα κῦδος 'Αχαιῶν,
νῆα κατάστησον, ἵνα νωϊτέρην ὄπ' ἀκούσῃς.
οὐ γάρ πώ τις τῇδε παρήλασε νηὶ μελαίνῃ,
πρίν γ' ἡμέων μελίγηρυν ἀπὸ στόματος ὄπ' ἀκοῦσαι,
ἀλλ' ὅ γε τερψάμενος νεῖται καὶ πλείονα εἰδώς.
ἴδμεν γάρ τοι πάνθ' ὅσ' ἐνὶ Τροίῃ εὐρείῃ
'Αργεῖοι Τρῶές τε θεῶν ἰότητι μόγησαν·
ἴδμεν δ' ὅσσα γένηται ἐπὶ χθονὶ πουλυβοτείρῃ.

Come closer, famed Odysseus, great glory of Akhaians,
stay your ship, so you can listen to our voice.
For no one ever sails by this place in his black ship
until he hears the honeyed voice from our mouths,
takes his pleasure and sails off knowing even more.
For we indeed know everything that in wide Troy
the Argives and Trojans suffered by the will of the gods,
and we know everything that happens on the fertile earth.

The degree to which this passage raises the intimately related issues of poetic utterance (189-91), sweetness of voice (187), pleasure from song (188)—through which the Sirens are assimilated to the Muses themselves—and the risk of Detention (185) is obvious.[67] What deserves closer treatment, especially in relation to the figure of Nestor, are how the Sirens characterize themselves and, specifically, the content of the song they promise to sing for the Visitor.

To begin with, it has been noted that the Sirens' claim to knowledge rivals what is attributed to the Muses in the famous invocation at the beginning of the *Catalogue of Ships* (§25); with the anaphora of #ἴδμεν... (*Od.* 12.189, 191) compare ἴστε τε πάντα# [you know everything] (*Il.* 2.485). Its range also corresponds—if disproportionately, given their quasi-divine status—to the temporal scope of the knowledge traditionally assigned in the poems to the type of the Elder. We have seen (Chapters 1.2, 3.2) that the aged Halitherses (*Od.* 2.188), Ekheneos (*Od.* 7.157) and Nestor himself (*Od.* 24.51) are all qualified by the phrase παλαιά τε πολλά τε εἰδώς# [knowing many ancient things], in an attribution unique to these three figures. The same association of greater knowledge with greater age is gnomically expressed by the endline formula ἐπεὶ πρότερος γενόμην καὶ πλείονα οἶδα# [since I am older than you and know more] (*Il.* 19.219, 21.440)—a fact that Nestor makes much of in his lecture to Agamemnon and Akhilleus in the opening of the *Iliad* (*Il.* 1.259), as well as in his qualified praise of Diomedes several books later in the poem (*Il.* 9.53-59 = §2).

The kind of knowledge to which advanced age gives special access is that of the past. This is not to discount the fact that Elders may also command a strictly practical wisdom that is oriented to the range of possibilities offered in the present; after all, Nestor himself is the outstanding proponent of μῆτις [practical intelligence] in the *Iliad* (cf. *Il.* 7.323-24 = 9.92-93, 10.18-19, 14.106-08, 23.313-18).[68] Still, their minds turn chiefly toward what has happened before, thanks to which they "know many ancient things" and enjoy their capacity for "circumspection." This is what guarantees their role as guardians of tradition, whether at the level of specific moral conventions—issuing in their greater sense of propriety and of what is "right and fitting"—or else more generally, at the level of the ethnic and cultural memory of the group to which they belong. It will be recalled that Nestor himself also figures as the keeper of the inventory of *all* the Greeks who came to Troy (*Il.* 7.128 = §23); and that his inaugural narrative in the *Odyssey* summarily invokes the Iliadic tradition as a whole (§§26-27). Elders typically embody the link between their present community and the narrative lines that define it and shape its moral horizons. The direction of their vision is therefore essentially the same as that of both Siren and Muse, even if its scope and range are not coterminous with theirs.

The character of these narratives is the second point worth noting. What the Sirens offer to tell Odysseus is of course precisely the tale of the *Iliad* itself: πάνθ' ὅσ' ἐνὶ Τροίῃ εὐρείῃ | Ἀργεῖοι Τρῶές τε θεῶν ἰότητι μόγησαν [everything that in wide Troy the Argives and Trojans suffered by the will of the gods] (*Od.* 12.189-90). This is the same song that the Muses inspire the Iliadic narrator to tell—unless what these creatures promise to sing is even more comprehensive, since the *Iliad* as such is clearly just one fragment of a far broader narrative tradition.[69] As Pucci (1987:212; with note 7) observes:

> The Sirens, Muses of Hades, have the same power of *thelgein* as the Iliadic, epic Muses. . . . Even their poetic themes become contiguous: because the Sirens are Muses of Hades, their promise to sing of all that happens in Troy sounds like a polemic intimation by the *Odyssey* that the epic cycle of the Trojan War is obsessionally involved with what today we would call the "beautiful death" of the heroes. . . . I suggest that the *Odyssey* presents the Sirens as the embodiment of the paralyzing effects of the Iliadic poetics because their song binds its listeners obsessively to the fascination of death.

Nestor's tales have a similar resonance, and are identical at least in tenor and substance, with the larger narratives in which they are mimetically embedded. On the one hand, most reach back into a pre-Iliadic antiquity, such as that of the κλέα ἀνδρῶν that Akhilleus sings as the Embassy approaches his compound (*Il.* 9.189). In this sense, they are metonyms of the unrecorded narrative tradition out of which poems like the *Iliad* arise. Others (cf. *Od.* 3.118-200; 254-312) evoke the process of storytelling after the sack of Troy—with which the *Odyssey* is self-reflexively concerned—that details the homecomings of the heroes. In both instances, the act of their narration is in some respects an icon of the performance of the story by Homer's *aoidos*. Could their overall function be similar, too? Do the old man's songs likewise inspire in the listener much the same obsessive "fascination" with the past? Is Nestor's logorrhea—tenacious and interminable—itself a figure for "the paralyzing effects of the Iliadic poetics"? Both the values they promote and the ends they serve are indeed closely linked with the kind of heroically "beautiful" death around which epics traditionally center. This is evident in the case of the affect his *Nestoris* has on Patroklos in *Iliad* 11. It lures the young man to emulate precisely the paradigm to which true Iliadic warriors aspire: an utterly splendid *aristeia*, culminating in unequivocal victory and glory such as an immortal enjoys—πάντες δ' εὐχετόωντο θεῶν Διὶ Νέστορί τ' ἀνδρῶν [all glorified Zeus among the gods, and Nestor among men] (*Il.* 11.761).[70] The fact that Nestor himself has somehow safely negotiated the passage from *ergon* into *mythos*, and now lives on to tell his own story in a tent two generations afterwards, whereas Patroklos' more treacherous crossing takes him in the opposite direction—from *mythos* into *ergon* and failure, self-sacrifice and death—is only one among a number of sinister ironies touching this scene.

What the preceding discussion has also suggested is that the scene in which Telemakhos avoids meeting Nestor a second time raises issues no less troubling. For all the parody that shapes it, his trial at Pylos (and earlier at Sparta) is an analogue of his father's with the Sirens; the role the old man and these creatures play is essentially one and the same. Two travelers bent on homeward journey encounter in the welcome rites of Hospitality on distant shores a hidden threat—a hand that takes one's own and then will not let go, a narrative that lures and stuns, a strange sweet food that saps the body and the will for home. Forewarned, and bound securely to a mast, the father can safely expose himself to the delicious agony of what his Hosts offer; the son, on the other hand, has learned that few bonds are stronger than the ritual ties that bind Visitor to Host, and altogether shuns the meeting. Frame (1978:81-113) relies on linguistic reconstructions and comparative mythology to argue that Nestor is the literary avatar of an Indo-European god named "Who-Brings-Home" (**nes-tôr*), who leads his people out of night's dread darkness and into the full splendor of sunrise.[71] Whatever the status of the evidence here—which relies chiefly on Nestor's own tale in *Iliad* 11—as well as the implicit view of the nature of myths, our discussion of passages would suggest that Nestor often ironically serves just the opposite function. Like the Sirens, he is a sweet and potentially deadly Detainer, a figure of Death rather than *nostos*. His lucid, flowing, honey-sweet song of the fabled past—no less than theirs—actually threatens to keep his Guest from ever reaching home again.

For it is clear that the fare Nestor serves his Visitor within the ritual framework of *xenia* is chiefly the rich food of traditional narrative—no less appetizing for all its age than what Sirens offer, and (in its interminability) just as great an obstacle to his Guest's journey. In both cases, the Visitor is invited to dine on honeysweet epic tales—tales of the vanishing past, where through some strange alchemy *ergon* is decocted into everflowing *mythos* and warriors purchase deathless fame by sacrificing life on the altar of Memory—tales that like the *Iliad* itself begins and ends with a funeral. Both Nestor and the Sirens explicitly embody a view of epic song that exposes the great risks involved in lingering to listen too long to the voice of traditional tales. Both offer their guests weird fare that, in the very different, unIliadic world traversed by Odysseus and his son—a world where desire has its seat in "shameless belly" (*Od.* 7.216-221; cf. 15.343-45, 17.468-76), which drives men restlessly across unharvestable oceans (17.286-89)—only dishes up detention, loss of *nostos*, and death.

NOTES

1. Kirk (1985:116-17), and for a contrary view, de Jong 1987:211-12.

2. Wace and Stubbings 1962:442;451, Kakridis 1963:86-88, Finley 1979:99-102.

3. Edwards 1975:61-62, Arend 1933:28-63. Arend isolates three kinds of Arrival Scene: (1) *Einfache Ankunft* (pp. 28-34), (2) *Besuch* (pp. 34-53) and (3) *Botschaft* (pp. 54-63). The syntax of *Einfache Ankunft*, the basic type, and essentially comprises the description of a character's (I) setting out, (II) arrival, (III) encounter with the person sought, (IV) taking a position beside him and (V) speech. In the *Besuch* Scene, element IV is elaborated by the description of the character's reception. Arend (p. 34f.) contrasts *Einfache Ankunft* with *Besuch* as follows: "in den Ankunftsszenen tritt der Ankommende sogleich näher (T[eil]. IV) und bringt sein Anliegen vor (T[eil]. V), in den Besuchsszenen aber werden vorher ausführlich Aufname und Bewirtung geschildert, vor T[eil]. V treten also verschiedene neue Erzälungsteile" (quoted also by Edwards, p. 62).

4. This list is adapted from Edwards 1975:62, who in turn freely translates Arend's analysis (1933:35). See now also Reece 1993:15-28.

5. Foley 1990:248-77, Reece 1993:33.

6. Kirk (1985:122) notes that "ἤ θέμις ἐστί is a formular expression (6X *Il.*, 4X *Od.* in this exact form) . . . to designate proper behaviour, including that of a ritual and family kind. . . . It can also serve, vague as it is, to justify a kind of behaviour which a character—or the poet himself—does not wish to spend time in elaborating further." On "zero degree," see Barthes 1970.

7. Kirk 1990:204. The doubling of the sequence of {Request—Refusal} (Alexandros:Hektor/Helen:Hektor) in *Iliad* 6 further suggests the presence of a more abstract narrative pattern in which a character resists being deflected—by Hospitality or anything else that would cause him to turn aside—from his present purpose. Compare the scene in *Iliad* 19, in which Agamemnon's proposal that Akhilleus hold back from battle until the compensatory gifts have been

brought to his tent—#εἰ δ' ἐθέλεις, ἐπίμεινον... [But if you are willing, wait . . .] (142)—is rejected (146-50).

8. The address-formula used here—τὴν δ' ἠμείβετ' ἔπειτα μέγας κορυθαίολος ῾Εκτωρ (*Il.* 6.359)—as in the remaining cases of Hospitality Declined to be examined, contains no prolepsis of the Visitor's refusal.

9. On the similarity between these two scenes as indices of Hektor's *ethos*, though not in terms of their formulaic responsion, see Redfield 1975:121-22; Reinhardt (1961:262-63) notes their structural identity.

10. Kirk (1990:196) compares the use of γυιόω [make lame] at *Il.* 8.402;416, but fails to mention that the closing hemistich of 265—μένεος ἀλκῆς τε λάθωμαι#—recurs (with slightly different syntax) at *Il.* 22.282, in the Trojan's words to Akhilleus.

11. Foley 1991:156-89.

12. Arend 1933:54-63.

13. Foley 1991:174-89.

14. Bölte 1934, Cantieni 1942:9-22, Vester 1956:54-74, Reinhardt 1961:258-64, Austin 1966, Lohmann 1970:70-75, Pedrick 1983 and especially Schadewaldt 1987:74-94.

15. The problem was noted by the scholiasts. See Schadewaldt 1987:75, Reihnardt 1961:259.

16. See Schadewaldt 1987:74-94 for an extensive analysis, with summary of prior scholarship. Though he accepts the status of the scene as an "inset" ("Zwischenstück"), he nonetheless treats it as a "Verbindungsstück" rather than a mere "Einlage," and convincingly shows how it is organically— and so deliberately ("kompositorisch")—related to the narrative as a whole. Reinhardt (1961:263-64) also argues against the claim that it represents a mere interpolation by the hand of the "Ordner der Ilias."

17. Wilamowitz (1920:200): "Machaon hat für den Dichter nur die Bedeutung, den Nestor zum Frühstück zu bringen und von Achill gesehen zu werden, damit Patroklos zu Nestor geschickt wird." Reinhardt (1961:259) remarks, *apropos* of Makhaon's wound, that "Es scheint sich um Machaon zu handeln, in Wahrheit handelt us sich um Nestor. Idomeneus ist einzig dazu da, um Nestor in sein Zelt zu schicken. . . . Der Sorge nach ist die Verwundung schwer—wozu auch sonst die eilige Fahrt?—

nachher ist sie wie nicht mehr vorhanden. . . . [D]er nackte Befund ist, dass die Wunde da ist, wo sie der Dichter braucht, und nicht mehr da ist, wo er sie nicht mehr braucht. Die Erklärung ergibt sich aus der Situation."

18. Pedrick (1983:67).

19. See Monro 1884:374, Leaf 1900 (at 609); and Page (1959:305), to whom "it seems very obvious that these words were not spoken by an Achilles about whose knees the Achaeans were in fact standing in supplication on the previous evening; an Achilles who had rejected their prayers, who had made it clear that we would never accept apology or compensation, but would wait until Hector was killing the Greeks in their tents and burning their ships." For the response, see the summary in Hogan 1979:184; and Willcock 1978:131, to whom "[i]t seems . . . perfectly human for Achilles, who is still angry," to speak as he does.

20. Compare *Il.* 11.508-15, in which this assertion is made. Reinhardt (1961:261) remarks: "Aber in welchem Missverständnis steht dazu der Auftrag? Was macht es ihm aus, ob er den Namen, den er mutmasst, sicher weiss? Den Namen nicht eines der Grossen, des Agamemnon oder des Odysseus, sondern des belanglosen Machaon?   Aber so lieben Trägodien zu beginnen: belanglos."

21. Reinhardt 1961:261.

22. For these elements and conventions, see Cantieni 1942:53, Fenik 1968:113 and Krischer 1971; for their application to Nestor's speech, see Pedrick 1983:63-65.

23. Pedrick (1983:64) notes: "The great Iliadic aristeiai normally continue with the wounding of the hero, his restoration by a god, and his final duel with an enemy warrior. The subsequent battle over the corpse establishes a boundary for the hero's glory, since he is regularly prevented from capturing it . . . by a god. Nestor's glory, however, culminates in complete victory over his enemies—something which none of the Iliadic warriors can achieve."

24. Bölte 1934, Cantieni 1942, Vester 1956; Willcock 1976:132-33 summarizes the view "that it is an excerpt from some other poem about the legends of Pylos, with Nestor as hero, inserted here in the *Iliad*."

25. Willcock 1976:133.

26. Cp. Schadewaldt 1987:87; and see Pedrick 1983:57-62 for instances in which Nestor's *paradeigma* both does and does not fit the circumstances in which both Akhilleus and Patroklos find themselves.

27. Lines 762-84 were athetized in antiquity; see Leaf 1886:393-94, Schadewaldt 1987:87.

28. Reece 1993:22-23; Fenik 1974:234 notes the "standard practice in Homer, when two groups of persons come together, for the actions of the one at the moment of meeting to be described fully—typical epic expansion"; compare, for example, *Od*. 3.5ff., 15.222-23. In *Iliad* 11, of couse, this "expansion" occurs at a *secondary* diegetic level.

29. Reinhardt 1961:263, Gaisser 1969:9-13.

30. Contrast Nestor's paraphrase (*Il.* 11.783-84) of Peleus' words to Akhilleus, which Odysseus (*Il.* 9.254-58) directly quotes when addressing Akhilleus himself. Note also Willcock's observation (1977:45) that speeches in which one character quotes another "are directly related to . . . the particular circumstances of the person who is addressed." His conclusion (46-47) that both Odysseus and Nestor *invent* the speeches they quote indeed seems—as de Jong (1987:174) remarks—"rather extreme."

31. Thus of the Akhaians' response to Agamemnon's proposal to abandon the war (*Il.* 2.142); of Helen to the disguised Aphrodite's summons on behalf of Alexandros after the Duel (*Il.* 3.395); of Makhaon, upon hearing that Menelaos has been wounded (*Il.* 4.208); of Aineias, to news of the death of his brother-in-law Alkathoös (*Il.* 13.468); and of Penelope, to Telemakhos' report that Odysseus is rumored to be alive but held captive by Kalypso (*Od.* 17.150).

32. *En route* back to Akhilleus' tent, Patroklos allows himself to be deflected from his course once again, this time to minister to the wounded Eurypylos (*Il.* 11.806-848, 15.390-404). This scene—essentially single, though dispersed over two widely separated places in the narrative—is interesting in light of the pattern of Hospitality Declined + Haste to Depart examined above, and in fact suggests that the pattern might itself be a species of a more generic pattern structuring responses to invitations of any type. On Eurypylos in this scene, see Reinhardt 1961, Schadewaldt 1987:78, Janko 1992:270-72.

33. Schadewaldt 1987:75.

34.   De Jong 1987:180-92.

35.   On the motifs, see Thompson 1955: type L10, and 1977:125-30.

36.   Pedrick (1983:64, with note 45) observes that the exaggeration is one "commonly associated with an older generation of heroes," and cites *Il*. 4.393, 6.244, 23.147 and 24.495. What she does not mention is that such inflation is a function of the degree to which a community's access to its "older generation" comes more or less through *narrative*.

37.   His failure to fulfill that paradigm is prefigured, of course, in Patroklos' inability to heft Akhilleus' spear at *Il*. 16.140-44. See Armstrong 1958; and Sinos 1980:32ff., on the degree to which his success is always contingent on his ability to impersonate the Hero.

38.   De Jong 1987:86-89, Janko 1992:320-21, 397 and references.

39.   In this it resembles, for example, the encounter of Odysseus with the shade of Elpenor in *Odyssey* 11 and his request for proper burial, whose actual function in the logic of the story is to motivate Odysseus' return to Aiaia for specific instructions on how to get home. See Peradotto 1980.

40.   On the significance of the motif of departure vs. detainment or unwillingness to leave in the *Odyssey*, see Taylor 1960-61; and Apthorp 1980:12-16, who remarks (12) that "central to the temptation theme in the *Odyssey* is the conflict between *forgetting* home and *remembering* home."

41.   Delebecque 1958, Taylor 1960, Rose 1971, Apthorp 1980. On other parallels between father and son in the *Odyssey*, see e.g. Clarke 1967:40-44, Austin 1975:181-200, Powell 1977:50-56 and references.

42.   Apthorp 1980:13-15, Bergren 1981, Marsh 1979.

43.   Reece 1993:67-69 and 84-99, Delebecque 1958:26, Apthorp 1980:19-20 and Rose 1971:511-13.

44.   To be sure, the language of §9 implies that in the opposition between *polemos* (war) and *nostos*, the latter term would normally be expected to enjoy a higher value; this is what makes the infusion of strength or *menos* so extraordinary.

45.   See Heubeck-West-Hainsworth 1988:51-66, 229 (on *Od*. 4.594ff.) and 231-32 (on *Od*. 4.621-24), along with Heubeck-Hoekstra 1989:231 (on *Od*. 15.1-3), on the problems associated with this shift. Apthorp 1980—drawing principally on

Delebecque 1958 and Taylor 1960—argues that the narrative chronology "keeps moving" despite this "suspension," i.e. that the actual departure of Telemakhos from Sparta in Book 15 occurs roughly one month after the scene in Book 4. See Reece 1993:71-72 for a brief summary of scholarship.

46. Apthorp 1980:5-6, 12-13.

47. Heubeck-Hoekstra 1989:231.

48. Rose 1971:513-14, Bergren 1983, Dimock 1989; for a contrary view, Reece 1993:73-74.

49. Page 1955 and Austin 1969.

50. Delebecque 1958:25-26 attributes Telemakhos' forgetfulness of aim to his "ravissement" by the "coqueterie" of Helen. Apthorp 1980:13 (with note 57) is too offended by the Frenchman's "tasteless view," which "goes well beyond the bounds of Homeric hospitality," to acknowledge that the line between erotic and verbal seduction is often hard to draw in Homer; see Marsh 1979, Parry 1992.

51. Rose (1971:513) locates the irony elsewhere, noting that the disruption of the normal sequence of formulas in the scene of Telemakhos' departure from Sparta (*Od.* 15.145-84) serves to characterize Menelaos himself as "obtuse" and "overly hospitable." On the awkward departure from Sparta, see Gunn 1970, Edwards 1975, Reese 1990:97-98.

52. Apthorp (1980:20) remarks: "After his difficulty in escaping from Menelaos' hospitality it is hardly surprising that Telemachus should appear almost paranoid in his fear lest Nestor should *hold him back* (κατέσχη) against his will." See also Rose (1971:511-13), who draws attention to the parallels between Telemakhos in Sparta and Pylos on the one hand, and Odysseus among the Phaiakians on the other; and notes (513) that "Telemachus' eagerness to return home and his difficulties in breaking away [from Sparta] make his concern to avoid a second visit with Nestor even more understandable." Clarke (1967:39) refers to "Nestor's oppressive hospitality," Reece (1993:67) to his "overzealousness."

53. Compare *Od.* 8.156, where Odysseus remarks on the fact that he sits in the middle of the Phaiakian assembly "though longing for home" (νόστοιο χατίζων#); and also *Od.* 11.350.

54. On the impression made by the fabulous luxury of the Spartan and Phaiakian courts on Telemakhos and Odysseus, respectively, see Apthorp 1980:21; and compare Odysseus'

statement (§62) that home is still sweetest, even if the traveller lives in a *rich house* (πίονα οἶκον) far from his land.

55. Note that their arrival and welcome—with only slight variation, given the fact that the encounter takes place out of doors—conform to the basic pattern for Hospitality: *Od.* 3.31 = §47(a); 34-39 = (b)-(f); 40-41 = (g).

56. Compare Dimock 1989:45. Reece 1993:31-32 identifies this as a distinct element ("XVI: Visitor asks to be allowed to sleep") of the Hospitality scene.

57. Heubeck-West-Hainsworth 1988:160; see also Reece 1993:59.

58. Taylor 1960 and Frame 1978; on the issue of polemics, Pucci 1987.

59. Cp. Reese 1993:67.

60. By way of contrast, note the prominence with which the issue of gifts figures in his dealings with Menelaos (*Od.* 4.589-619, 15.75-132); on which see Rose 1971:511-12. On the convention of gift-exchange, see Coldstream 1983, M. Finley 1978:73ff. and Donlan 1982.

61. For an introduction to views of poetry and pleasure represented in Homer, see e.g. Thalmann 1984:147-49, Walsh 1984:3-21 and Pucci 1987:193-96, 201-04. The bibliography on this theme is extensive; for summary and references, see Goldhill 1990:1-68. On the Hesiodic view that poetry acts as a remedy for present anxieties by deflecting the listener's attention from immediate (particular) cares to monuments of universal order—hence through an evocation of memory that simultaneously induces forgetfulness—see Walsh 1984:22-36 and Pucci 1977, especially pp. 22-27.

62. De Romilly 1975, Marsh 1979, Apthorp 1980:16-19, Dickson 1986:129-31, Parry 1992.

63. In addition to the passages discussed above, see e.g. *Od.* 4.239, 8.367-69;487-91, 9.3-4, 13.1-2, 17.513-21.

64. **Sirens**: *Od.* 12.160;185;187;192; **Muses**: *Il.* 1.604, *Od.* 24.60 (cf. *Theog.* 41, 68); **Kalypso**: *Od.* 5.61; **Kirke**: *Od.* 10.221; **various gods**: *Il.* 7.53, 2.182, 10.512, 14.150, 20.380, *Od.* 24.535.

65. The loud cry of Poseidon (*Il.* 14.150) turns the Akhaians from thoughts of retreat and inspires them with courage, while Akhilleus' voice (*Il.* 18.222) strikes paralyzing fear into the Trojans; and fear is also the immediate response of Hektor to

Apollo's voice (*Il.* 20.380). On the role of the voice in inducing the fascination associated with binding-spells, see Marsh 1979: Chapter 1. Also compare Clay 1974 and Ford 1992:172-97, for a discussion of various terms for "voice" in Homer.

66. Walsh 1984:14-21, Pucci 1987:193-94, Suzuki 1989:72-73; Reece 1993:179-80.

67. For discussion and bibliography, see Pucci 1979, 1980, 1987:209-13.

68. Vester 1956:18-23, Detienne-Vernant 1974:11-26.

69. Pucci (1987:211) also implicitly recognizes this possibility, though with reference chiefly to the second claim made by the Sirens, on which he notes that the Sirens' song "is infinite in scope: the Sirens tell Odysseus that he will learn not only all that happened in Troy but also all that happens in the world." Despite his acknowledgment (17-18) that the process of evolution of both poems follows the dynamics of oral composition, much of his language at times ("text", "writing", "reader") seems to imply the status of the *Iliad* as a relatively fixed *text* against which the *text* of the *Odyssey* launches its "polemic." This language is of course encouraged by his claim (26-27) that the nature of written and oral semiosis is identical; see further pp. 209-213. The "strictly Iliadic diction" of the Sirens' song is the subject of Pucci 1979; see also Buschor 1944, Pollard 1965:137-45, Segal 1983:38.

70. On this line, see Frame 1978:81-115.

71. Cf. Dimock 1989:45.

5

Conclusion

At Telemakhos' first landfall, on the beach at sandy Pylos, Nestor responds to the young man's request for news of his father with a sweeping gesture that seems to evoke the *Iliad* tradition in its entirety (*Od*. 3.103-19 = §26), from the early raiding sorties to the sack of Troy itself and its aftermath in a summary Catalogue of Fallen Heroes. We have already (Chapter 2.3) briefly assessed this passage in terms of its symmetry with Nestor's earlier catalogue of Greeks at the beginning of the Trojan expedition, to which the passage at *Iliad* 7.125-28 (= §23) alludes. At least in terms of the story's overall chronology, I suggested, there is a sense in which the *Iliad* is bracketed by these two simple acts of enumeration. As the former initiates its history as a narrative by introducing the names around which and through whose agency its own tale is constructed, the latter effectively brings the story that the *Iliad* only partially relates to a conclusion. This is a conclusion all more proper and fitting if only because it is more final, as meeting the limit of certain *nostos* or else that of sooner and no less certain death. Moreover, in these balanced evocations of quick and dead, Nestor's bare lists themselves seem to touch very close to the bones, as it were, of traditional epic. This is at least insofar as heroic *epos* is devoted above all other aims to the perpetuation of heroic identity by simple repetition of the hero's name.[1] As the *loci* of specific tales in the sense discussed earlier (Chapter 1.3)—namely, as the dense textual sites of "narrative potential," now mostly realized and catalogued duly—the names of the dead are a shorthand embodiment of the fuller narrative traditions that preserve them in storied memory.[2] One has the sense that Nestor, bardlike, is quite capable of unfolding the complete tale out of this mere enumeration of semes.

At the same time, Nestor's response to Telemakhos also officially inaugurates the tradition of return tales from which the *Odyssey* takes its own point of departure (*Od.* 3.130-98), providing both the general and also the specific narrative

background for the major accounts of homecoming—those of
Menelaos (276-303), Agamemnon (303-16), Telemakhos,
Odysseus—with which this "newest" of poems is concerned. For
all its abbreviation, then, and even despite the fact that it
really provides no concrete information at all about
Telemakhos' father, his speech here contextualizes the
Odyssey in much the same way as his narratives in the *Iliad*
provide a kind of frame for that poem. For that matter, this
contextualization may well indeed be all the more successful
given precisely Nestor's failure to have something certain to
say about the whereabouts and ultimate fate of Odysseus. For
in thus far having resisted the closure to which many of his
comrades have already long ago succumbed—those who are now
forever fixed in Nestor's *Catalogue of Fallen Heroes*, all
bodiless now, their selves gone on crepuscular wings to Hades,
their names dactylic rhythm on an old man's honeyed lips—
Odysseus at the opening of this his own story paradoxically
(and characteristically, too) remains well out of earshot. Here
he initially—as perhaps also ultimately, depending on both
how and where one finds the "end" of this poem—lies far
beyond the range of the *kleos* that would finally fully
narrativize him too.[3]

Nestor's position is therefore a privileged and unique—and
also a very powerful—one. Our earlier discussions (Chapter
1.4) emphasized his intermediate status, slung midway as he is
between generations, thus between a heroic present and the past
to which it still looks for the standards of its heroism. He is
thereby able to offer guidance along the passage from *ergon* to
mythos that all warriors would undertake. He does this first
through reference to his own career, since his superannuation
makes him simultaneously agent, sole surviving witness and
therefore by necessity the *aoidos* of his accomplishments.
Throughout the *Iliad*, Nestor is engaged in the essentially
autobiographical act of composing and recomposing his own
history out of the tales he tells others; we hear him in the
process of constructing himself and thereby of becoming his own
song, so to speak, through a metamorphosis in many respects
analogous to the one that controls the natural transformation of
the Elders in the *Teikhoskopia* into sweet-voiced cicadas (*Il.*
3.146-53). The body wastes away, but the finer matter of the
voice is thereby refined and purified; the dense flesh of a life
becomes sensual music. As such, his activities are a figure of

heroic *kleos* in the course of its formation as heroic narrative, as an ongoing and continuous process of oral performance influenced by the rules of traditional patterning as well as by personal history, private motives and the specific, rhetorical needs of the immediate occasion. He also fulfils the same role *per exemplum* for his warrior peers, to whom he offers his own course of life as a paradigm for them to emulate and his tale as a model of the glorious story they themselves should all strive to become. This is true notwithstanding how ironized and sinister a turn this emulation may well take, as in the death of Patroklos and in Telemakhos' near detention (Chapter 4), and no matter even how ultimately fragile a thing is the very *kleos* itself Nestor purveys and to which most of his audience so ardently aspire.

This last possibility must be confronted before we finally turn to a summary of Nestor's place in the *Odyssey*. Much of this study has relied on insight gained from narratological perspectives to situate Nestor both within the texts of the poems and also in relation to the oral narrative tradition out of which both texts were produced. Chapter 2 in particular focused on the high degree of extradiegetic narration that is attributed to him as one among several signs that his characterization suggests a planned resemblance of the oral poet, making Nestor an icon of the traditional bard. In that context, his mention in *Iliad* 7 (§23) of the catalogue delivered by him at Phthia while recruiting for the Trojan expedition was identified as his farthest-reaching analepsis—indeed, as a reference that stretches back beyond and enframes the very narrative within which it is made (§24). That this statement ranges the farthest is not entirely true, however, since another analepsis of even greater reach is also attributed to Nestor. For that matter, it may well even mark the greatest range of any "flashback" reference made in either of the poems, short of strictly mythological allusions to divine affairs *in illo tempore*, such as the autobiographical embarrassment at which Hephaistos gestures at the end of the first book of the *Iliad* (*Il.* 1.584-94). I discount these latter, as verging on the qualitatively different time of origins, and to which narratives *sui generis* accrue. The farthest of *human* analepses, then, is instead put into Nestor's mouth in *Iliad* 23, in the scene in which he instructs his son, Antilokhos, on how best to negotiate the turning-post set by Akhilleus for the chariot-race that will help to commemorate Patroklos in his funeral games (326-33):

§70

σῆμα δέ τοι ἐρέω μάλ' ἀριφραδές, οὐδέ σε λήσει.
ἕστηκε ξύλον αὖον ὅσον τ' ὄργυι' ὑπὲρ αἴης,
ἢ δρυὸς ἢ πεύκης· τὸ μὲν οὐ καταπύθεται ὄμβρῳ,
λᾶε δὲ τοῦ ἑκάτερθεν ἐρηρέδαται δύο λευκὼ
ἐν ξυνοχῇσιν ὁδοῦ, λεῖος δ' ἱππόδρομος ἀμφίς·
ἤ τευ σῆμα βροτοῖο πάλαι κατατεθνηῶτος,
ἢ τό γε νύσσα τέτυκτο ἐπὶ προτέρων ἀνθρώπων,
καὶ νῦν τέρματ' ἔθηκε ποδάρκης δῖος 'Αχιλλεύς.

I will give you an unequivocal sign (*sêma*), and it will not
    escape you.
There is a dry stump standing up from the ground about two
    arms' stretch high,
of oak or else of pine. The rain has not rotted it away,
and on either side two white stones lean against it,
at the juncture of the way, and with smooth driving around it.
It is either the tomb (*sêma*) of someone who died long ago,
or was set up as a racing-goal by men who lived before us.
Now swift-footed brilliant Akhilleus has made it the turning-
    point.

The relatively trivial uncertainty over whether the stump is pine or oak (328) prefigures the far more critical question (331-32) of what precisely this *sêma* signifies—or whether, for that matter, it should be regarded as a *sêma* at all. To be sure, it should be recognized first that the "unequivocal sign" (σῆμα . . . μαλ' ἀριφραδές) to which Nestor refers in the formulaic line (326; cf. *Od.* 11.126, 21.217, 23.73;225;273, 24.329) that opens this passage is not the sign to which his doubt soon thereafter (331-32) attaches. Instead, it is initially the sign of his own making at the moment of this utterance, namely the one he has just then selected for the practical advice he will impart to his son, and around which that advice will turn. At the same time, his act of sign-making or semiosis also initially points to the transient nature of all signs. For whether or not it was ever some hero's tomb or else the racing-goal used by an earlier generation of men, it has now been doubly coopted, first by Akhilleus (333) and now by Nestor (326), to signify other things. The landscape thus presents itself as a field of signs that might well bear dense meanings, potentially over-layered many times; their referents shift over time, and as a consequence these *sêmata* exhibit an unsettled, even disposable character.

Nestor thus appropriates what may well be an arbitrary and inherently insignificant aspect of their surroundings and turns it into a *sêma* to which Antilokhos must now pay close attention if he is to win the race and thereby gain additional glory (*kleos*) both for himself and Patroklos. For we must not forget the context within which this new act of meaning takes place. The competition among individual contestants for personal *kleos*—often fierce and potentially divisive, even lethal—unfolds within the framework of the *kleos* thereby made and indirectly conceded to another, absent hero. The games are meant to consecrate his memory and collectively ensure the perpetuation of his name. They contribute just as much (if not more) to the erection of the dead warrior's *sêma* or tomb as does the actual raising of a mound that will "shine from far away . . . for men now alive and those hereafter" (*Od.* 24.83-84).[4] Here if nowhere else as clearly in this society of heroes—witness the utopian strains with which the Funeral Games of Patroklos are generally discussed—such *kleos* would seem to underwrite and somehow even justify itself in the name of the community gathered to celebrate and remember its dead. Moreover, granted the practical success with which Antilokhos soon makes use of his father's advice, this first *sêma* is unequivocal (ἀριφραδές) indeed. This is notwithstanding even the pair of disputes to which that use gives rise (*Il.* 23.532-613)—and perhaps even thanks to them, as providing an occasion for what is generally taken as a wise adjudication by Akhilleus (539-65) and a magnanimous sacrifice on Menelaos' part (566-613). Despite the tensions, harmony prevails and everyone gets his due share of glory.

It is of course additionally a testament to the practical intelligence (μῆτις) that Nestor eulogizes earlier (311-18) in his speech and that he himself elsewhere often embodies (*Il.* 7.323-24 = 9.92-93; 10.18-19, 14.106-08).[5] In this respect, his Iliadic *sêma* differs from the "unequivocal" Teiresian sign in

Odyssey 11 only in that the material body of the former is already present at hand, right out there in the Trojan landscape, not subject to some perhaps merely contingent realization at some distant and indefinite time hence in some fabled place not yet on any known map, the stuff of an ἀμέτρητος πόνος (*Od.* 23.249).[6] Apart from that, one might even indeed be tempted to acknowledge a kind of symmetry in this pair of scenes, which are in fact the only two in the poems to share the line σῆμα δέ τοι ἐρέω μάλ' ἀριφραδές, οὐδέ σε λήσει [I will give you an unequivocal sign, and it will not escape you] in common (*Il.* 23.326 = *Od.* 11.126). On the one hand, the dead seer's prophecy of the saltless folk and the winnowing-fan opens out for the character Odysseus upon a future in whose real uncertainty the proper end of the Odyssean narrative itself is inscribed.[7] To this extent, it marks that narrative's ultimate prolepsis, offering the vision of an end simultaneously posited but within the actual bounds of the tale itself forever held in suspension. It foreshadows that end only by keeping it unmeasureable, tentative and, in fact, shadowy; it hints at closures but never fully closes the narrative frame.

On the other, the stump of oak or pine in *Iliad* 23 incorporates a reach of analogous and also analogously disturbing length, though a reach in just the opposite direction. The real question it poses of course involves less its present use as a sign as whether this feature of the landscape may have ever meant something *prior* to its appropriation now. The old man is unsure if his sign-making has just then touched upon a thing already touched by some other act (or acts) of meaning, specifically upon the *sêma* (tomb) of a hero dead long ago, hence the product of an even earlier semiosis. Both Nagy and Peradotto rightly draw attention to how this latter doubt seems to undercut the ideology of *kleos* supporting not only the institutionalized behavior depicted within the *Iliad* and the Iliadic poems of the *Cycle*—the heroic code; the fragile semiotics of the *gerata* that are meant to signify individual worth; the choreography of arming, flyting, and the kill; the rationalization itself of war—but the narrative tradition as well that would guarantee the duration of heroic identity over time.[8] For the irony affecting this scene is precisely the inability—*and precisely Nestor's*—to say whether this oak (or pine) and rock embodies a memory at all. That it is Nestor's memory that fails here makes the irony correspondingly much sharper, since we have already (Chapter 2.2) noted how his powers of recollection are represented as in significant respects far greater than those of the principal narrator. Given the fact that Nestorian memory tends to be identified with the whole oral narrative tradition as such, what does it mean that the old man cannot unequivocally read this one sign?

This unexpected limit on authorial memory, the terrible forgetfulness on which it appears to verge as it reaches deeper into the past than can be certified by its own autopsy or else at least rumored about in the narratives of others once present at that original time, marks an analepsis far more extensive than any other offered in either of the poems. This is not just another instance of the kind of extradiegetic gesture with which Nestor elsewhere often remembers and cites events long before the narrative that includes his act of recollection. Mirroring the tentative, Teiresian prolepsis of an ending for the *Odyssey*—which points to an unequivocal sign translated nonetheless into a context riddled by sheer contingency—it is in fact less a sure reach back at all than a kind of groping at the very margins both of memory and meaning. At this distance, the landscape becomes increasingly harder (nearly impossible) to read, broken up as it is by worn lumps of wood or stone of radically equivocal import. These are vague shapes now that perhaps indeed were conspicuous trophies once, the far-shining (Τηλεφανές) inscription of memory, the famous hero's splendid tomb, but that might also just as well have always been simply natural things from the beginning, unmarked by human hand or voice, mere things whose own elemental features—(is it pine or oak?)—are not even themselves immune from time's erosion. At this ultimate limit, once memory has failed and all narrative and naming along with it, *kleos* surely must fail as well.

In this context, Ford's argument (1992:131-71) that this and similar passages in the *Iliad* speak to an oral tradition's fundamental hostility to the kind of permanence the new (and in some respects, rival) technology of writing claims to ensure seems persuasive. As I have suggested elsewhere with reference to the far more overt contrast between voice and sign in Pindar,[9] it is precisely the *muteness* of the visual token that is seen to render it opaque, occluding its referent, and that causes it to be regarded with suspicion, as a *sêma* that condemns its signified to perpetual silence rather than broadcasting it for all subsequent generations to hear and repeat. Though *seen*, it remains paradoxically invisible unless it is also *heard*. For it is indeed only by the act of *voicing* the sign—by naming the hero whose conspicuous but ultimately mute tomb is seen from afar on the headland, by speaking the stone inscription aloud, or else even by having the inscribed sign compellingly appropiate our own voice as transient readers[10]—that this silence can be overcome and the hero's name preserved from sheer oblivion. The equivocal *sêma* on the Trojan plain in *Iliad* 23 therefore marks a terrible failure of *kleos* only in the sense that the corpse it may well designate did not find another voice to keep its fame alive. Its hero somehow never achieved complete transformation into narrative, never successfully made the passage over from *ergon* into everliving *mythos*. If this *sêma* incorporates an additional irony, then, it is not one that necessarily undermines the oral narrative tradition as such, but instead one that in fact touches closest and most threateningly on Nestor's own position within it. For having outlived every prior witness to his glory, every *other* voice that might maintain his *kleos* and his name in living memory, he must either continue always to speak or else fall ultimately as mute as the *sêma* about whose meaning and nature he expresses such doubt. This is the need from which his logorrhea issues.

To appreciate the full extent of this position, we must also acknowledge the part played by Nestor in his first appearance in the *Odyssey*. Here he stands at the pivotal center of a narrative tradition that orients itself by two cardinal points of reference—*The Grief Abroad* and *The Return*—that together define the Trojan War story. His direct experience, memory and powers of narration, even despite the conventional disclaimer he makes (*Od.* 3.113-19), effectively seem to negotiate the transition from one to the other. This is Mediation on a grander scale than that of the scenes examined in Chapter 3. There, as we saw, Nestor reflects the storyteller's control over the plot by intervening editorially at critical points in its development to help motivate other characters to move down one narrative path or another. In this role he is chiefly an agent of closure, an actor in the service of the abstract story that steers the concrete tale toward its predetermined end, even if that role was later seen (Chapter 4.3) to conflict with the far more tentative kind of closure at which the *Odyssey* aims. It is in fact from the specifically Iliadic closure with which Nestor is identified that this conflict gains much of its value as a tension between basic narrative types.[11]

Here, moreover, he is represented as exercising a far more comprehensive kind of narrative influence, namely control over the very *transmission* of the stories in which he himself also figures. In one sense, of course, this dual status as both participant and chronicler is no longer, as it generally was in the *Iliad*, especially unique to him; it is instead merely one instance illustrative of a number of themes—the narrative construction of identity, the role of storytelling in social intercourse, perhaps even what might be called the ethnography of discourse—that acquire an increasingly prominent place in the *Odyssey* as a whole. Menelaos, Helen, Penelope, Odysseus himself *par excellence*, along with a host of minor characters (Eumaios, Euryklea, Theoklymenos), are all depicted to greater or lesser degrees in acts of autobiographical narration. Moreover, it is more often than not the specifically rhetorical dimension of their storytelling that enjoys emphasis; its illocutionary and perlocutionary features are sometimes just as (if not even more) important than its actual content. The tale with which Odysseus patently aims to extract a warm cloak from Eumaios (*Od.* 14.462-517) comes immediately to mind, since the issue of narrative as a means to some end other than simple exposition is explicitly addressed here (457-61). Ulterior motivation, however, of course pervades most of the other tales as well; most if not all speakers in the poem deliberately manipulate what they say with implicit reference to personal interests and aims.[12] Helen's tale of Odyssean espionage in Troy (*Od.* 4.239-64), for instance, is no less tailored to the character and expectations of her audience, no less moved by her desire to depict herself in a favorable light before her husband and their Ithakan guest, than are the *Wundererzählungen* Odysseus tells the isolationist, credulous Phaiakians (Books 9-12). Further, the added depth that ulterior motivation gives to their stories also implicitly affects how the enframing tale itself is received, thus finally enabling questions to be raised about the overarching narrative tradition as a whole. As a consequence, the *Odyssey* offers a view of narrative and the act of narration as events far more complex and potentially more problematic than what they seem to be in the *Iliad*, where narrative is generally—and however disingenuously—presented as if it were a perfectly transparent medium, a clear window providing a relatively unobstructed and undistorted view of the past.[13]

What distinguishes Nestor from this group is first the sheer breadth of his narrative, which reflects the scope of his prodigious memory. Others in the *Odyssey* tell their own tales, from within their own limited perspectives; Nestor suggests—again, granted the trope of his disclaimer—that he has access to the story as a whole, namely to everything the Akhaians suffered before and during and (to a lesser extent) also after the sack of Troy. This disclaimer in fact warrants closer scrutiny. It will be remembered that, in the invocation preceding the *Catalogue of Ships*, the Iliadic narrator disavows the possibility that he could recount the names of the multitude (πληθύν), even if he had "ten tongues, ten mouths, an unbreakable voice and a breast of bronze" (*Il.* 2.488-90). On the contrary, Nestor's *recusatio* in *Odyssey* 3 might instead be taken to suggest that his inability to recount *The Grief* in its entirety is less a function of his powers of memory and speech than of the length of time a full narration would require, given the sheer number and detail of the events that would need to be told. His words are worth quoting again (*Od.* 3.113-19; cf. §26):

§71

　　　　　　　　　. . . τίς κεν ἐκεῖνα
πάντα γε μυθήσαιτο καταθνητῶν ἀνθρώπων;
οὐδ' εἰ *πεντάετές* γε καὶ *ἑξάετες* παραμίμνων
ἐξερέοις ὅσα κεῖθι πάθον κακὰ δῖοι 'Αχαιοί·
πρίν κεν ἀνιηθεὶς σὴν πατρίδα γαῖαν ἵκοιο.
εἰνάετες γάρ σφιν κακὰ ῥάπτομεν ἀμφιέποντες
παντοίοισι δόλοισι . . .

Who among mortal men could recount them all?
Not even if you stayed here *five years or six*
could you ask about as many evils as the bright Akhaians
　　　suffered there;
you would return home, worn out, before then.
For we contrived against them intently for *nine years*
with all kinds of stratagems. . .

It may not be unreasonable to see in this disproportion between *five or six years* of inquiry-and-answer and the *nine years* that the events themselves took to unfold an implicit assumption that the two should be equal for the account to be complete and *a fortiori* genuine. That is to say, the *narrated time* should ideally be matched by the *time of narration*, and events that filled nine years could not be recounted in anything less than that exact number. This is narrative that would deny its own status as such, *diegesis* that aims to *recreate* rather than simply to relate its object;[14] and this is of course the deeper risk involved in stopping to hear it. For when the time of narration replicates the time that is narrated, and the story in its fullness is isomorphic with what it would tell, an essential boundary vanishes. Like Patroklos or Telemakhos, the listener unwittingly crosses out of a world of practical aims and needs into one of sheer, seductive *mythos*, in which the present is wholly denied or overwhelmed and the past fully reclaimed, not as a set of equivocal, "mute" signs but somehow instead as a complete reality. At this point, the burden of the song becomes too heavy—indeed, even oppressive and lethal.

The same compulsion that motivates Nestorian logorrhea also makes for the repletion and saturation of his narratives. For the need constantly to repeat a past of which he is himself the only witness is at the same time a compulsion to deny the difference entailed by every repetition, to deny the mediation that narrative provides and to insist instead on the literal reinstantiation of that past. This amounts to an aesthetics of exhaustiveness whose affect on its audience is utter exhaustion. After *five or six* years, Nestor says, you would return home both wearied and disheartened (ἀνιηθείς, cf. *Il.* 2.291), simultaneously worn down by the length of the tale and also deeply aggrieved that it still remained incomplete. What then would happen after *nine*, once the narrative had not just signified but instead fully evoked its referent? After *nine* years—after "eleven or twelve more days" (cf. *Od.* 4.587-92)— would *nostos* or even the desire for home be any longer possible at all?

NOTES

1. Nagy 1979, Svenbro 1988.

2. Or perhaps not. One thinks here less of the conspicuously "heroic" dead (Sarpedon, Hektor), around whom the tradition has woven its primary tale, than of the relatively "anonymous" ones, so to speak. By this I mean the very many characters who survive in name alone, who seem to appear *in nomina propria*—along with patronymic, sometimes also with the name of a place that is their home—only so their deaths at others' more fabled hands can be registered, and whose so-called "fuller narratives" (assuming they exist at all) perhaps never grew much beyond local or even clan and familial traditions. As the voice of that "higher," "pan-hellenic"—or better, *monoglossic* (Bakhtin 1981)—narrative tradition, Nestor has nothing to say about any but the chiefs.

3. On the problem of the end of the Odyssey, see e.g. Wender 1978 and Peradotto 1986; on the general theme of disguise, Murnaghan 1987.

4. The use of the adjective ἀριφραδές [unequivocal, clear] to refer formulaically to the *sêma* Nestor promises Antilokhos, placed here in the context of the *sêma* or tomb of Patroklos and Akhilleus, elsewhere described as τηλεφανές [far-shining], also recalls the use of ἀριφραδέα (*Il.* 23.240) with reference to Patroklos' bones after his corpse has been burnt. Akhilleus tells Agamemnon (236-48) that they are easy to recognize, since they stand apart conspicuously from those of the horses and men burnt along with him.

5. Detienne-Vernant 1978:11-26; on Nestor and νόος, see Nagy 1983.

6. Peradotto 1986.

7. Peradotto 1986, 1990:59-93.

8. See Nagy 1983, Lynn-George 1988:265-70, Peradotto 1993. Peradotto (159) comments: "So precarious and impermanent is the *kleos* it was meant, if it was a *sêma*, to preserve beyond its hero's death. In the context of this mute, unclear, and merely possible sign of heroic endeavor, are we meant to read ironically the ultimate fate of the . . . *sêma* of Achilleus and Patroclus . . . ?" See also Ford 1992:144-45.

9. Dickson 1990.
10. Burzachechi 1962, Raubitschek 1968, Svenbro 1988, esp. 44-63.
11. Peradotto 1986.
12. Most 19891, 1989b.
13. Conte 1986, Ford 1992:6.
14. Ford 1992:55 comments: "Though epic is by definition poetry of the past, it is poetry that claims to transport us into an *au delà*, not a beyond buried in the vault of recollection but a place as present as our own, though elsewhere."

Bibliography

Accame, S. 1963. "L'invocazione alla Musa e la verità in Omero e in Esiodo." *Rivista di Filologia e di Instrizione Classica* 41:257-81, 385-415.

Alexiou, Margaret. 1974. *The Ritual Lament in Greek Tradition*. Cambridge: Cambridge University Press.

Andersen, Øivind. 1975. *Paradeigmata. Beiträge zum Verständnis der Ilias*. Dissertation, University of Oslo.

———. 1978. *Die Diomedesgestalt in der Ilias. Symbolae Osloensis* 25. Oslo: Bergen.

——— . 1987. "Myth, Paradigm and 'Spatial Form' in the *Iliad*." In *Homer: Beyond Oral Poetry. Recent Trends in Homeric Interpretation*, edited by J. Bremmer, I. de Jong, and J. Kalff, pp. 1-13. Amsterdam: Gröner.

Apthorp, M.J. 1980. "The Obstacles to Telemachus' Return." *Classical Quarterly* 30:1-22.

Arend, Walter. 1933. *Die Typischen Scenen bei Homer*. Berlin: Weidmann.

Armstrong, James. 1958. "The Arming Motif in the *Iliad*." *American Journal of Philology* 79:337-54.

Atchity, Kenneth. 1978. *Homer's Iliad: The Shield of Memory*. Carbondale and Edwardsville: Southern Illinois University Press.

Auerbach, Erich. 1953. *Mimesis: The Representation of Reality in Western Literature*. Trans. W. Trask. Princeton: Princeton University Press.

Austin, Norman. 1966. "The Function of Digressions in the *Iliad*." *Greek, Roman and Byzantine Studies* 7:337-54.

———. 1969. "Telemachus polymechanos." *California Studies in Classical Antiquity* 2:46-52.

———. 1975. *Archery at the Dark of the Moon*. Berkeley: University of California Press.

Bakhtin, Mikhail. 1981. *The Dialogic Imagination*. Trans. C. Emerson and M. Holinquist. Austin: University of Texas Press.

Bal, Mieke. 1981. "Notes on Narrative Embedding." *Poetics Today* 2:41-59.

———. 1985. *Narratology: Introduction to the Theory of Narrative*. Toronto: University of Toronto Press.

Barck, Christophorus. 1976. *Wort und Tat bei Homer*. Hildesheim: Olms.

Barmeyer, Eike. 1968. *Die Musen. Ein Beitrag zur Inspirationstheorie*. Munich: Fink.

Barthes, Roland. 1970. *Writing Degree Zero and Elements of Semiology*. Trans. A. Lavers and C. Smith. Boston: Beacon Hill Press.

————. 1972. *Mythologies*. Trans. A. Lavers. New York: Hill & Wang.

————. 1974. *S/Z*. Trans. R. Miller. New York: Hill & Wang.

Bassett, S.E. 1923. "The Proems of the *Iliad* and the *Odyssey*." *American Journal of Philology* 44:339ff.

————. 1938. *The Poetry of Homer*. Berkeley: University of California Press.

Bauman, Richard, ed. 1977. *Verbal Art as Performance*. Prospect Hts., Ill.: Waveland Press.

————. 1986. *Story, Performance and Event: Contextual Studies of Oral Narrative*. Cambridge: Cambridge University Press.

Becker, O. 1937. *Das Bild des Weges*. Berlin: Weidmann.

Bergren, Ann. 1981. "Helen's 'Good Drug': *Odyssey* 4.1-305." In *Contemporaty Literary Hermeneutics and Interpretation of Classical Texts*, edited by S. Krésic, pp. 201-14. Ottawa: Editions de l'Université.

————. 1983. "Odyssean Temporality: Many (Re)Turns." In *Approaches to Homer*, edited by C. Rubino and C. Shelmerdine, pp. 38-73. Austin: University of Texas Press.

Beye, Charles. 1993. *Ancient Epic Poetry: Homer, Apollonius, Virgil*. Ithaca: Cornell University Press.

Bleicher, Josef. 1980. *Contemporary Hermeneutics: Hermeneutics as Method, Philosophy and Critique*. London: Routledge and Kegan Paul.

Block, E. 1982. "The Narrator Speaks: Apostrophe in Homer and Vergil." *Transactions of the American Philological Association* 112:7-22.

Boedeker, Deborah. 1984. *Descent from Heaven: Images of Dew in Greek Poetry and Religion*. Chico: Scholars Press.

Bölte, F. 1934. "Ein pylisches Epos." *Rheinisches Museum* 83:319-47.

Bourdieu, Pierre. 1972. *Outline of a Theory of Practice*. Trans. R. Nice. Cambridge: Cambridge University Press.

Bowra, Cecil. 1930. *Tradition and Design in the Iliad*. Oxford: Oxford University Press.

————. 1952. *Heroic Poetry*. Oxford: Oxford University Press.

Braswell, Bruce. 1971. "Mythological Innovation in the *Iliad*." *Classical Quarterly* 21:16-26.

Bremer, J., I. de Jong, and J. Kalff, eds. 1987. *Homer Beyond Oral Poetry: Recent Trends in Homeric Interpretation*. Amsterdam: Grüner.

Burzachechi, M. 1962. "Oggetti parlanti nelle epigrafi greche." *Epigraphica* 24:3-54.

Buschor, Ernst. 1944. *Die Musen des Jenseits*. Munich: Bruckmann.

Bynum, David. 1969. "The Generic Nature of Oral Epic Poetry." *Genre* 2:236-58.

Calhoun, G.M. 1938. "The Poet and the Muses in Homer." *Classical Philology* 33:157-66.

Cantieni, Räto. 1942. *Die Nestorerzälhung im XI. Gesang der Ilias (V 679-762)*. Dissertation, University of Zurich.

Carpenter, Rhys. 1962. *Folk Tale, Fiction and Saga in the Homeric Epics*. Berkeley: University of California Press.

Chambers, Ross. 1984. *Story and Situation: Narrative Seduction and the Power of Fiction*. Minneapolis: University of Minnesota Press.

Chatman, Seymour. 1978. *Story and Discourse: Narrative Structure in Fiction and Film*. Ithaca: Cornell University Press.

————. 1990. *Coming to Terms: The Rhetoric of Narrative in Fiction and Film*. Ithaca: Cornell University Press.

Cixous, Hélène. 1974. "The Character of 'Character'." *New Literary History* 5:383-402.

Clarke, Howard. 1967. *The Art of the Odyssey*. Englewood Cliffs, N.J.: Prentice-Hall.

————. 1981. *Homer's Readers. A Historical Introduction to the Iliad and the Odyssey*. Newark: University of Delaware Press.

Clay, Jenny Strauss. 1974. "*Demas* and *Aude*: The Nature of Divine Transformation in Homer." *Hermes* 102:129-36.

————. 1983. *The Wrath of Athena: Gods and Men in the Odyssey*. Princeton: Princeton University Press.

Clifford, James and George Marcus, eds. 1986. *Writing Culture: The Poetics and Politics of Ethnography*. Berkeley: University of California Press.

Coldstream, J.N. 1976. "Hero-Cults in the Age of Homer."
    Journal of Hellenic Studies 96:8-17.
————. 1983. "Gift Exchange in the Eighth Century B.C." In
    *The Greek Renaissance of the Eighth Century BC: Tradition
    and Innovation*, edited by R. Hägg, pp. 201-06. Stockholm:
    Aström.
Collins, Leslie. 1988. *Studies in Characterization in the Iliad.*
    Athenaeum: Frankfurt am Main.
Combellack, F.M. 1950. "Contemporary Unitarians and Homeric
    Originality." *American Journal of Philology* 71:337-64.
————. 1959. "Milman Parry and Homeric Artistry."
    Comparative Literature 11:193-208.
Connerton, Paul. 1989. *How Societies Remember.* Cambridge:
    Cambridge University Press.
Conte, Gian Biago. 1986. *The Rhetoric of Imitation.* Trans. E.
    Segal. Ithaca: Cornell University Press.
Davies, M. 1986. "Nestor's Advice in *Iliad* 7." *Eranos* 84:69-75.
Delebecque, Edouard. 1958. *Télémaque et la Structure de
    l'Odyssée.* Aix-en-Provence: Editions Ophrys.
Detienne, Marcel. 1967. *Les maîtres de vérité dans la grèce
    archaïque.* Paris: Maspero.
Detienne, Marcel and Jean-Pierre Vernant. 1974. *Cunning
    Intelligence in Greek Culture and Society.* Trans. Janet Lloyd.
    Atlantic Highlands, N.J.: Humanities Press.
Dickson, Keith. 1986. "*Damasiphrôn khrysos*: Act, Implement
    and *Tekhê* in Pindar." *Ramus* 15:122-42.
————. 1990a. "A Typology of Mediation in Homer," *Oral
    Tradition* 5.1:37-71.
————. 1990b. "Voice and Sign in Pindar." *Ramus* 19.2:109-29.
————. 1992a. "Orality and *Auctoritas* in Homer." *Humanitas*
    16.2:28-35.
————. 1992b. "Kalkhas and Nestor: Two Narrative
    Strategies in *Iliad* 1." *Arethusa*: 25.3:327-58.
————. 1993. "Nestor Among the Sirens." *Oral Tradition*
    8.1:21-58.
Dimock, G.E. 1989. *The Unity of the Odyssey.* Amherst:
    University of Massachusetts.
Dindorf, W., ed. 1855. *Scholia Graeca in Homeri Odysseam.*
    Oxford: Oxford University Press.
————. 1875. *Scholia Graeca in Homeri Iliadem.* Oxford:
    Oxford University Press.

Docherty, Thomas. 1983. *Reading (Absent) Character: Towards a Theory of Characterization in Fiction.* Oxford: Oxford University Press.

Donlan, Walter. 1973. "The Origin of *Kaloskagathos.*" *American Journal of Philology* 94:365-74.

————. 1979. "The Structure of Authority in the *Iliad.*" *Arethusa* 12:51-70.

————. 1980. *The Aristocratic Ideal in Ancient Greece.* Lawrence, Kansas: Coronado Press.

————. 1982. "The Politics of Generosity in Homer." *Helios* 9:1-15.

Dover, Kenneth. 1975. *Greek Popular Morality in the Time of Plato and Aristotle.* Oxford: Clarendon Press.

Doyle, R. 1970. "Ὄλβος, κότος and ἄτη from Hesiod to Aeschylus." *Traditio* 26:283-303.

Duckworth, G.E. 1933. *Foreshadowing and Suspense in the Epics of Homer, Apollonius, and Vergil.* Princeton: Princeton University Press.

Ducrot, O. and T. Todorov. 1979. *Encyclopedic Dictionary of the Sciences of Language.* Baltimore: Johns Hopkins University Press.

Dukat, Zdeslav. 1976. "Parry, Propp and Literary Studies." *Ziva antika* 26:149-59.

Dunbar, H. 1962. *A Complete Concordance to the Odyssey of Homer. Completely revised and enlarged by B. Marzullo.* Hildesheim: Olm.

Durante, M. 1960. "Richerche sulla preistoria della lingua poetica graeca. La terminologia relativa alla creazione poetica." *Rendiconti della Classe di Scienze morali, storiche e filologiche dell'Accademia dei Lincei* 15:231-49.

————. 1971. *Sulla preistoria della tradizione poetica graeca, parte prima: Continuità della tradizione poetica dall' età Micenea ai primi documenti.* Roma: d'Ateneo.

————. 1976. *Sulla preistoria della tradizione poetica graeca, parte seconda: Risultanze della comparazione indoeuropea.* Roma: d'Ateneo.

Eagleton, Terry. 1983. *Literary Theory: An Introduction.* Minneapolis: University of Minnesota Press.

————. 1990. *The Ideology of the Aesthetic.* Oxford: Blackwell.

Edmonds, Susan. 1990. *Homeric Nepios.* New York: Garland.

Edwards, Anthony. 1985. *Achilles in the Odyssey.* Königstein/Ts.: Hain.

Edwards, Mark. 1966. "Some Features of Homeric Craftsmanship." *Transactions of the American Philological Association* 97:115-79.

———. 1969. "On Some 'Answering' Expressions in Homer." *Classical Philology,* 64:81-87.

———. 1970. "Homeric Speech Introductions." *Transactions of the American Philological Association,* 74:1-36.

———. 1975. "Type-Scenes and Homeric Hospitality." *Transactions of the American Philological Association,* 105:51-72.

———. 1980. "Convention and Individuality in *Iliad* 1." *Transactions of the American Philological Association,* 84:1-28.

———. 1986. "Homer and Oral Tradition: The Formula, Part I." *Oral Tradition* 1:171-230.

———. 1987a. "Homer and Oral Tradition: The Formula, Part II." *Oral Tradition* 3:11-60.

———. 1987b. "*Topos* and Transformation in Homer." In *Homer: Beyond Oral Poetry. Recent Trends in Homeric Interpretation,* edited by J. Bremer, I. de Jong, and J. Kalff, pp. 47-60. Amsterdam: Gröner.

———. 1987c. *Homer: Poet of the Iliad.* Baltimore: Johns Hopkins University Press.

———. 1991. *The Iliad: A Commentary. Volume V: Books 17-20.* Cambridge: Cambridge University Press.

Erbse, Harmut, ed. 1969. *Scholia Graeca in Homeri Iliadem.* Berlin: de Gruyter.

Falkner, Thomas. 1989. Ἐπὶ γήραος οὐδῷ: Homeric Heroism, Old Age and the End of the *Odyssey.*" In *Old Age in Greek and Latin Literature,* edited by T. Falkner and J. de Luce, pp. 21-67. Albany: State University of New York Press.

Felson-Rubin, Nancy. 1987. "Penelope's Perspective: Character from Plot." In *Homer: Beyond Oral Poetry. Recent Trends in Homeric Interpretation,* edited by J. Bremer, I. de Jong, and J. Kalff, pp. 61-83. Amsterdam: Gröner.

Fenik, Bernard. 1968. *Typical Battle Scenes in the Iliad.* Wiesbaden: Steiner.

———. 1974. *Studies in the Odyssey.* Wiesbaden: Steiner.

——. ed. 1978. *Homer: Tradition and Invention*. Leiden: Brill.

Ferrari, Giovanni. 1987. *Listening to the Cicadas: A Study of Plato's Phaedrus*. Cambridge: Cambridge University Press.

Fine, Elizabeth. 1984. *The Folklore Text: From Performance to Print*. Bloomington: Indiana University Press.

Finkelberg, Margalit. 1987. "Homer's View of the Epic Narrative: Some Formulaic Evidence." *Classical Philology* 82:135-38.

Finley, John H., Jr. 1978. *Homer's Odyssey*. Cambridge, MA.: Harvard University Press.

Finley, Moses I. 1978. *The World of Odysseus*. New York: Viking Press.

Finnegan, Ruth. 1970. *Oral Literature in Africa*. Oxford: Oxford University Press.

——. 1977. *Oral Poetry: Its Nature, Significance, and Social Context*. Cambridge: Cambridge University Press.

——. 1992. *Oral Traditions and the Verbal Arts: A Guide to Research Practices*. London and New York: Routledge.

Foley, John Miles. 1977. "The Traditional Oral Audience." *Balkan Studies* 18:145-54.

——, (ed.). 1981a. *Oral Traditional Literature: A Festschrift for Albert Bates Lord*. Columbus: Slavica.

——. 1981b. "Oral Texts, Traditional Texts: Poetics and Critical Methods." *Canadian-American Slavic Studies* 15:122-45.

——. 1985. *Oral-Formulaic Theory and Research: An Introduction and Annotated Bibliography*. New York: Garland Press.

——. 1986a. "Tradition and Collective Talent: Oral Epic, Textual Meaning, and Receptionalist Theory." *Cultural Anthropology* 1:203-22.

——. 1986b. *Current Issues in Oral Litarature Research: A Memorial for Milman Parry*. Columbus: Slavica.

——. 1986c. *Oral Tradition in Literature: Interpretation in Context*. Columbia: University of Missouri Press.

——. 1988. *The Theory of Oral Composition: History and Methodology*. Bloomington: Indiana University Press.

——. 1990. *Traditional Oral Epic: The Odyssey, Beowulf, and the Serbo-Croatian Return Song*. Berkeley: University of California Press.

————. 1991. *Immanent Art: Aesthetics and Traditional Oral Epic*. Bloomington: Indiana University Press.

Ford, Andrew. 1992. *Homer: The Poetry of the Past*. Ithaca: Cornell University Press.

Foucault, Michel. 1970. *The Order of Things*. Trans. A. Sheridan. London and New York: Vintage Books.

————. 1972. *The Archaeology of Knowledge and The Discourse on Language*. Trans. A. Sheridan. New York: Pantheon Books.

Frame, Douglas. 1978. *The Myth of Return in Early Greek Epic*. New Haven and London: Yale University Press.

Freidenberg, Olga. 1930. "Tersit." *Japheticeskii Sbornik* 6:231-53.

Gadamer, Hans-Georg. 1975. *Truth and Method*. London: Sheed.

Gaisser, Julia. 1969. "A Structural Analysis of the Digressions in the *Iliad* and the *Odyssey*." *Harvard Studies in Classical Philology* 73:1-43.

Geertz, Clifford. 1973. *The Interpretation of Cultures*. New York: Basic Books.

Genette, Gérard. 1968. "Vraisemblance et motivation." *Communications* 11:5-21.

————. 1980. *Narrative Discourse: An Essay in Method*. Trans. J. Lewin. Ithaca: Cornell University Press.

————. 1982. *Figures of Literary Discourse*. Trans. M.-R. Logan. New York: Columbia University Press.

————. 1988. *Narrative Discourse Revisited*. Trans. J. Lewin. Ithaca: Cornell University Press.

Gentili, Bruno. 1988. *Poetry and its Public in Ancient Greece: From Homer to the Fifth Century*. Trans. T. Cole. Baltimore: Johns Hopkins University Press.

Gernet, Louis. 1981. *The Anthropology of Ancient Greece*. Trans. J. Hamilton, S. Nagy, and B. Nagy. Baltimore: Johns Hopkins University Press.

Goffman, E. 1959. *The Presentation of Self in Everyday Life*. Garden City, N.J.: Doubleday Anchor.

Goldhill, Simon. 1991. *The Poet's Voice: Essays on Poetics and Greek Literature*. Cambridge: Cambridge University Press.

Goody, Jack. 1977. *The Domestication of the Savage Mind*. Cambridge: Cambridge University Press.

————. 1986. *The Logic of Writing and the Organization of Society*. Cambridge: Cambridge University Press.

———. 1987. *The Interface Between the Written and the Oral.* Cambridge: Cambridge University Press.

Goody, Jack and Ian Watt. 1968. *Literacy in Traditional Societies.* Cambridge: Cambridge University Press.

Gouldner, Alvin. 1965. *Enter Plato: Classical Greece and the Origins of Social Theory.* New York: Harper and Row.

Greene, W. C. 1951. "The Spoken and the Written Word." *Harvard Studies in Classical Philology* 60:23-59.

Greindl, M. 1938. *KLEOS, KUDOS, EUCHOS, TIME, PHATIS, DOXA: Eine bedeutungs-geschichtliche Untersuchung des epischen und lyrischen Sprachgebrauches.* Dissertation, University of Erlangen: Lengerich.

Gresseth, G. 1975. "The Gilgamesh Epic and Homer." *Classical Journal* 70:1-18.

Griffin, Jasper. 1980. *Homer on Life and Death.* Oxford: Clarendon Press.

Gundert, Hermann. 1935. *Pindar und sein Dichterberuf.* Klostermann: Frankfurt-am-Main.

Gunn, David. 1970. "Narrative Inconsistency and the Oral Dictated Text in the Homeric Epic." *American Journal of Philology* 91:192-203.

———. 1971. "Thematic Composition and Homeric Authorship." *Harvard Studies in Classical Philology* 75:1-31.

Gutmann, D. 1977. "The Cross-Cultural Perspective: Notes Toward a Comparative Psychology of Aging." In *Handbook of the Psychology of Aging*, edited by J. Birren and K. Schaie, pp. 302-26. New York: Academic Press.

Haft, Adele. 1992. "τὰ δὴ νῦν πάντα τελεῖται: Prophecy and Recollection in the Assemblies of *Iliad* 2 and *Odyssey* 2." *Arethusa* 25.2:223-40.

Hainsworth, Brian. 1993. *The Iliad: A Commentary. Volume III: Books 9-12.* Cambridge; Cambridge University Press.

Hainsworth, J. 1964. "Structure and Content in Epic Formulae: The Question of the Unique Expression." *Classical Quarterly* 14:155-64.

———. 1968. *The Flexibility of the Homeric Formula.* Oxford: Oxford University Press.

Hansen, William. 1972. *The Conference Sequence: Patterned Narration and Narrative Inconsistency in the Odyssey.* Berkeley: University of California Press.

Harriot, R. 1969. *Poetry and Criticism before Plato*. London: Methuen.

Harris, William. 1989. *Ancient Literacy*. Oxford: Clarendon Press.

Havelock, Eric. 1963. *Preface to Plato*. Cambridge, MA: Harvard University Press.

———. 1982. *The Literate Revolution in Greece and Its Cultural Consequences*. Princeton: Princeton University Press.

———. 1986. *The Muse Learns to Write: Reflections on Orality and Literacy from Antiquity to the Present*. New Haven: Yale University Press.

Held, George. 1987. "Phoinix, Agamemnon and Achilleus: Parables and Paradeigmata." *Classical Quarterly* 37:245-61.

Heubeck, Alfred, Stephanie West, and John Hainsworth. 1988. *A Commentary on Homer's Odyssey, Volume I: Introduction and Books I-VIII*. Oxford: Clarendon Press.

Heubeck, Alfred, and A. Hoekstra. 1989. *A Commentary on Homer's Odyssey, Volume II: Books IX-XVI*. Oxford: Clarendon Press.

Higbie, Carolyn. 1994. *Heroes' Names, Homeric Identities*. New York: Garland Publishing.

Hogan, James. 1979. *A Guide to the Iliad*. Garden City: Anchor Press.

Holoka, James. 1973. "Homeric Originality: A Survey." *Classical World* 66:257-93.

———. 1979. "Homer Studies 1971-1977." Special Survey Issue: *Classical World* 73.

———. 1983. "'Looking Darkly' (ΥΠΟΔΡΑ ΙΔΩΝ): Reflections on Status and Decorum in Homer." *Transactions of the American Philological Association*, 113:1-16.

Holub, R. 1984. *Reception Theory: A Critical Introduction*. London: Methuen.

Hooker, J. T. 1989. "Gifts in Homer." *British Institute of Classical Studies* 36:79-90.

Humphries, Sarah 1978. *Anthropology and the Greeks*. London: Routledge and Kegan Paul.

Huxley, G. L. 1969. *Greek Epic Poetry*. Cambridge, MA: Harvard University Press.

Ingalls, Wayne. 1982. "Linguistic and Formular Innovation in the Mythological Digressions in the *Iliad*." *Phoenix* 36:201-08.

Iser, Wolfgang. 1974. *The Implied Reader: Patterns of Communication in Prose Fiction from Bunyan to Beckett.* Baltimore: Johns Hopkins University Press.

———. 1978. *The Act of Reading. A Theory of Aesthetic Response.* Baltimore: Johns Hopkins University Press.

Janko, Richard. 1992. *The Iliad: A Commentary. Volume IV: Books 13-16.* Cambridge: Cambridge University Press.

Jauss, Hans. 1982. *Aesthetic Experience and Literary Hermeneutics.* Trans. M. Shaw. Minneapolis: University of Minnesota Press.

Jensen, Minna. 1980. *The Homeric Question and the Oral-Formulaic Theory.* Copenhagen: Tusculum 1980.

Jong, Irene de. 1985. "*Iliad* 1.366-392: A Mirror Story." *Arethusa* 18.1:5-22.

———. 1987. *Narrators and Focalizers: The Presentation of the Story in the Iliad.* Amsterdam: Grüner.

Junther, Julius. 1930. "Kalokagathia." In *Charisteria Alois Rzach zum achtzigsten Geburtstag dargebracht.* Reichenberg: Gebrüder Stiepel.

Kakridis, H. J. 1963. *La notion de l'amité et de l'hospitalité chez Homère.* Salonika: Biblioteke tou philologou.

Karp, Andrew. 1977. "Homeric Origins of Ancient Rhetoric." *Arethusa* 10:237-58.

Kelly, Stephen. 1990. *Homeric Correption and the Metrical Distinctions Between Speeches and Narrative.* New York: Garland Publishing.

King, Helen. 1986. "Tithonos and the Tettix." *Arethusa* 19.1:15-35.

Kirby, John. 1990. "The 'Great Triangle' in Early Greek Rhetoric and Poetics." *Rhetorica* 8:213-28.

Kirk, G.S. 1971. "Old Age and Maturity in Ancient Greece." *Eranos* 40:123-58.

———. 1985. *The Iliad: A Commentary. Volume I: Books 1-4.* Cambridge: Cambridge University Press.

———. 1990. *The Iliad: A Commentary. Volume II: Books 5-8.* Cambridge: Cambridge University Press.

Koller, H. 1965. "ΘΕΣΠΙΣ ΑΟΙΔΟΣ." *Glotta* 43:277-85.

Krischer, Tilman. 1965. "Die Entschuldigung des Sängers (*Ilias* B 484-493)." *Rheinisches Museum* 108:1-11.

———. 1971. *Formale Konventionen der homerischen Epik.* Munich: Beck.

Kullmann, W. 1952. *Das Wirken der Götter in der Ilias. Untersuchungen zur Frage der Entstehung des homerischen "Götterapparats".* Dissertation, Berlin University.

Lang, Mabel. 1969. "Homer and Oral Techniques." *Hesperia* 38:159-68.

———. 1983. "Reverberation and Mythology in the *Iliad.*" In *Approaches to Homer,* edited by C. Rubino and C. Shelmerdine, pp. 140-64. Austin: University of Texas Press.

Leaf, Walter, ed. 1886. *The Iliad.* London: Macmillan.

———. 1892. *Companion to the Iliad.* London: Macmillan.

Lenz, A. 1980. *Das Proöm des frühen griechischen Epos.* Bonn: Habelt.

Lesher, J. H. 1981. "Perceiving and Knowing in the *Iliad* and *Odyssey.*" *Phronesis* 26:1-24.

Lévi-Strauss, Claude. 1966. *The Savage Mind.* Chicago: Chicago University Press.

Lloyd, Michael. 1987. "Homer on Poetry: Two passages in the *Odyssey.*" *Eranos* 85:85-90.

Lohenstam, Steven. 1981. *The Death of Patroklos: A Study in Typology.* Königstein/Ts.: Hain.

Lohmann, Dieter. 1970. *Die Komposition der Reden in der Ilias.* Berlin: de Gruyter.

Lord, Albert B. 1960. *The Singer of Tales.* Cambridge, MA: Harvard University Press.

———. 1967. "Homer as Oral Poet." *Harvard Studies in Classical Philology* 72:1-46.

———. 1974. "Perspectives on Recent Work on Oral Literature." *Forum for Modern Language Studies* 10:187-210.

———. 1991. *Epic Singers and Oral Tradition.* Ithaca: Cornell University Press.

Lynn-George, Michael. 1988. *Epos: Word, Narrative and the Iliad.* Atlantic Highlands, N.J.: Humanities Press International.

MacLeod, Colin. 1983. *Collected Essays.* Edited by. O. Taplin. Oxford: Clarendon Press.

Marsh, Teri. 1979. *Magic, Poetics, Seduction: An Analysis of ΘΕΛΓΕΙΝ in Greek Literature.* Dissertation, State University of New York at Buffalo.

Martin, Richard. 1989. *The Language of Heroes. Speech and Performance in the Iliad.* Ithaca: Cornell University Press.

Martino, Francesco de. 1977. "Omero fra narrazione e mimesi."
    Belfagor 32:1-6.

Medda, E. 1981. "῎Ηρατο τῶν ἀπεόντων. Prosperità e
    limitezza umana in una gnome Pindarica," in *Scritti Buratti*,
    pp. 295-309. Pisa: Pacini.

Minton, W.W. 1960. "Homer's Invocations of the Muses."
    Transactions of the American Philological Association
    91:292-309.

————. 1962. "Invocation and Catalogue in Hesiod and
    Homer." *Transactions of the American Philological Association* 93:188-212.

Mitchell, Stephen. 1991. *Heroic Sagas and Ballads*. Ithaca:
    Cornell University Press.

Mondi, Robert. 1978. *The Function and Social Position of the
    κῆρυξ in Early Greece*. Dissertation, Harvard University.

Monod, Jacques. 1970. *Le hasard et la nécessité. Essai sur la
    philosophie naturelle de la biologie moderne*. Paris:
    Editions de Seuil.

Moran, W. 1975. "*Mimneskomai* and 'Remembering' Epic Stories
    in Homer and the Hymns." *Quaderni Urbinati di Cultura
    Classica* 20:195-211.

Morson, Gary, ed. 1986. *Bakhtin: Essays and Dialogues on his
    Work*. Chicago: University of Chicago Press.

Morson, Gary, and Catherine Emerson. 1990. *Mikhail Bakhtin:
    Creation of a Prosaics*. Stanford: Stanford University Press.

Most, Glen. 1989a. "The Stranger's Strategem: Self-Disclosure
    and Self-Sufficiency in Greek Culture." *Journal of Hellenic
    Studies* 109:114-33.

————. 1989b. "The Structure and Function of Odysseus'
    Apologoi." *Transactions of the American Philological
    Association* 119:15-30.

Muellner, Leonard. 1976. *The Meaning of Homeric ΕΥΧΟΜΑΙ
    Through its Formulas*. Innsbruck: Becvar.

Mugler, C. 1980. "La loquacité sénile chez Homère." *LAMA
    (Centre de recherches comparatives sur les Langues de la
    Méditerranée ancienne)* 3:428-38.

Munro, D., ed. 1884. *Homer: Iliad.* Oxford: Clarendon Press.

Murnagham, Sheila. 1987. *Disguise and Recognition in the
    Odyssey*. Princeton: Princeton University Press.

Murray, Penelope. 1981. "Poetic Inspiration in Early Greece."
    Journal of Hellenic Studies 101:87-100.

Nagler, Michael. 1974. *Spontaneity and Tradition: A Study in the Oral Art of Homer.* Berkeley: University of California Press.

Nagy, Gregory. 1979. *The Best of the Achaeans: Concepts of the Hero in Archaic Greek Poetry.* Baltimore and London: Johns Hopkins University Press.

————. 1990a. *Pindar's Homer: They Lyric Possession of an Epic Past.* Baltimore: Johns Hopkins University Press.

————. 1990b. *Greek Mythology and Poetics.* Ithaca: Cornell University Press.

Nash, L.L. 1978. "Concepts of Existence: Greek Origins of Generational Thought." *Daedalus* 107:1-21.

Notopolous, J. 1938. "*Mnemosune* in Oral Literature." *Transactions of the American Philological Association* 69:465-93.

Ong, Walter. 1967. *The Presence of the Word: Some Prolegomena for Cultural and Religious History.* New Haven: Yale University Press.

————. 1977. *Interfaces of the Word: Studies in the Evolution of Consciousness and Culture.* Ithaca: Cornell University Press.

————. 1982. *Orality and Literacy. The Technologizing of the Word.* London: Methuen.

O'Nolan, K. 1987. "Doublets in the *Odyssey*," *Classical Quarterly* 28:23-27.

Owen, E.T. 1946. *The Story of the Iliad.* Toronto: University of Toronto Press.

Page, Denys. 1955. *The Homeric Odyssey.* Oxford: Clarendon Press.

————. 1959. *History and the Homeric Iliad.* Berkeley: University of Califoria Press.

Pagliaro, A. 1951. "La terminologia poetica di Omero e l'origine dell'epica." *Richerche linguistiche* 2:1-46.

Parks, Ward. 1990. *Verbal Dueling in Heroic Narrative: The Homeric and Old English Traditions.* Princeton: Princeton University Press.

Parry, Adam. 1972. "Language and Characterization in Homer." *Harvard Studies in Classical Philology* 76:1-22.

Parry, Hugh. 1992. *THELXIS: Magic and Imagination in Greek Myth and Poetry.* Lanham: University Press of America.

Parry, Milman 1971. *The Making of Homeric Verse: The Collected Papers of Milman Parry.* Edited by A. Parry. Oxford: Clarendon Press.

Pavel, Thomas. 1979. "Fiction and the Causal Theory of Names." *Poetics* 8:179-91.

Pedrick, Victoria. 1983. "The Paradigmatic Nature of Nestor's Speech in *Iliad* 11." *Transactions of the American Philological Association* 113:55-68.

Pelling, Christopher, ed. 1990. *Characterization and Individuality in Greek Literature.* Oxford: Clarendon Press.

Peradotto, John. 1974. "*Odyssey* 9.564-571: Verisimilitude, Narrative Analysis and Bricolage. *Texas Studies in Literature and Language* 15.5:803-32.

———. 1983. "Texts and Unrefracted Facts: Philology, Hermeutics and Semiotics." *Arethusa* 16:15-33.

———. 1986. "Prophecy Degree Zero: Tiresias and the End of the *Odyssey*." In *Oralità: Cultura, Letteratura, Discorso,* edited by B. Gentili and G. Paioni, pp. 429-59. Atti del Convegno Internazionale, Urbino 1980. Rome: Atenei.

———. 1990. *Man in the Middle Voice: Name and Narration in the Odyssey.* Princeton: Princeton University Press.

Pollard, J. 1965. *Seers, Shrines, and Sirens.* London: Allen & Unwin.

Post, L. 1939. "The Moral Pattern in Homer." *Transactions of the American Philological Association* 70:158-90.

Pötscher, Walter. 1986. "Das Selbstverständnis des Dichters in der Homerischen Poesie." *Literaturwissenschaftliches Jahrbuch* 27:9-22.

Powell, Barry. 1977. *Composition by Theme in the Odyssey.* Meisenheim am Glan: Hain.

Pratt, Louise H. 1993. *Lying and Poetry from Homer to Pindar: Falsehood and Deception in Archaic Greek Poetics.* Ann Arbor: University of Michigan Press.

Prendergast, G.L. 1962. *A Complete Concordance to the Iliad of Homer. Completely revised and enlarged by B. Marzullo.* Hildesheim: Olm.

Prince, Gerald. 1987. *A Dictionary of Narratology.* Lincoln: University of Nebraska Press.

Propp, Vladimir. 1968. *Morphology of the Folktale.* 2nd ed. Trans. L. Scott. Austin: University of Texas Press.

Pucci, Pietro. 1977. *Hesiod and the Language of Poetry.* Ithaca.

———. 1979. "The Song of the Sirens." *Arethusa* 12:121-32.

———. 1980. "The Language of the Muses." In *Classical Mythology in 20th Century Thought and Literature*, edited by W. Aycock and T. Klein. Proceedings of the Comparative Literature Symposium, Texas Tech University, vol. 11. Lubbock: Texas Tech University Press.

———. 1987. *Odysseus Polytropos: Intertextual Readings in the Odyssey and the Iliad*. Ithaca: Cornell University Press.

Querbach, Carlyn. 1976. "Conflicts between Young and Old in Homer's *Iliad*." In *The Conflict of Generations in Ancient Greece and Rome*, edited by S. Berman. Amsterdam: Grüner. pp. 55-64.

Rabinow, Paul, ed. 1984. *The Foucault Reader*. New York: Pantheon Books.

Ramnoux, C. 1960. "L'amour du lointain," *Revue de la Méditerranée* 20:435-59.

Raubitschek, Anthony. 1968. "Das Denkmal-Epigram." In *L'Epigramme Grecque*. Geneva: Fondation Hardt. pp. 1-36.

Redfield, James. 1975. *Nature and Culture in the Iliad: The Tragedy of Hector*. Chicago: University of Chicago Press.

———. 1979. "The Proem of the *Iliad*: Homer's Art." *Classical Philology* 74:95-110.

Reece, Steve. 1993. *The Stranger's Welcome: Oral Theory and the Aesthetics of the Homeric Hospitality Scene*. Ann Arbor: University of Michigan Press.

Reinhardt, Karl. 1961. *Die Ilias und ihr Dichter*. Göttingen: Vandenhoeck.

Richardson, Nicholas. 1993. *The Iliad: A Commentary. Volume VI: Books 21-24*. Cambridge: Cambridge University Press.

Richardson, Scott. 1990. *The Homeric Narrator*. Nashville: Vanderbilt University Press.

Ricoeur, Paul. 1974. *The Conflict of Interpretations: Essays in Hermeneutics*. Edited by D. Ihde. Evanston: Northwestern University Press.

———. 1976. *Interpretation Theory: Discourse and the Surplus of Meaning*. Forth Worth: Texas University Christian Press.

———. 1992. *Oneself as Another*. Trans. Kathleen Blamey. Chicago: University of Chicago Press.

Rimmon-Kenan, Shlomith. 1983. *Narrative Fiction: Contemporary Poetics*. London: Methuen.

Ritoók, Zs. 1989. "The Views of Early Greek Epic on Poetry and Art." *Mnemosyne* 42:331-48.

Bibliography 243

Romilly, Jacqueline de. 1975. *Magic and Rhetoric in Ancient Greece*. Cambridge: Cambridge University Press.

Roochink, David. 1990. "Homeric Speech Acts: Word and Deed in the Epics." *Classical Journal* 85:289-99.

Roscher, W. 1924-37. *Ausführliches Lexikon der griechischen und römischen Mythologie*. Leipzig: Tebuner.

Rose, Gilbert. 1971. "*Odyssey* 15.143-82: A Narrative Inconsistency?" *Transactions of the American Philological Association* 102:509-14.

Rose, Peter. 1988. "Thersites and the Plural Voices of Homer." *Arethusa* 21:5-25.

———. 1992. *Sons of the Gods, Children of Earth. Ideology and Literary Form in Ancient Greece*. Ithaca: Cornell University Press.

Rosner, Judith. 1976. "The Speech of Phoenix: *Iliad* 9.434-605." *Phoenix* 30:314-27.

Russo, Joseph. 1968. "Homer against His Tradition." *Arion* 7:275-95.

———. 1976. "How, and What, Does Homer Communicate? The Medium and the Message of Homeric Verse." *Classical Journal* 71:289-99.

Rüter, K. 1969. *Odysseeinterpretationen: Untersuchungen zum ersten Buch und zur Phaiakis*. Götingen: Vandenhoeck and Ruprecht.

Sachs, Eva. 1933. "Die Meleagererzählung in der *Ilias* und das mythische Paradeigma." *Philologus* 88:16-29.

Sacks, Richard. 1987. *The Traditional Phrase in Homer: Two Studies in Form, Meaning and Interpretation*. Leiden: Brill.

Schadewaldt, Wolfgang. 1965. *Von Homers Welt und Werk*. Stuttgart: Koehler.

———. 1987. *Iliasstudien*. Darmstadt: Wissenschaftliches Buchgesellschaft.

Schein, Seth. 1984. *The Mortal Hero*. Berkeley: University of California Press.

Scodel, R. 1982a. "The Achaean Wall and the Myth of Destruction." *Harvard Studies in Classical Philology* 82:33-50.

———. 1982b. "The Autobiography of Phoenix: *Iliad* 9.444-95." *American Journal of Philology* 103:128-36.

Scully, Stephen. 1981. "The Bard as the Custodian of Homeric Society: *Odyssey* 3,263-272." *Quaderni Urbinati di Cultura Classica* n.s. 8:67-83.

244   *Bibliography*

————. 1986. "Studies of Narrative and Speech in the *Iliad*." *Arethusa* 19:135-53.

Segal, Charles. 1971. "Nestor and the Honor of Achilles (*Iliad* 1.247-84)." *Studi Micenei ed Egeo-Anatolici* 13:90-105.

————. 1983. "*Kleos* and its Ironies in the *Odyssey*." *Acta Classica* 52:22-47.

Sheppard, John. 1922. *The Pattern of the Iliad*. London: Haskell.

Sheridan, Alan. 1980. *Michel Foucault: The Will to Truth*. London: Tavistock Publications.

Sinos, Dale. 1980. *Achilles, Patroklos and the Meaning of Philos*. Innsbruck: Beiträge Sprachwissenschaft.

Shipp, G.P. 1972. *Studies in the Language of Homer*. Cambridge: Cambridge University Press.

Shive, David. 1987. *Naming Achilles*. Oxford: Oxford University Press.

Simpson, R., and J. Lazenby. 1970. *The Catalogue of the Ships in Homer's Iliad*. Oxford: Clarendon Press.

Solmsen, Friedrich. 1954. "The 'Gift' of Speech in Homer and Hesiod." *Transactions of the American Philological Association* 85:1-15.

Stanford, W.B. 1958-59. *The Odyssey of Homer*. 2 vols. London: St. Martin's Press.

Stock, Brian. 1983. *The Implications of Literacy: Written Language and Models of Interpretation in the Eleventh and Twelfth Centuries*. Princeton: Princeton University Press.

————. 1990. *Listening for the Text*. Baltimore: Johns Hopkins University Press.

Stockinger, Hildebrand. 1959. *Die Vorzeichnen im homerischen Epos*. Munich: EOS Verlag.

Stolz, Benjamin, and Richard Shannon, eds. 1976. *Oral Literature and the Formula*. Ann Arbor: University of Michigan Press.

Sulzberger, M. 1926. "Ὄνομα ἐπώνυμον. Les noms propres chez Homère et dans la mythologie grecque." *Revue des études grecques* 39:381-447.

Suzuki, Mihoko. 1989. *Metamorphoses of Helen: Authority, Difference and the Epic*. Ithaca: Cornell University Press.

Svenbro, Jesper. 1976. *La parole et le marbre: Aux origines de la poétique grecque*. Dissertation: Lunds Universitet.

———. 1993. *Phrasikleia: An Anthropology of Reading in Ancient Greece.* Ithaca: Cornell University Press.

Taylor, Charles. 1960. "The Obstacles to Odysseus' Return." *Yale Review* 50:569-80.

Thalmann, Gregory. 1984. *Conventions of Form and Thought in Early Greek Epic Poetry.* Baltimore: Johns Hopkins University Press.

———. 1988. "Thersites: Comedy, Scapegoats and Heroic Ideology in the *Iliad*." *Transactions of the American Philological Association* 118:1-28.

Thomas, Rosalind. 1989. *Oral Tradition and Written Record in Classical Athens.* Cambridge: Cambridge University Press.

Thompson, Stith. 1955. *Motif-Index of Folk-Literature.* Bloomington: Indiana University Press.

———. 1977. *The Folktale.* Berkeley: University of California Press. (Reprint of 1946 edition.)

Thornton, Agathe. 1984. *Homer's Iliad: Its Composition and the Motif of Supplication.* Göttingen: Vandenhoeck and Ruprecht.

Tigay, Jeffrey. 1982. *The Evolution of the Gilgamesh Epic.* Philadelphia: University of Pennsylvania Press.

Todorov, Tzvetan. 1977. *The Poetics of Prose.* Trans. R. Howard. Ithaca: Cornell University Press.

———. 1981. *Introduction to Poetics.* Trans. R. Howard. Minneapolis: University of Minnesota Press.

———. 1984. *Mikhail Bakhtin: The Dialogic Principle.* Trans. W. Godzich. Minneapolis: University of Michigan Press.

Tornow, W. 1893. *De apium mellisque significatione symbolica et mythologica.* Berlin: Weidmann.

Tracy, Stephen. 1990. *The Story of the Odyssey.* Princeton: Princeton University Press.

Van Groningen, B. A. 1946. "The Proems of the *Iliad* and the *Odyssey*." *Mededeelingen der Koninklijke Nederlandshe Akademie von Wetenschappen* 9.8:279-94.

Vansina, Jan. 1985. *Oral Tradition as History.* Madison: University of Wisconsin Press.

Vernant, Jean-Pierre. 1965. *Mythe et pensée chez les grecs.* Paris: Maspéro.

———. 1982. "La belle mort et le cadavre outragé." In *La Mort: Les morts dans les sociétés anciennes,* edited by G. Gnoli and J.-P. Vernant, pp. 45-76. Cambridge: Cambridge University Press.

Vester, H. 1956. *Nestor: Funktion und Gestalt in der Ilias.* Dissertation, Tübingen University.

Vivante, Paolo. 1970. *The Homeric Imagination. A Study of Homer's Poetic Perception of Reality.* Bloomington: University of Indiana Press.

———. 1975. "On Homer's Winged Words." *Classical Quarterly* 25:1-22.

———. 1982. *The Epithets in Homer: A Study in Poetic Values.* New Haven: Yale University Press.

Wace, Alan, and Frank Stubbings, eds. 1962. *A Companion to Homer.* London: Macmillan.

Walsh, George. 1984. *The Varieties of Enchantment: Early Greek Views of the Nature and Function of Poetry.* Chapel Hill: University of North Carolina Press.

Wender, Dorothea. 1978. *The Last Scenes of the Odyssey. Mnemosyne* Supplement 52. Leiden: Brill.

West, Martin. 1966. *Hesiod: Theogony.* Oxford: Clarendon Press.

———. 1969. "The Achaean Wall." *Classical Review* 19:255-63.

———. 1978. *Hesiod: Works and Days.* Oxford: Clarendon Press.

Whallon, William. 1961. "The Homeric Epithets." *Yale Classical Studies* 17:97-142.

———. 1969. *Formula, Character, and Context: Studies in Homeric, Old English, and Old Testament Poetry.* Cambridge, MA: Harvard University Press.

Whitman, Cedric. 1958. *Homer and the Heroic Tradition.* Cambridge, MA: Harvard University Press.

Wilamowitz-Moellendorff, Ulrich von. 1916. *Die Ilias und Homer.* Berlin: Weidmann.

Willcock, Malcolm. 1964. "Mythological Paradeigmata in the *Iliad.*" *Classical Quarterly* 14:141-54.

———. 1976. *A Companion to the Iliad.* Chicago: University of Chicago Press.

———. 1977. "*Ad hoc* Invention in the *Iliad.*" *Harvard Studies in Classical Philology* 81:41-53.

Yates, Francis. 1966. *The Art of Memory.* London: Routledge and Kegan Paul.

Young, David. 1968. *Three Odes of Pindar.* Leiden: Brill.

Zumthor, Paul. 1990. *Oral Poetry: An Introduction.* Trans. K. Murphy-Judy. Minneapolis:University of Minnesota Press.

Passages
Discussed

General Index